Murderous Mothers

German Studies in America

No. 78

PETER LANG
Oxford • Bern • Berlin • Bruxelles • New York • Wien

Claire E. Scott

Murderous Mothers

Late Twentieth-Century Medea Figures and Feminism

PETER LANG
Oxford • Bern • Berlin • Bruxelles • New York • Wien

Bibliographic information published by Die Deutsche Nationalbibliothek
Die Deutsche Nationalbibliothek lists this publication in the Deutsche Nationalbibliografie; detailed bibliographic data are available on the Internet at http://dnb.ddb.de.

A catalogue record for this book is available at the British Library.

Library of Congress Control Number: 2022028114

Cover image: Medea, 2009, painting by Marie Hines Cowan.
www.mariehinescowan.com mhc@mariehinescowan.com.
Cover design by Peter Lang Ltd.

ISSN 0721-3727
ISBN 978-1-80079-413-9 (print)
ISBN 978-1-80079-414-6 (ePDF)
ISBN 978-1-80079-415-3 (ePub)

Published by Peter Lang Ltd, International Academic Publishers,
Oxford, United Kingdom
oxford@peterlang.com, www.peterlang.com

This book has been peer reviewed.

This book is dedicated to all the women who have mothered me through this world, especially Lori Scott. I would not be here without you.

Contents

Acknowledgments

The idea for this book began as I was searching for a dissertation topic. I found my way to Medea amid representations of reproductive healthcare, including abortion. Although I ultimately wrote about violence in my dissertation, this interest in Medea has never waned. My research for this book, at least seven years in the making, is the result of numerous support systems, some of which I want to acknowledge here.

I am grateful for the financial support that I received throughout my time in graduate school including a Duke Graduate School Summer Research Fellowship, the Robert K. Steel Family Graduate Fellowship at Duke University, and the Duke Women's Studies Dissertation Fellowship. The dissertation that started this process was also awarded the Coalition of Women in German's annual dissertation prize in 2017. Most recently, I received a Provost Faculty Research Award from Kenyon College to support the final editing stages of this monograph. I am honored that this book won the 2020 Peter Lang Young Scholars Competition for German Studies in America and thankful for the team that helped me through the publication process, especially Laurel Plapp.

I am extremely grateful to the colleagues and friends who have generously given me feedback on this book: Kata Gellen, Stefani Engelstein, Maria Stehle, Vanessa Plumly, Sara Jackson, Priscilla Layne, Dick Langston, Holly Yanacek, Rebekah Slodounik, Steffen Kaupp, BethAnne Dorn, and Ian McLean.

I especially want to thank Kata, who was there from the very, very beginning and who I can always count on to ask the tough questions. You convinced me not to write my dissertation only about Medea and I am glad that you did, because this book is so much richer since I started somewhere else.

Special thanks also go to Stefani. Being around you helped me to understand the type of scholar and teacher that I want to be. I am grateful for how you let me bring all of myself into our conversations and how you always get to the heart of the matter.

I am also deeply grateful to my creepiest friend, Steffen Kaupp, for his loyalty, unwavering support, and (most directly) for the hours spent double-checking German quotations and translations.

I want to thank the students in my mythology seminar at Kenyon College, Katie, Hayden, Elena, and Israel, for putting up with my overly enthusiastic discussion of some of these texts and for teaching me to look at them with fresh eyes.

Much gratitude to my official copyeditor Sam Brawand for her attention to detail, and to my favorite copyeditors, my parents Lori and Tom Scott. Thanks also to Steve Moore for assistance with the index.

To the Diversity, Decolonization, and the German Curriculum Dissertation to Book Writing Group: thanks for helping me across the finish line.

I wrote this book during some very difficult years. This project was a beacon of hope within a great deal of uncertainty, and I would be remiss if I did not also acknowledge some of the people who lifted me up during these challenging, yet rewarding, times.

I am grateful to Ann Marie Rasmussen for being one of the best listeners I have ever known and for giving me professional and personal advice that will stand the test of time.

To Anne Schaffer for being there through all the highs and lows. You understand me better than almost anyone and consequently, you do not let me get away with anything. Knowing you connects me to the person that I was and to the person that I am becoming.

To BethAnne Dorn for reminding me that I am capable of many things and that I am enriched by, rather than defined by, my work. Thank you for always believing in all of me.

To the Changelings: Brianna, Liana, and Kelly. You are amazing people, scholars, and teachers. I learn from you every day and you make me happy to just be myself.

To Flora and Bill McCormick for helping me to live out my dreams and for convincing me that this was possible.

Finally, my thanks and love go to Mom, Dad, Eric, and Tommy for going through this process alongside me. You inspire me every day to be the best version of myself by giving me a space where I can just be myself. Writing a book is no small thing. Finishing the writing of a book amid precarious situations of all kinds—professional, personal, and physical—is a feat that requires love. My deepest thanks to everyone who provided the love that got me here.

Introduction

"Auf ihren Leib jetzt schreibe ich mein Schauspiel"

—Müller 78

["It is on her body that I write my play"]

—Weber 131

In Heiner Müller's post-dramatic theatrical text *Verkommenes Ufer Medeamaterial Landschaft mit Argonauten* (*Despoiled Shore Medea Material Landscape with Argonauts*) (1982–1983) the mythological figure of Medea casts herself as an author. Although Medea is probably best known for killing her children—as a destroyer of life, of legacy, and of family—it is essential to remember that Medea also creates. She has children, heals disease, and in this case, even makes art. This juxtaposition of positive and negative forces is deeply gendered. Because of their physical and symbolic reproductive functions, women's bodies often bear the responsibility for nurturing life (as mothers) and for inspiring art (as muses). Furthermore, Müller's Medea makes it clear that men are not the only perpetrators of violence against women and that establishing solidarity between women is a difficult undertaking. In this moment of authorship, Medea describes in graphic detail how she will burn her ex-husband Jason's new wife alive. The play that Medea will write is notably an affective one, in the sense that her extreme violence has intertwined physical and emotional consequences. In *Murderous Mothers* I seek to articulate and better understand the connections between women as bodies and women as subjects within the Medea story as it was employed in response to contemporaneous feminist theory and politics. I analyze Germanophone adaptations of Medea from the late twentieth century to ask what kind of plays women create when they write Medea stories, and on whose bodies such texts might be figuratively transcribed.

The Medea stories I discuss in this book offer an alternative vision of agency and power, one that aligns more with classicist Mary Beard's vision when she describes how feminist power "means thinking collaboratively about the power of followers not just of leaders. It means, above all, thinking about power as an attribute or even a verb [...], not as a possession" (87). Instead of power existing as something that one has, I argue that Medea's feminist power is something that she becomes through the process of repeated, polyvocal storytelling. In her analysis of Christa Wolf's Medea story, Helen Bridge describes how "myth is no longer just a political tool, employed deliberately to influence the way others think; it is now also a layer of unconscious self-deception. Wolf's interest has shifted from the effects of myth to the human needs which enable it to exert power" (38). Germans in the postwar and eventually the post-Reunification periods certainly had a collective need for myth, for stories that defined or redefined their identities. In this book, I trace one specific piece of this much larger process by analyzing the role that Medea stories played in defining German women and their relationship to feminism.

During the last few decades of the twentieth century, German women authors turned to the Medea story as a means for working through their own uncertain feelings within the developing feminist political landscape of the New Women's Movement in West Germany, and later the unified Federal Republic of Germany. In *Murderous Mothers*, I look closely at how authors adapted the Medea story, arguing that German feminist Medea adaptations provide space for engaging with contradictions and ambiguities within feminist ideas, especially feminist conceptions of language and of narration. The aesthetic representation of these Medea figures generates nuanced conversations about reproductive rights, intersectionality, bodily autonomy and empowerment, colonialism, racism, gender performativity, and numerous other topics that continue to hold relevance for feminist movements well into the twenty-first century. Ultimately, Medea stories by Germanophone women generate a feminist form of *Gewalt* (a German word meaning both violence and power) that simultaneously dismantles and reconstructs understandings of gender identity and literary representations of violence.

Euripides: Ending or Beginning?

In Euripides's *Medea*, which serves as a foundational text for many subsequent Medea adaptations, Medea is the epitome of the calculating and vengeful woman scorned. In his version of this mythological story, Medea is a princess and sorceress from Colchis who assists Jason, the leader of the Argonauts, in capturing the Golden Fleece (a woolen pelt from a winged ram that symbolizes kingly authority). Medea marries Jason, runs away with him to Corinth, and gives birth to twin sons. As the play opens, however, Medea discovers that Jason is planning to marry Glauce/Creusa, the daughter of King Creon, in order to increase his own political position and power. In anticipation of her wrath, Creon tries to send Medea into exile, but he makes the mistake of giving her twenty-four hours to get her affairs in order. Medea uses that day to exact her violent revenge on Jason, poisoning Creon and his daughter with a gift of golden robes, and killing her own children, so that Jason will have no progeny. In the end, she escapes triumphantly to Athens to take refuge at the court of Aegeus, promising to cure his infertility. This basic plotline in which Medea betrays her family to run away with Jason, only to be betrayed by him in turn before exacting her revenge is a common thread to most (but certainly not all) Medea adaptations.

When invoking this mythological story, Medea's brutal and triumphant exit from Corinth is typically not the first scene that comes to mind. More commonly, readers are captivated by the horror of Medea's previous deeds, making the story's final scene seem inconsequential in comparison. However, it is significant that Euripides, one of this myth's best-known authors, ultimately depicts Medea as triumphant. At the very end of Euripides's drama Medea sits aloft in a golden chariot pulled by dragons, a gift from her grandfather, the sun god Helios. The bodies of her dead children by her side, she looks down at Jason, her former lover and husband, who now begs her to leave the corpses with him, so that he can bury them. "οὐκ ἔστι· μάτην ἔπος ἔρριπται" [It cannot be. Your words are uttered in vain] (Euripides 412, 413) she insists before taking off into the sky. The stage directions in the Loeb Classical Library edition of Euripides's

Medea indicate that when first performed in 431 BCE the *mechane* (a crane used for special effects in the ancient Greek theater, such as making the gods fly) was used to hoist Medea above the stage, providing evidence of a visually marked, highly dramatic, and exalted exit (403). Despite her violent actions, Medea is no criminal who slinks away into exile. She is a woman who has reclaimed herself from a traumatic marriage, albeit at an extremely high cost to both her and to the people around her. She is physically placed on a higher plane from her now former husband, Jason, and from the Corinthian chorus. Medea is exceptional. She is different from the people around her in ways that have both extremely positive and negative connotations; she is victorious and she suffers, she is cold and stoic, as well as nurturing and emotional.

Medea's final words in Euripides's play also confront the limits of language itself. "Your words are uttered in vain" (413), Medea says. Classicist C. A. E. Luschnig describes this "visually and morally astonishing moment" as one in which both character and author "assert godlike control over the fates of the characters in the story" (84). Even though Jason and the chorus speak the play's actual final words, Medea, in her god-like position, undermines them by declaring beforehand that the speech of those who would malign her is ineffectual. Ironically, she uses language to render their utterances harmless. If words were indeed in vain, then she could not effectively declare them so in a speech act. As Luschnig alludes, a victorious Medea, who confronts the power of language, draws our attention to the complexity of Euripides's role as author and the contradictory nature of narrative itself. As Heike Bartel and Anne Simon write in the introduction to their own volume on Medea adaptations, "Medea's conflicting elements challenge our thinking and [...] form a tense, emotionally and intellectually challenging oxymoronic structure which resists reduction to a single—and therefore safely defusable [sic]—facet" (2). Medea is both victim and perpetrator, brutal killer and triumphant heroine. Because of these contradictions, Medea upsets established beliefs and critiques binary thinking. Mythology relies on repeated storytelling. If a myth is not repeated, it ceases to be normalized or to have the same power and influence. When Medea challenges the ability of words to perform their intention, she calls into question the very process of repetitive storytelling and mythologization that produced her. As Yixu Lü articulates, because of these contradictions "es gibt keinen kanonischen Medea-Mythos" [there is no canonical Medea-myth] (*Medea* 11; translation mine).[1]

Medea's ability to circumvent binary distinctions and to reveal the process through which social categories are normalized through myth makes her relevant as a representative figure for social justice movements, including feminism. During the late twentieth century, transatlantic feminist movements experienced a *second wave*, as women in North America and in Europe developed a deeper understanding of gender and of sex, and used it to fight for their rights and to carve out new spaces for women in a post-suffrage world. In her 1976 essay on the figure of Medusa (a name linguistically related to Medea), French feminist theorist Hélène Cixous described gendered oppression as inherent in language, writing that

> if woman has always functioned "within" the discourse of man [...] it is time for her to dislocate this "within," to explode it, turn it around, and seize it; to make it hers, containing it, taking it in her own mouth, biting that tongue with her very own teeth to invent for herself a language to get inside of. (Cixous 887)

The aggression in Cixous's metaphors as she articulates the challenges facing feminist writers mirrors the brutality and the triumph exhibited by Medea as she makes her escape from Corinth. All of the authors under discussion in *Murderous Mothers*—Ursula Haas, Christa Wolf, Dagmar Nick, Dea Loher, and Elfriede Jelinek—use Medea stories to take up Cixous's call for women to generate a language of their own. Much like the difficult process described by Cixous, they all struggle, succeed, and fail in different ways and to different degrees. Whether or not these authors self-identify as feminists (and some of them, particularly Dagmar Nick and Christa Wolf, publicly resisted such a political connection[2]), my analysis proves

1 All translations are my own unless otherwise noted.

2 Wolf's principled commitment to socialism is one likely reason for her resistance to the term "feminist." Such a label was regarded as bourgeois under the state socialism of the GDR. However, as many scholars have already pointed out, "her work engaged women-centered issues in transnationally relevant ways" (Klocke and Hosek 33).

that their works can and should be contextualized within contemporaneous feminist discourses and debates.

Medea is a fascinating figure to examine in a feminist context because of her own ambiguous gender identity and/or gender presentation. Depending on which version of the story one reads, Medea can range from hyper-feminine to hyper-masculine and anywhere in between. She is feminine and romantic, suffering for love, as well as a masculine cold-hearted killer, desperate for revenge. In Seneca's "Medea" from around 50 CE, King Creon describes this dynamic saying that Medea has "a woman's evil willingness to dare anything, along with man's strength, and no thought of reputation" (341). King Creon's misogynistic equation of women with evil aside, scholarly critics are similarly divided in terms of how to classify Medea's gender. Lü, like Seneca's Creon, highlights Medea's confusing combination of masculine and feminine qualities, writing that Medea exhibits "einmal ein typisch weibliches, dann wieder ein ausgesprochenen männliches Verhalten" [a sometimes typically feminine and then other times a decidedly masculine manner] (*Medea* 219). Luschnig marvels that Medea "is at least the equal of any man, in intelligence, courage, creativity, and lack of modesty or restraint" (7). Although not all of these are positively connotated qualities, as Beard reminds us, during the time period when the Medea story was first written down, "public speech was a—if not *the*—defining attribute of maleness" (17). By merely opening her mouth, Medea transgresses gendered boundaries. Britta Schmierer searches for a middle road and contends that Medea is "nicht ausschließlich weiblich, sondern hermaphrodit" [not exclusively feminine, but rather hermaphroditic] (147). Medea's gender fluidity or androgyny makes her an ideal figure through which to investigate the connection between literature, gender theory, and politics.

Despite her gender-bending and brutal acts of violence, Medea is often portrayed as more noble and successful than the unfaithful Jason. For instance, Barbara Feichtinger argues that Euripides warns his society not to be like Jason (227), because through his betrayal Jason loses "das Recht auf Weiterleben für sich und seine Nachkommenschaft" [the right to continued life for himself and his descendants] (231). Even in Euripides's play, Jason is clearly in the wrong. Although he is often juxtaposed with

Medea, our moral judgment of these two characters cannot be as simple as saying that one is good and the other is bad. In their analysis of feminist Medea stories, Astrid Messerschmidt and Eva Peters write of the contrast between "die Entwicklungsfähigkeit der Protagonistin" [the protagonist's ability to evolve] and the "statischen Charakter Jasons" [static character of Jason] (528), arguing that the depiction of Medea and Jason as opposites is especially characteristic of adaptations by female authors. Rather than any inherent goodness or purely evil nature, a crucial difference between Jason and Medea is that one is open to the possibility of change, of starting over, and the other is not. What does it mean for female authors to generate sympathy for and attachment to a dynamic, collaborative, change-oriented Medea, rather than a static, power-hungry, immovable Jason? I argue that the answers to this question reveal how German feminists confronted the ambiguities and internal divisions within women's movements and sought, but were not necessarily able to fully realize, solidarities between different marginalized groups.

Medea in Germanophone Literature

Medea has a unique place in Germanophone literary history because she is both an example of and an exception to a long-standing German interest in Ancient Greek culture. Notable German adaptations of *Medea* begin in the seventeenth century with the *Singspiele* [musical comedies] of Friedrich Christian Bressand (1692) and Johann Gottlieb Kleist (1752). These were followed closely by a very successful melodrama written by Friedrich Wilhelm Gotter in 1775. Although Medea adaptations appeared regularly in these genres of popular theater, she was often overlooked in intellectual circles. Starting in the eighteenth century, German thinkers, most prominently Johann Joachim Winkelmann (1717–1768) and Gotthold Ephraim Lessing (1729–1781), valorized classical art, crafting aesthetic theories based on the beauty, grandeur, and emotion displayed in ancient works of statue and of theater. Medea, however, was often an outlier in this glorious history of Ancient Greek artistic accomplishment.

Georg Wilhelm Friedrich Hegel (1770–1831), for example, favored Sophocles's *Antigone* as the paradigmatic Greek tragedy, calling it "one of the most sublime and in every respect most excellent works of art of all time" because "everything in this tragedy is logical" (Hegel 464). In contrast to this high praise, Hegel viewed all of Euripides's works as the opposite of what good Greek tragedies should be, never even mentioning *Medea* (Hegel 229; Lü, *Medea* 90). Medea's contentious reception contrasts with that of other female mythological characters, who were lauded during Weimar Classicism including (in addition to Antigone) Iphigenia, popularized by the canonical 1779 play by Johann Wolfgang von Goethe (1749–1832). As Lü remarks, in contrast to Iphigenia, Medea is "kein einfaches Bild der Weiblichkeit" [not a simple image of womanhood] (*Medea* 94). Medea's violence, passion, and her use of magic represent a challenge to neo-classical understandings of femininity and beauty in art. I agree with Lü when she argues that Medea stories directly conflict with aesthetic goals, such as those expressed by Winkelmann, because, "Medea who is nothing if not passionate, had scant attraction for playwrights seeking to incarnate 'noble simplicity and calm grandeur'" (*edle Einfalt und stille Größe*) (Lü, "Transformations" 154). In other words, Medea has the feminist potential to be a metaphorical fly in the ointment for a variety of social, aesthetic, and intellectual traditions.

Despite their preference for other ancient dramas, the pull of the intriguing Medea mythology proved impossible for German philosophers and artists to completely ignore. In fact, over two decades before the production of Goethe's Iphigenia play, Lessing himself wrote *Miss Sara Sampson* (1755), a theatrical work loosely based on the Medea material. This *bürgerliches Trauerspiel* [bourgeois tragedy] focuses on the domestic competition between two women, Sara (the demure woman/Glauce figure) and Marwood (the aggressive Medea figure). The womanliness of Sara serves as a positive contrast to the androgynous Marwood. In the German theater, the story of Medea developed into a compelling frame for discussions of gender and of other social issues, even if aesthetically it was not as revered as other Ancient Greek dramas. Most of the best-known German adaptations of the Medea material continued to come out of the theater, with especially notable plays appearing from Franz Grillparzer in 1821[3] and Hans Henny Jahnn in 1925. Lü calls Grillparzer's Medea trilogy the first modern German Medea play in that it breaks free from the conventions of both Weimar Classicism and the German Enlightenment (*Medea* 143). This is just one example within a long history in the German-speaking world of writers using Medea to innovate on the levels of form and of content.

Taking the Medea plays of Grillparzer and Jahnn as early examples, it is clear that German-speaking Medeas are deeply tied to interrelated discourses surrounding motherhood, colonialism, xenophobia, and desire. In Ancient Greek and Roman texts, Medea's children are mostly silent. However, in both Grillparzer and Jahnn's plays the children have significant speaking parts. In the German context especially, abandonment by her children becomes a significant part of Medea's struggle, thereby emphasizing her role as a mother. Lorraine Daston argues that the motives of Grillparzer's Medea "are made consistently and inexorably maternal" (385). It is difficult to argue with this conclusion when Grillparzer's Medea bemoans the fact that when given the choice, her children elect to stay with their new mother figure, Creon's daughter Kreusa, rather than go away into exile with Medea. Schmierer describes how in Grillparzer "Kreusas Einfluss zerstört die natürliche Mutter-Kind-Beziehung und verursacht für Medea den Verlust ihres Mutterdaseins bereits vor dem Kindermord" [Kreusa's influence destroys the natural mother-child-relationship and causes Medea's loss of her being as a mother already before the child murder] (130). After her children fail to come to her, Grillparzer's Medea disowns them saying brutally, "Sie sind Jasons Kinder! Ihm gleich an Gestalt, an Sinn, Ihm gleich in meinem Haß" [They are Jason's children. Identical to him in stature and mind, identical to him in my hate] (Act 4). Medea is obviously even more hurt by the betrayal of her children than by the betrayal of her husband Jason. This allows Grillparzer to give her a more concrete reason for including filicide in her revenge plans.

3 For more on Grillparzer's engagement with female figures from the classical world, I recommend Alicia E. Ellis's book, *Gender and Identity in Franz Grillparzer's Classical Dramas* (2021).

Instead of becoming enemies, in Jahnn's play, Medea and her sons are allies and Jason betrays them all. This makes Medea's eventual murder of the sons more, rather than less, unexpected. Jahnn's Jason goes to woo Creon's daughter on behalf of his son, but decides to marry her instead. This alteration of the classical plot, combined with abundant incestual themes, makes Jahnn's play a meditation on inappropriate desire. Furthermore, Jahnn transplants Medea's homeland from the Caucus Mountains to the continent of Africa. Sometimes played in blackface, Jahnn's Medea is described using racial slurs, as when Creon exclaims: "Laß dies dich trösten, niemals hätt ich eingewilligt, daß mein geliebtes Kind als Bettgenoss nem halben N[---] beigegeben würde" [let yourself be comforted by this, never would I agree to my beloved child being given as the bedfellow of a half-N---] (31; censorship mine). By sexualizing and racializing the Medea story, Jahnn adds new elements to the reception of Medea in the German-speaking world. In this play, Medea's efforts to be a good mother are explicitly complicated by her outsider status as a dark-skinned African woman. Inge Stephan writes that in the subtext of Jahnn's drama "'Afrikanisches,' 'Jüdisches' und 'Homoerotisches' in merkwürdiger Weise mischen" [the "African," "Jewish," and "homoerotic" mix in strange ways] (63). Combined discourses of marginalization are not a unique feature of Jahnn's Medea play, but rather a general trend in German-language Medea stories.

In the twentieth century, the trajectory of German Medea adaptations starts to expand in terms of content and of medium. Medea stories range from Anna Seghers's short story "Das Argonautenschiff" (The Ship of the Argonauts) (1948), to Helga M. Novak's poems, to Ula Stöckl's film *Der Schlaf der Vernunft* (The Sleep of Reason) (1984). As Medea expands beyond the stage, she symbolically extends her reach into a wider variety of political contexts. My primary interest in this book is the large number of German and Austrian women who chose to (re)write the Medea story, especially in the final few decades of the century. In her analysis of multi-media Medea stories, Stephan identifies a peak in female adapters of the Medea material around 1989 (5). In *Murderous Mothers*, I examine five Germanophone Medea stories from this same time frame: Ursula Haas's *Freispruch für Medea* (Acquittal for Medea) (1987), Christa Wolf's *Medea. Stimmen* (1996) (*Medea. A Modern Retelling*) (1998), Dagmar Nick's *Medea. Ein*

Monolog (Medea: A Monologue) (1988), Dea Loher's *Manhattan Medea* (1999), and Elfriede Jelinek's *Lust* (1989 [13th ed. 2012]). These texts generally fall into two categories—works that highlight Medea's violent actions in order to present her as a gender-defying figure of (im)possible feminist empowerment and works that dismiss Medea's violence, declaring her a feminine victim of malicious misinformation.

Authors such as Nick and Wolf refer to source texts other than Euripides (often Eumelos's fragmentary epic poem *Korinthiaka* from the eighth century BCE and Apollonius of Rhodes's *Argonautika* from the third century BCE) and present their readers with a sensitive and hyper-feminized Medea. In these texts, Medea is framed for the murder of her children and does not, in fact, enact the bloody revenge around which Euripides's play hinges. Significantly, a Medea who does not commit filicide also does not have the opportunity to triumphantly fly away from Corinth. In Wolf's text, for example, Messerschmidt and Peters argue that what is missing is "das Fluchtmoment der Transzendenz. Die Protagonistin bleibt an die Welt gefesselt" [the transcendental moment of escape. The protagonist stays chained to the world] (541). One question surrounding adaptations in which Medea is not a murderer is: what is at stake for feminist politics in light of a Medea figure who is literally and figuratively grounded?

Simultaneously, other authors, including the playwright Loher and the author and librettist Haas, stake out a different kind of feminist territory for Medea, one that does not rely on presenting her as a victim of scapegoating and misinformation, but instead depicts her as an androgynous, creative, and manipulative figure intent on violently exposing society's double standards and injustices. For instance, Loher's Medea performs acts of self-harm and murders her child on stage to draw attention to her traumatic past and to the guilt she shares with Jason. By comparing Medea figures from these two groups, I demonstrate how these vastly different feminist strategies for engaging with the Medea material work together toward critiquing and imagining alternatives to the repetitive and normalizing storytelling model of the myth. While definitely falling short of their progressive potential, especially in terms of ethnicity and race, German feminist Medea stories productively explore anxieties about changing notions of both gender and national identities.

Highlighted at the beginning of this introduction, another important Medea text during this time period is Heiner Müller's *Verkommenes Ufer Medeamaterial Landschaft mit Argonauten* (*Depoiled Shore Medea Material Landscape with Argonauts*). This theatrical work represents a postmodern shift in how Medea is represented in the German context. Müller engages in a critique of the violence of colonialism and the environmental destruction of modern technologies, locating his "despoiled shore" in Straußberg, East Germany, and describing how women are used as baby factories: "Kinder ausstoßend in Schüben gegen den Anmarsch der Würmer" (73) ["Ejecting babies in batches against the advance of maggots"] (Weber 127). In addition to this invocation of reproductive rights, Müller's text sets the stage for other discourses on Medea that will be taken up by the women writers highlighted in this book. For example, when Jason argues that he gave Medea two sons in exchange for her brother, Müller's Medea bemoans that "Alles an mir dein Werkzeug alles aus mir / Für dich hab ich getötet und geboren" (75) ["All of me is your tool and all things from me / For you I killed for you I did give birth" (Weber 129)]. Medea's regret after giving up her biological family for Jason underscores how this mythological story continues to be used to critique the institution of marriage in texts by other twentieth-century German writers. Eventually Müller's Medea wipes Jason from her memory, ending her monologue by asking "Amme Kennst du diesen Mann" (80) ["Nurse Do you know this man"] (Weber 133). Medea eliminates Jason from history and from her own memory in an act of defiance against his imperial and patriarchal dominion. In this way, Müller establishes a precedent for using the Medea story to engage with contemporaneous concerns surrounding gender politics.

Despite the effort made by Müller's Medea to dis-remember Jason, he is still a relevant figure in this mythological story, one whose position as a contrast to Medea sets up many of the discourses on gender, ethnic, or social difference that I will explore more in this book. Unsurprisingly then, the history of the Medea material in the twentieth and twenty-first centuries also contains numerous examples of texts and films that center Jason. The 1963 Anglo-American film *Jason and the Argonauts* is perhaps the best-known example, but in the German-speaking context one should also include texts such as Seghers's short story and most recently Christoph

Hein's novella *Das Goldene Vlies* (The Golden Fleece) (2005). Generally, adaptations that focus on Jason or the Golden Fleece marginalize Medea, or even exclude her entirely, presenting us only with independent, masculine heroes. As Stephan writes, Jason-centric stories usually present him as "jung, dynamisch, mutig, offen und edel von Gesinnung" [young, dynamic, brave, with an open and noble disposition] (114). Contrastingly, in stories with Medea at the center, Jason is often ignoble and unlikable. Especially in feminist Medea stories, Jason fails to measure up to the dramatic and exciting Medea. While Medea shows passion and nobility when she loses herself for the love of him, "Jason dagegen verliere neben aller Zuneigung seine Ziele, Macht, Herrschaft, Heldentum, nie aus den Augen" [Jason contrastingly, despite all affection, would never lose sight of his goals, power, authority and heroism] (Feichtinger 210). Even going all the way back to Euripides it is clear that, although readers may not always sympathize with Medea, they almost always are led to dislike Jason because of his arrogance and cold, brutish attitude.

In addition to highlighting Jason's selfishness and his role as a perpetrator of masculine violence, Hein's retelling of the origins of the Golden Fleece introduces readers to a related heroic protagonist, Phrixos. Instead of aggressive and masculine, Hein represents Phrixos as naïve and effeminate. Like Medea, Phrixos had to flee his homeland because of a threat to his life. Unlike the accurately accused Medea, Phrixos is unjustly accused of betraying his family ties. His aunt sleepwalks into his bedroom and attempts to have sex with the incredibly attractive young man, later claiming that Phrixos tried to rape her. The narrator insists that Phrixos "sich nicht zu verteidigen verstand" [did not understand how to defend himself] (23), thereby placing him in a position of innocence usually reserved for female characters. After his escape, Phrixos comes to live with two farmers panning for gold, for whom he will "als Frau dienen" [serve as a woman/wife] (35). He cooks and cleans for them and is raped by them before eventually running away to Colchis with the titular gold-bespeckled fleece. He presents this stolen tool used for panning for gold to the king (Medea's father) as a gift from Zeus, thereby falsely imbuing the object with even greater value than the flecks of gold trapped in the wool. The story ends with the narrator listing the people who have suffered or died because of this remarkably unremarkable object:

> fünf Halbgötter, einundzwanzig Giganten, zwölf Könige, sieben Königinnen, eintausendvierhundert Helden, siebenundzwanzig adlige Damen und fünf hochgeborene Säuglinge. Vergewaltigt wurden neunhundertsiebenundvierzig edle Frauen verschiedenen Alters, dreiunddreißig von ihnen verfielen in Wahnsinn… (59–60)
>
> [five half-gods, twenty-one giants, twelve kings, seven queens, one thousand four hundred heroes, twenty-seven noble ladies and five highborn infants. Nine hundred forty-seven noble women of various ages were raped, thirty-three of whom fell into madness…]

In the world of Hein's novella all passions, whether lustful or violent, are impossible to control. Cycles of violence continue without end and innocent victimhood knows no gender. The attention to sexual violence and emasculating deception of Phrixos in Hein's novella make it a clear addendum to the politically engaged Medea stories of the twentieth century.

Around the same time as Hein was crafting his origin story of the Golden Fleece, scholarly interest in Medea adaptations within the field of German Studies also peaked. During the first decade of the twenty-first century, several notable monographs on the Medea material were published including Christoph Steskal's *Medea und Jason in der deutschen Literatur des 20. Jahrhunderts* (Medea and Jason in German Literature of the 20th Century) (2001), Britta Schmierer's *Motivation in Medeatragödien der Antike und der Neuzeit* (Motivation in Medea Tragedies from Antiquity through the Modern Age) (2005), Inge Stephan's *Medea: Multimediale Karriere einer mythologischen Figur* (Medea: Multimedia Career of a Mythological Figure) (2006), and Yixu Lü's *Medea unter den Deutschen* (Medea among the Germans) (2009). Most of these works offer a trajectory of Medea stories, providing a catalog of adaptations and how they have changed over time. This group of scholarly works succeeds in giving us a broad overview of the development of Medea adaptations across the centuries, within multiple national contexts, and through a variety of media. While these approaches were incredibly useful for me at the beginning of this project, as I put together a corpus of Germanophone Medea stories and thought about the wide-ranging history of this myth, this methodology has the limitation of not allowing scholars much opportunity to perform close readings of these rich texts. By focusing on a smaller subset of material, I build on this previous scholarship, offering a level of specificity and contextualization not possible in the survey-like format of these previous monographs. Rather than providing an overview of numerous Medea stories, I draw connections between a specific subset of Medea texts and contemporaneous transatlantic feminist theories, ideologies, and political strategies.

It is also noteworthy that most of this scholarship on Medea reception in the German context comes from outside of the United States (Australia, Great Britain, and Germany), where there is often a greater integration and overlap between the field of *Germanistik* and what is known in North America as Classics or Classical Studies. Another goal of this book is to bridge the gap between these scholarly contexts and my own North American one. I am a millennial and a white, settler-scholar of German Studies in the United States. As such, I have a degree of distance in terms of time and space from this material, both the Medea stories themselves and the contemporaneous feminist theories I engage here. My work in this book approaches this material from a new perspective, namely one in which feminist studies and cultural studies (i.e., the connections between cultural products and social institutions) is the methodological background for my analysis. By connecting my close readings of these Medea stories to contemporaneous feminist theory, I engage in a detailed analysis of these texts on their own terms and within the intellectual context in which they were written.

With polarization and political divisions currently growing in both Europe and North America, I believe it is a productive time to revisit the Medea material because of what it teaches us about unassuageable rifts between people who are different from one another. No matter which Medea story you read, it is always clear that Medea and Jason are irreconcilably different. Whether this difference is ultimately attributed to gender, race, culture, class status, etc., depends on the adaptation. However, these two characters represent opposite ends of a binary and this divide intercedes in their union. Today we are faced with numerous differences and partisan divisions that seem impossible to overcome. In fact, if Medea stories are to be believed, overcoming them is not even a realistic goal. The question then becomes how we live within such a framework: How do we (re)act when the differences between us prove to be irreconcilable?

Medea as Murderous

The title of this book, *Murderous Mothers*, reflects a dual emphasis on representations of violence and of motherhood in the Medea story. These two focal points, and the often-contradictory combination thereof, serve as guiding forces for my analysis. In the remainder of this introduction, I will explicate the two parts of this title and how they each play a role in my readings of the Medea mythology.

Although filicide is often the primary focus of her story, this is far from the only instance of murder attributed to Medea. In different versions of her story Medea is responsible for killing her brother and throwing his body piece by piece into the sea, manipulating King Pelias's daughters into chopping him up, poisoning King Creon and his daughter, and killing her children. In 1992, writing just after a peak in German Medea stories by women, Feichtinger argues that Medea's acts of violence are futile describing how, "wiederholt tötet Medea für Jason, doch keine Tat begreift sie als das, was sie ist, einen sinnlosen Mord" [repeatedly Medea kills for Jason, but she does not recognize any deed for what it is, a senseless murder] (218). Feichtinger reads Medea's murderous behavior as something that, from a feminist perspective, needs to be overcome. According to Feichtinger, a feminist Medea recognizes that violence is not in her best interest because it only serves a patriarchal power structure. If Medea's violence is pointless, however, her story also loses some of its edge. While Feichtinger may be correct that Medea's violence sometimes appears ineffectual (as we will see in Haas, Nick, and Jelinek's Medea stories), I argue that in the larger context of feminist literature, Medea's murderous nature is not pointless and that it functions on a variety of levels.

Medea's act of filicide is sometimes explained as atonement for her past violence against her family, especially her brother. For instance, Seneca's Medea laments: "If only *he* [Jason] had a brother! He has a wife: let the sword be thrust into her. Is this sufficient for my wrongs?" (327; emphasis in original). Violence in *Medea* is cyclical. By killing Jason's family (even when that family is now her family as well), Medea hopes to avenge the old family she has already destroyed. As Stephan explains: "Es entsteht eine Spirale der Gewalt, die sich durch Blut fortzeugt und einen Gegensatz zur Sphäre der Familie bildet" [a spiral of violence develops, which is sired by blood and forms a contrast within the sphere of the family] (72). The cycles of domestic violence that form the foundation of the Medea story call into question straightforward understandings of marriage, family, and motherhood. A murderous Medea is a Medea who both dutifully affirms and simultaneously resists her role as wife and as mother. Jason and Medea are from different places, yet they come together through the act of stealing the Golden Fleece, only to see their uneven partnership splinter amidst cycles of violence. To a contemporary reader this deep skepticism around familial roles also calls the structure of the traditional nuclear family into question.

Medea becomes murderous when she acts with the intent to kill, but it is crucially important to recognize that her decision to murder her children often springs from the maternal feelings one might expect this act to negate. In Euripides's play, Medea reasons that her children will pay the ultimate price if she goes through with her plans to kill Creon and his daughter. Rather than see them suffer at the hands of someone else, she determines to kill them herself. Medea laments that "they must die in any case. And since they must, the one who gave them birth shall kill them" (Euripides 381). In Wolf's version of the story, Medea's children are indeed killed by an angry mob, thereby lending credence to this threat as a potential driving force for Medea's act of filicide (Wolf 223). Later, Euripides's Medea articulates her internal debate as follows: "I know well what pain I am about to undergo, but my wrath overbears my calculation, wrath that brings mortal men their gravest hurt" (383). Despite the pain to herself, Medea's murderous nature wins out. Jennifer Jones describes Medea's crimes as a "carefully reasoned response to an insane situation" (98). A murderous Medea presents audiences with a contrast between the logical and the emotional, allowing this mythological figure to ambiguously fluctuate between these two poles. According to Luschnig, the story of Medea demonstrates that "the worst evil is logical, carefully planned, and carried out methodically" (84). While I agree that Medea is most often portrayed as rational in her actions, I disagree with the idea that her deeds are meant to depict evil. In the German feminist texts I examine here, it matters not only whether or how Medea kills, but also why. The motivation for Medea's murderousness opens this figure up to numerous political interpretations that make her story a fruitful foundation for a wide variety of adaptations. A murderous Medea is a political Medea, a Medea whose actions are rooted in a network of systems of power that demands careful scrutiny.

Medea's murderousness also reveals itself in aesthetic concerns. Stephan articulates the potential consequences of an understanding of Medea's violence as atonement writing, "Damit verschmelzen die vier wichtigsten Männer—Geliebter, Bruder, Söhne—in Medeas Wahrnehmung tendenziell zu einer Figur" [with that the four most important men—lover, brother, sons—tend to fuse together into one figure in Medea's perception] (39). This interpretation of the connections between Medea's acts of violence also prompts aesthetic questions about narrative voice(s), who gets to speak, and how stories are told. When understood as a condensation of the many into one, Medea's murderous behavior becomes a universalizing gesture in which Medea reductively lumps all men into a single category. This accusation (often itself leveled against feminism) is true of these Medea stories to some degree. However, this context also generates space for authors to experiment with polyvocal narratives and for new models for feminist solidarity to emerge. Loher's *Manhattan Medea* is the primary work of theater that I analyze in this book, but all of these texts use theatrical aesthetic techniques, including Brechtian *Verfremdung* [alienation], monologue, and collaborative performance to generate a multiplicity of voices and perspectives. In feminist Medea stories, the oscillation between the many and the one plays out on the level of plot and on the level of form.

Medea's aggressive behavior also applies to gender roles. In an essay on Lars von Trier's film *Medea* (1988), Barbara Bollig connects the contradictions of the figure of Medea with feminist politics writing:

> Doch ist sie nicht die kalte, emotionslose Rächerin, auch nicht die affektierte Wahnsinnige, als die sie teils dargestellt wird; vielmehr ist sie Erduldene, Leidende und doch Entschlossene, Schöpferin von Leben und Zerfall gleichermaßen—und damit eine Frau, die auch die ihr oktroyierte bürgerliche Geschlechterkategorie aufbricht. (Bollig 132)
>
> [She is actually not the cold, emotionless avenger, not the affected lunatic, as she is sometimes portrayed. More often she is the patient, suffering, and yet decisive and simultaneous creator of life and collapse. And in so being, she is a woman who breaks out of the societal gender category that is forced on her.]

Medea is murderous in the actions that she undertakes on the page and the stage, as well as in her direct confrontation of binaries, especially the gender binary. Medea's murderousness goes far beyond her most notable act of filicide to encompass a wide range of destructive and deconstructionist practices. Medea's murderous deeds place her outside of our contemporary expectations for motherly love and affection, and Medea's act of filicide, likely itself the invention of Euripides, is often difficult to justify. This prompts some feminist Medea adaptations to deny Medea's responsibility for this murder entirely. Regardless of how many people Medea does or does not kill, she always attacks established beliefs and gender roles. All Medea stories must engage with the high-stakes question of what it means for a mother to kill her children, whether or not they give or absolve their Medea of culpability for this deed. Even when she does not explicitly kill, Medea is always murderous because the act of filicide haunts every adaptation. When retelling Medea stories, Bartel and Simon remind us that we are "in search of a discourse that can accommodate, without fracturing, acts that our own society and sensibilities may condemn" (11). The thin line that Medea walks, between generating change from within and blowing up the system, is a line with which all social justice movements, including feminism, must engage.

Medea as Mother

In a review of George Tabori's play *M. Nach Euripides* (M. According to Euripides) (1984) in the *Frankfurter Allgemeine Zeitung*, Georg Hensel writes that "Wer Medea den Mord nimmt, verkleinert sie: er macht aus einem Mythos eine Mama" [whoever takes murder away from Medea reduces her; he makes a mama out of a myth] (cited in Stephan 8). I argue instead that Medea always has been both murderous and a mother. As much as Medea is linked to destruction and violence, she is also known for her nurturing capacity as a mother, as a restorer of youth, and as an herbalist healer. Euripides's Jason criticizes Medea because in his eyes "sie ihr Frausein über ihre Mutterschaft stellt" [she places her womanhood above her motherhood] (Feichtinger 229). It is true that these two sides of Medea, the destructive and the (re)productive, initially seem at odds with one another, as when Messerschmidt and Peters argue that "in Medea zeigt sich das zerstörerische Potential der Frau, die die Zuschreibung des Mütterlichen, ihre ureigenste Rolle zurückweist" [In Medea, the destructive potential of [a] woman is shown, a potential that rejects the attribution of the maternal, her most distinct role] (526). However, Medea actually gives life almost as frequently as she takes it: she nurses her father back to health, she cultivates healing plants, she restores Jason's youth, and she gives birth to children. Motherhood is indeed Medea's most distinctive role, but not only through its negation in filicide.

Instead of denying motherhood, the Medea story reveals an unexpected, but no less crucial side to this social role. Stephan writes, "Als umstrittene Täterin und maßlos gedemütigtes Opfer erinnert sie an die dunklen, tabuisierten Seiten des Eros und der Mutterliebe" [as disputed perpetrator and excessively humiliated victim, she reminds us of the dark, taboo sides of Eros and motherly love] (1). Medea is no less, and in many adaptations surprisingly more, of a mother because of, not in spite of, her violence. Seneca's Medea attributes the strength required to perform her violent deeds to the increased stakes brought about by her motherhood saying, "My bitterness must grow more weighty: greater crimes become me now, after having given birth" (321). Medea tries, but she does not always succeed at being a protective mother and in doing so, she highlights motherhood as a condition that raises the stakes for how one cares for others. For instance, Seneca's Medea insists that motherhood increases one's capacity for a full spectrum of emotions, including both love and hate.

In previous scholarship, Medea's supposed failures as a mother have been tied to her androgyny or to her bitterness over no longer being viewed as a beautiful woman. For instance, Steskal writes that:

> Medea beklagt ihre Altershäßlichkeit zusätzlich als allgemeines Schicksal der Frau, die durch Schwanger- und Mutterschaft frühzeitig ihre Attraktivität verliere und damit schon rein äußerlich dem natürlichen Kreislauf von Werden und Vergehen unterworfen sei. (Steskal 129)
>
> [Medea additionally complains about the ugliness of her aging as a universal fate of women, who through pregnancy and motherhood prematurely lose their attractiveness and because of which they are, already in a purely exterior way, subjected to the natural cycle of growth and decay.]

Such argumentation removes blame for the situation from Jason, Creon, and the other men involved, suggesting that Medea actually suffers from unrealistic expectations about her vitality and feminine beauty, expectations which are directly thwarted when she has children. While it is true that when she restores Jason's youth it does little to help their romantic relationship, the feminist adaptations of the Medea story in this book suggest that Medea's actions cannot be reduced to so petty an explanation. Medea's magical powers ultimately come from her ability to control and to manipulate the same natural process of growth and decay that Steskal places outside of her grasp. Why would she resent a process that she repeatedly proves through her healing arts that she has mastered? Medea cures diseases, ends famines, and reverses infertility. Instead of feeling limited by natural processes, Medea as a murderous mother repeatedly takes hold of the cycles of both violence and reproduction, bending them to her will.

This is not to say that Medea is a perfectly self-actualized feminist heroine either. Medea's role as a mother is unique because of its often fatal consequences, but her role as a wife is where much of Medea's resentment and dissatisfaction actually lies. Stephan writes bitterly: "Als 'bedeutende Frau' könnte Medea eine feministische Ikone sein, ihre Liebe zu einem 'mittelmäßigen Mann' macht sie jedoch zu einer problematischen Bezugsfigur für den feministischen Diskurs um 1900" [As a "meaningful woman" Medea could be a feminist icon, but her love for a "mediocre man" actually makes her a problematic figure of reference in feminist discourses after 1900] (158). In many respects, it is Medea's marriage rather than her motherhood or her aging body that causes her the most grief. Even though she gives up her own family to demonstrate her love for Jason, he does not stand by her when it matters most. In feminist adaptations of the Medea material, the issue is not so much that Medea is a bad mother, but that she falls in love with an exploitative and abusive man who refuses to fulfill his obligation to her when she is demeaned and cast out of Corinth. A feminist Medea is always a mother, but often comes to regret or reject being a wife.

Medea as Outsider

Authors of Medea adaptations frequently try to justify Jason's betrayal of Medea by emphasizing her status as an outsider. First, Medea finds herself at odds with her father and her homeland, prompting her to run away with Jason. Despite her best efforts, she never fits into Jason's world either. In one of his final lines to Medea in Euripides's play, Jason slanders her based on her background saying, "No Greek woman would have dared to do this, yet I married you in preference to them" (405). Medea's differences are exotic and attractive up until the point at which they become difficult or inconvenient for him. No matter where she is, Medea is both exalted and reviled for simply being herself. She is so foreign, so strange, that she is almost unimaginable. Other characters equate Medea with danger long before she even considers killing her children. As Kevin J. Wetmore Jr. describes in his work on Black Medeas, there are a number of Greek words used to describe Medea's Otherness: she is "*xenon* (a stranger), *apolis* (without a city or home), *barbaroi* (a non-Greek speaking foreigner), and *agrioi* (a savage)" (3). Medea comes across to the people around her as strange and sometimes as less than human, a perception that makes it impossible for her to find a home.

Turning to Medea in late twentieth-century Germany also meant engaging with Germany's postwar identity crisis and even more significantly the political, economic, and social conditions surrounding German Reunification in 1990. Medea epitomizes the dangerous foreigner and therefore plays into what Susanne Zantop (also writing in the 1990s) called "colonial fantasies." Zantop defines the intellectual effects of colonialism on Germany as "the desire to venture forth, to conquer and appropriate foreign territories, and to (re)generate the self in the process formed in subtle and indirect ways" (2). Extending Zantop's argument, German Medea stories highlight an incomplete reckoning with Germany's colonial past and often promote an understanding of the absorption of East Germany into West Germany as a colonial takeover. Wolf's opposition to German Reunification is well known. Speaking about *Medea. Stimmen*, Lü writes that Wolf illustrates "*how* myths arise which divide societies into hostile factions by blurring the unpalatable truths of the past" ("Myth and Apologia" 17). In Germany this situation is made even more complex because some of those unpalatable truths are better known and more established in cultural and political discourses than others. For example, the Holocaust is ubiquitous in German discourse and media, whereas the genocide perpetrated by German colonizers against the Herero and Namaqua peoples in Africa is much less frequently referenced. The portrayal of the people of Colchis (Medea's homeland) and Corinth (Jason and Medea's new home) is crucial in terms of determining whether or not an adaptation of Medea upholds or disrupts the understanding (shared by Wolf, Günter Grass, and other notable intellectuals) of the *Wende* as a period of neocolonialism in which the West colonized the East.

In addition to these colonial narratives, Medea's status as a foreign threat is intertwined with her failure to fit in with the established gender roles of the Corinthian community. As Messerschmidt and Peters articulate,

> Da Medea bedrohlich ist mit ihrem Wissen und Selbstbewußtsein, muß sie als Fremde markiert werden. Sie muß die Andere sein, von der man sich distanzieren kann. Medea befindet sich in der Spannung zwischen dem, was sie ist, und dem, was andere aus ihr machen. (536)
>
> [Since Medea is threatening with her knowledge and self-confidence, she must be marked as a stranger. She must be the Other, from whom one can distance oneself.

> Medea finds herself in the tension between what she is and what others make out of her.]

Medea is a cipher for the distinction between how those with privilege view people who are different and how historically excluded people view themselves. As Feichtinger puts it, Medea stories demonstrate that "eine Gesellschaft, die einen Teil ihrer Mitglieder unterdrückt, mit bedingungslosen Haß zu rechnen hat" [a society that oppresses a group of its members must contend with unconditional hate] (234). Medea's inability to overcome discrimination often makes her angry, and her frustration becomes a productive means for talking about difference in general and about the violence that sometimes results when people are dehumanized and pushed to their limits.

Although this was not necessarily the intention behind labeling Medea as a barbarian in the ancient world, in the modern era the terminology used to malign her often invokes colonialist and imperialist tropes. This is one of the most prominent features of the Medea story as it is translated into more contemporary settings. In an effort to make Medea's Otherness legible to white Western audiences, the Medea mythology frequently becomes a colonial story. As I mentioned when discussing Jahnn's play, Medea's homeland of Colchis, which lies in the Caucus Mountains, is sometimes problematically and inaccurately depicted as African. This geographical displacement serves as a tool used by authors to explain why she is so marginalized. In my book, I highlight how this use of colonial rhetoric plays out specifically in the context of feminist movements in the German-speaking world. Authors such as Ursula Haas, end up limiting the progressive politics of their own feminist Medea projects when they continue to rely on racialized understandings of Medea's Otherness and then employ colonial rhetoric of the civilized versus the uncivilized to describe the differences between Corinth and Colchis. As Sabine Wilke articulates, in the German context "Medea ist nur denkbar als Konstrukt des orientalistischen Diskurses" [Medea is only conceivable as a construct of orientalist discourse] (Wilke 17).

As an outsider, Medea is further punished for her failure to assimilate. Rarely does Medea even try to fit into Corinthian culture, and when she does, she is quick to give up. For instance, in Grillparzer's *Medea*, she tries to learn Jason's favorite Corinthian song, but fails to produce a single note (Act 2). Even when the consequences are more dire, Medea has no choice but to be herself. She must create her own sense of self and her own morality within a system that was designed to exclude her. In the German context, framing Medea as a figure who fails to assimilate also connects her to Judaism and to the Holocaust. In her 1930–1931 story *Die jüdische Mutter* (The Jewish Mother), Gertrud Kolmar highlights the isolation felt by Jewish women in an antisemitic and patriarchal world. An accusation of Medea-ness is placed into the mouth of the titular character's romantic partner when he describes to his parents how, "sie ist imstande und tötet das Kind; das ist eine Medea!" [she is capable of killing the child, she is a Medea!] (Kolmar 22). Stephan argues that in this context Medea serves as a model for the failure of Jewish assimilation (174). In Kolmar's loose Medea adaptation, the Jewish mother is too foreign and cannot ever be "German." Other examples of Jewish Medea figures include Max Zweig's *Medea in Prag* (Medea in Prague) (1949) and Bertolt Brecht's Holocaust poem "Die Medea von Lodz" (The Medea of Lodz). Each of these examples draws attention to the false dichotomy between German and Jewish identities that continues to contribute to anti-semitism and xenophobia in Germany. Whether Medea is portrayed as African, Jewish, or Eastern European, she always distinguishes herself from the normalized, unmarked, Western European whiteness that wants to exclude her.

The final point I want to mention about Medea's outsider status is its connection to her mythologization. Medea is originally the creation of a Western, androcentric literary canon. Although her ambiguity leaves open the possibility that she might be used to deconstruct and to critique that same canon, she is still, to paraphrase Audre Lorde's 1979 essay, one of the master's tools and therefore cannot fully dismantle the proverbial master's house (41). Medea will always be a character that comes out of a Western male imaginary. In her 1979 scholarly investigation of literary femininity, German feminist Silvia Bovenschen, speaking about Frank Wedekind's Pandora figure (Lulu), articulates the problem as follows: "so wird Lulu einerseits zum Mythos dessen, was die männlichen Figuren in ihr sehen, andererseits ist sie konstruiert als eine Gestalt, die diese Bilder immer wieder zerstört" [in this way, Lulu on one level becomes a myth of what the male figures see in her. On the other hand, she is constructed as a figure that always repeatedly destroys these images] (48). Medea is forced into the position of an outsider within her diegetic world. However, the authors who adapt her story can also use her as a challenge to the very racist and androcentric discourses that become limiting for her within the plot. Adapting the Medea material with an eye toward feminist politics involves walking a thin line between representing Medea's oppression, while also depicting her as a challenge to hegemonic discourses and literary structures. Medea's mythological status lends her weight and credibility within the Western intellectual and literary canon, but her contradictions also push back against notions that any story can ever lead to one reified meaning or interpretation.

Chapter Summaries

At the end of her book, Bovenschen writes, "Die Geschichte der weiblichen Geschichtslosigkeit ernst zu nehmen, darf nicht heißen, sich dem Gegenstand in der Weise zu assimilieren, daß die Analyse selbst ahistorisch wird" [to take the history of feminine history-less-ness seriously, should not mean to assimilate the subject in such a way that the analysis itself is ahistorical] (265). This crucial articulation of feminist methodology is something that I adopt in this book, in which I pair Germanophone adaptations of the Medea story with contemporaneous feminist theory and politics. The context in which these Medea stories were written matters, not just in the sense of historical context, but also in the sense of intellectual and political context. My aim is to be mindful of the discourses that surrounded these texts when they were written, while also showing the continued relevance of these late twentieth-century feminist debates. Subtly is generally not a hallmark of the Medea story, hence its popularity in melodramatic theater and in numerous visually striking films. The title of this book, *Murderous Mothers*, embraces the provocative qualities of this mythology, while the content adds nuance and contextualization to previous characterizations of Germanophone Medea stories. My narrative of these Medea figures unfolds mostly chronologically from the 1980s to the year 2000. This allows me to establish the developing concerns represented in these texts from before and then after German Reunification. However, in the final chapter, I return to the late 1980s to look at a less explicit adaptation of the Medea story by Elfriede Jelinek. This serves as an example of how the developing literary landscape around Medea influenced contemporaneous Germanophone feminist literature more broadly. Even without explicitly engaging the Medea story, I argue that Jelinek's understandings of gender relations are shaped by many of the discourses that are central to the literary history of this myth.

To lay the groundwork for my eventual reading of Jelinek's *Lust* as a Medea story, I begin with one of the most explicitly feminist Medea stories written in German. In my first chapter, "Medea as Witch and Colonial Subject: Provocative Female Bodies in *Freispruch für Medea*," I delve into Ursula Haas's relatively unknown Medea story from 1987. Haas's Medea provides a foundation for several key concepts that link the Medea mythology with feminist movements in the German context, including reproductive rights, bodily autonomy, and the erasure of colonial history. Haas's emphasis on Medea's body, her feminine, seductive body, as well as her colonial body, highlights both the political potentials and the blind spots of the West German New Women's Movement. In her most significant departure from the classical Medea plot, Haas changes Medea's child-negating act from a filicide to an abortion, directly commenting on contemporaneous feminist political debates over the medicalization of reproductive healthcare. This emphasis on Medea's subversive corporeality also extends to Haas's characterization of her as both a witch and a colonial subject. When Medea uses her body to give as well as to take life, Haas emphasizes Medea's multi-valent and dangerously witchy corporeality. However, Haas undercuts her own message about female bodily autonomy by also relying on colonial stereotypes when depicting Medea's outsider status, thereby precluding possibilities for solidarity between groups of women.

The question of solidarity between women takes on a dimension of generational and political conflict in my second chapter "Can Medea Speak? Voice and Victimhood in Medea Stories by Dagmar Nick and Christa Wolf." In this section I examine stories in which Medea is not a murderer, but rather a victim of misinformation. In order to consider the interplay between voice, silencing, and victimization, I analyze Dagmar Nick's *Medea, ein Monolog* (Medea, a Monologue) (1988) and Christa Wolf's *Medea. Stimmen* (1996) (*Medea: A Modern Retelling*) (1998) alongside contemporaneous feminist and postcolonial theoretical texts by Gayatri Chakravorty Spivak (1988) and Luce Irigaray (1981; 1991). These four works interrogate the process of trying to capture the voices of people who have been marginalized. Read together, they paint a pessimistic picture about the ability of such voices to become comprehensible and the ability of such people to act and to speak as individuals. This understanding of victimhood as a gendered inheritance also ties into feminist concerns about the process of mythologization as enacted through repeated storytelling by universalized (white and male) subjects. This paradox is one that Wolf and Nick are only partially able to overcome. Wolf in particular hopes that these limitations can be transcended through the work of the female author, but ultimately Wolf detracts from her goal of freeing the voice of marginalized women by failing to create a truly polyvocal text. By depicting a Medea who is not violent, Wolf and Nick create a Medea who may speak, but who cannot be heard and, therefore, is fated to remain a victim of masculine power.

Questions of victimhood become even more intertwined with questions of identity in the third chapter of this book, titled "Performance and Gender Performativity in Dea Loher's *Manhattan Medea*." In her play from 1999, Loher increases the stakes for our understanding of feminist storytelling by putting the concepts of performance and of mythological adaptation themselves under the microscope. Loher's Medea lives up to the title of this book, and then some, as she engages in acts of performative self-harm and of dramatic violence in a play that ends with several people dead and a house in flames. Loher sets her Medea story in 1990s New York City, also issuing a critique of capitalist exploitation through the replacement of King Creon with the Sweatshop Boss. Loher's unique cast of characters also includes Velasquez, an artist who only makes copies, and Deaf Daisy, a gender-bending character with psychosomatic hearing loss. These unique characters push readers of this play to rethink how identity is constructed over time and through interactions with other people. With these themes in mind, I would be remiss if I did not to combine my reading of Loher's play with Judith Butler's contemporaneous work of the 1990s and 2000s on gender performativity. Butler and Loher explicate how grief, loss, guilt, and shame shared with an audience can generate collaborative performances both within and outside of gendered categories.

These connections between feminist political debates, language, storytelling, and Medea all come together in my final chapter, "A Forcible Return to the Womb: Elfriede Jelinek's Melodramatic Medea." Although Jelinek's controversial novel *Lust* (1989) does not engage as explicitly with the Medea mythology, I argue that it is a model for the broader implications of Medea figures in German-speaking contexts and of their interventions into feminist political debates. Jelinek's depiction of sexual violence mirrors the domestic conflict that serves as the backbone for the Medea story, while also connecting Medea's internal conflict to melodramatic tropes of the self-sacrificing mother. Most often read as a work of anti-pornography, I demonstrate how reading this novel as a melodramatic Medea story opens up interpretive possibilities that help explain the novel's final scene of filicide. Jelinek draws on numerous aspects of the Medea story in her characterization of the, often exploitative, relationship between men and women. In doing so, she pessimistically underscores the difficulty of escaping social constraints to imagine something different for ourselves and for our children. By crafting a melodramatic Medea story with a shifting narrative perspective, Jelinek encourages her readers to pause for self-reflection and to recognize their own complicity in systems of systemic oppression. Jelinek's Medea adaptation pushes us to see the violent extremes of the world as it is, ideally prompting us to work for change, however impossible the situation might seem. The legacy of feminist Medeas in the late twentieth-century German-speaking world underscores still unresolved tensions surrounding subjectivity, narrative, and intersectionality within the fight for gender equity.

Note on Names and Translation

Finally, I want to briefly draw attention to the various names and spellings of names that readers will encounter in this book. I do my best to align character names with how they appear in the primary text I am analyzing and/or the language in which I am writing. For added clarity I want to list some of these alternate names and spellings here. Medea (Μήδεια) is spelled the same in both English and German. However, Medea's husband is referred to as Jason or Iason and the woman he marries after Medea is alternately Glauce/Glauke (Γλαυκή), Creusa/Kreusa (Κρέουσα), or in Loher's more contemporary milieu, Claire. When code-switching between English and German Corinth (the destination of Jason and Medea's escape), Colchis (Medea's homeland) and King Creon (the ruler of Corinth) become Korinth, Kolchis, and Kreon respectively.

I also want to note that all translations of non-English texts are mine unless they are explicitly cited in translation. For example, in the second chapter, I draw on published translations of the works of Irigaray and Christa Wolf's *Medea. Stimmen*, while crafting my own translations of Dagmar Nick's *Medea. Ein Monolog*. I am extremely pleased that this material will be accessible to more people because of this translation work, both mine and others'. I hope that my translations manifest love and care rather than destruction with regard to the original language of these texts. Yet, as Medea demonstrates, love and destruction are often two sides of the same coin.

CHAPTER 1

Medea as Witch and Colonial Subject: Provocative Female Bodies in *Freispruch für Medea*

> Sie baten dringlichst um die Fruchtbarkeit der Felder und ihres eigenen Schoßes und hoben dabei Ährenbündel und Nachbildungen weiblicher Geschlechtsteile in die Luft.
>
> —Haas 114
>
> [They prayed most urgently for the fertility of the fields and their own womb and at the same time lifted bundles of wheat and replicas of female genitalia into the air.]

In this scene, the sorceress Medea leads a procession of naked women to Demeter's temple. Their goal is to end the famine that ravages Corinth. The narrator equates the fertility of the earth with the fertility of the womb and the women put their bodies on display in their attempt to end the crisis. This depiction of Medea as a provocative activist, unafraid to boldly use her body as a means to an end, is central to Ursula Haas's novel *Freispruch für Medea* (Acquittal for Medea).

Ursula Haas is a German feminist author, poet, and librettist. In 1987, Haas began a decades-long fascination with the Medea mythology. *Freispruch für Medea* marks the beginning of a series of Medea projects by Haas, which would span into the twenty-first century. The best known of these understudied adaptations are actually a series of operatic pieces with librettos by Haas and music by Rolf Liebermann. However, in this chapter my primary focus is the novel, Haas's original foray into the Medea material, because it represents a benchmark moment for the entanglement of German Medea adaptations and feminism. *Freispruch für Medea* is the earliest adaptation that I examine, and it also contains the most explicit and direct engagement with contemporaneous feminist politics. Haas extends the plot of her Medea story to include periods both before and after Medea's time in Corinth. She adds extensive descriptions of Medea's childhood in Colchis, the invasion of Medea's homeland by the Argonauts, Medea's escape to Athens after her revenge, and her eventual return to Colchis after also being exiled from the court of Aigeus (sometimes spelled Aegeus). This additional contextualization humanizes Medea and provides readers with more backstory through which to evaluate and understand Medea's actions.

Haas's Medea is quite murderous, contributing to the deaths of her brother and Jason's uncle, King Pelias. However, Haas also transforms Medea's filicide into an abortion, thereby explicitly invoking a major concern of the (then West German) New Women's Movement. A Medea who has an abortion engages directly in feminist political debates and emphasizes the corporeality of the pregnant body. I argue that this provocative physicality lies at the center of Haas's feminist critique. Haas creates a spectacle through explicit descriptions of female bodies in an effort to make a case for the empowerment of women. While this emphasis on physicality allows Haas to persuasively advocate for reproductive rights and bodily autonomy, her emphasis on corporeal spectacle also leads her to problematically reproduce feminine and colonial stereotypes, which detract from her calls for social equity.

In this chapter I use the terms "the female body" and "women's bodies." While the bodies of people who identify as women vary greatly, what constitutes a "female body" in Haas's novel is actually fairly narrow. Invoking feminist theoretical discourses that relate women and (bodily) fluids, female bodies in *Freispruch für Medea* are bodies that menstruate, bodies that have wombs, and bodies with the potential to bear children. While it is true that not all menstruating or pregnant bodies belong to people who identify as women and that not all women menstruate or give birth, in this chapter I use this terminology as it is used in the novel itself. The biological essentialism of this understanding of womanhood reads today as a failure to distinguish between gender and sex. Yet, such an understanding is taken for granted in Haas's novel and plays a central role in the articulation of her political goals. Nonetheless, much of Haas's overall argument could be adapted for all bodies that are culturally read as female, and it is productive to examine how Haas constructs her argument for feminist liberation through this specific understanding of the female body. This is especially true because Haas's emphasis on Medea's body contrasts with some of the German authors who follow her into the Medea mythology, including Dagmar Nick and Christa Wolf. As I will show in this and the following chapter, all three of these authors seek to humanize Medea by emphasizing her femininity and by giving their readers more background about Medea's life and decision-making. Rereading *Freispruch für Medea* today helps us better understand both the celebratory and the revolutionary, as well as the problematically limited nature of late twentieth-century German feminist discourses on the body.

In her journalistic book on female power, Sady Doyle writes that the ability to give birth imbues the female body with strength because this is "something only certain people can do, which is necessary to our collective survival" (118). Haas strives to articulate and to celebrate this kind of necessity through the women in her novel, especially Medea. Female bodies have power over life and death and in *Freispruch für Medea* the women who inhabit them express themselves through their bodies: dancing, having sex, excreting fluids, and yes, even eventually giving birth. These bodies are dangerous because they cannot fully be controlled, and yet they also prove extremely useful when they are instrumentalized by men. In Haas's novel, Medea helps Jason acquire the Golden Fleece, she avenges him against King Pelias, she ends the famine in Corinth, and she restores his youth. Many Medea stories leave out some of these opportunities for Medea to provide Jason direct assistance, but Haas's retelling includes them all. Her Medea does not miss out on any chance to use magic, channeled through her seductive body and her shrewd mind, to serve her husband's interests. Jason is both glad and wary of the fact that his wife is such a large contributor to his success. In the words of Seneca's Jason, he believes that he is ultimately justified in betraying his wife because "no gratitude is due for a life one is ashamed of receiving" (361). Jason's ego and inability to gratefully accept Medea's help is one of the main factors that drives the couple apart.

Furthermore, Haas represents the power of female bodies as natural and intrinsic, whereas male power derives from civic attachments that men build with others. For instance, female power extends to the feminine "bodies" of flowers. Plants, particularly the flowers of Colchis, Medea's native land, are the source of her magic, and she is initially uninterested in anything else: "wofür sie sich begeisterte, das waren das Einsetzen, Ziehen und Beobachten von Pflanzen und Kräutern" [that which made her excited was the planting, growing, and observation of plants and herbs] (17). All bodies described as feminine, whether human or plant, are threatening because of their ability to counteract the logical or predicted course of civic life. Such bodies are witch-like in their ability to create life, youth, or death where there was none before. That being said, this threat is also reduced by Haas's reliance on stereotypical rhetoric. Astrid Messerschmidt and Eva Peters argue that in *Freispruch für Medea*, Medea and Jason are set up as opposites in that, "Medea wird mit der Natur und dem Unbewußten, ihr männliches Gegenüber, Jason, mit Kultur und dem Bewußten gleichgesetzt" [Medea is equated with nature and the unconscious, while her male counterpart, Jason, is equated with culture and the conscious] (529). The equation of women with nature and of men with culture draws on both gendered and colonial stereotypes, thereby making it infertile ground for planting the seeds of true feminist empowerment.

In Haas's formulation of this story, Medea's mistake is ultimately using her corporeal power to help Jason, rather than in the service of her own goals and interests. Believing that love means completely overlapping her desires with his, Haas's Medea fails over and over again to find a home, a family, or a culture where she is valued for the power that she brings to the table through her body. She is and will always be an outsider and a foreigner, held back from the empowerment that she could seek, if only she would stop letting Jason pull the strings. Haas's Medea teaches readers that the concept of love is one of the things that keeps female bodies in line. As Lauren Berlant famously begins their influential monograph on *The Female Complaint*, "Everyone knows what the female complaint is: women live for love and love is the gift that keeps on taking" (1). As Creusa experiences firsthand, Medea knows all about "gifts" that take life, rather than adding to it. Without Medea's (fairly inexplicable) attachment to Jason, there is no telling what she might be capable of.

This gendered power dynamic is further complicated by the fact that Medea's body is not just a female body, but also a colonial body. Medea is consistently ostracized as foreign, and Haas embraces colonial rhetoric in her descriptions of Medea. For example, the narrator repeatedly refers to Medea as a "schwarzen Barbarin" [Black Barbarian] (Haas 68). In 1986, one year before Haas published this novel, Katharina Oguntoye, May Ayim (a.k.a. Opitz), and Dagmar Schultz released the volume *Farbe bekennen: Afro-deutsche Frauen auf den Spuren ihrer Geschichte* (*Showing Our Colors: Afro-German Women Speak Out*). This crucial and corrective text chronicles the history of Black Germans and documents contemporary anti-Black racism through interviews, essays, and poems. When describing the effects of German colonialism May Ayim, one of the coeditors and authors, writes, "auf vielfältige Weise wird das Bewußtsein von der weißen Hautfarbe als der besseren Hautfarbe und dem europäischen (=weißen) Bewußtsein als dem fortschrittlichen Denken vermittelt" [in many different ways, consciousness of the white skin color as the best skin color and the European (=white) consciousness as the most advanced thinking was conveyed] (43). The color of Medea's skin is not visible through words on the page and in German the term "black" was sometimes used to refer to a woman who simply has dark hair or eyes. However, the intended skin tone of Haas's Medea is far less important than the fact that the white European consciousness referenced by Ayim is clearly at work in this novel through the uncritical depiction of Medea as an exoticized colonial subject. In her history of the political organizing of Black German women, Tiffany N. Florvil describes how for activists during this time the category of Blackness was not exclusively used to refer to skin color: "For them, Blackness was not strictly tied to phenotype. It was a claim and a politically mobilizing strategy that united all marginalized minority communities in the nation" (135). Haas's Medea is then Black at the very least through her marginalized status in Corinth, if not also through her appearance.

Unfortunately, Haas, as a white German author, does not live up to the solidarity across difference that characterized the activism of Black German women during this time. By uncritically adopting colonial language in her descriptions of Medea, Haas normalizes white supremacy and reveals that there is a lack of solidarity between white German feminists and their Black German counterparts. Florvil describes how white Germans had "colonial amnesia" (131) and failed to recognize the "colonial afterlives" (94) still present within German culture. Florvil goes on to suggest that, "If the white German woman could put aside her preoccupation and fascination with people on the African continent and acknowledge her Afro-German compatriots, then perhaps a meaningful relationship could develop" (95). When Haas exoticizes Medea, she becomes one such white woman. This missed opportunity for mutual support between groups of women is especially striking in the context of a novel in which so many of the protagonist's struggles result from coupling herself to an undeserving male partner.

In *Freispruch für Medea*, female bodies have some power, but Haas is quick to instruct us that this does not mean they are empowered, that is, that individual female characters have the ability to make choices about their lives and to exercise full control over their spheres of influence. Haas wants her readers to understand women as having special, and in the case of Medea, magical abilities that mark them both as essential and as threats to the men exercising political power over them. In this regard, Haas's provocative depiction of women is similar to traditional depictions of witches as both dangerous and alluring. An exploration of how Haas eroticizes Medea is incomplete without also considering how she employs colonial rhetoric in ways that detract from her emancipatory goals. Through her Medea story, Haas outlines the stakes of debates surrounding bodily autonomy and reproductive rights within the West German New Women's Movement. Haas expresses a strong desire to carve out space and agency for female bodies, while contradictorily relying on colonial language that excludes Women of Color from this emancipatory potential.

Didacticizing the Medea Story

Using a strategy that will be repeated in other feminist Medea adaptations, Haas plays with the idea of Medea as an actual historical woman. This effort to didacticize Medea's fictional story begins with the paratext of Haas's novel. The inside cover of *Freispruch für Medea* features a map of Medea's journey away from and back to Colchis. The back cover depicts Medea's family tree and the final pages of the book include an explanation of the terms and names used throughout the novel. These paratextual materials would normally signal a non-fictional text, or perhaps a Sci-Fi text in which the author creates an alternate world. In either case, these elements lend such works an air of historicity. Although the story of Medea takes place in the ancient world, it is still (usually) located within a recognizable earthly geography. And yet, this story is a novel, by definition a work of fiction. Nevertheless, Haas and her editors make a concerted effort to blur the line between fiction and non-fiction in their presentation of Medea. They present themselves as having the authority to retell this story in a way that is more *accurate* than all of the adaptations that have come before.

Although Haas locates her novel in the ancient world, she uses the story of Medea as a vehicle for confronting the limitations placed on women in her contemporary setting. In the foreword to her novel, Haas describes a process of self-discovery through her engagement with the Medea story and a desire (not dissimilar from the desire that Christa Wolf will eventually articulate) to redeem this figure, whose reputation was supposedly tainted by Euripides. Haas describes how "der Kindsmord der Medea entsprang der Phantasie des Dichters Euripedes, den die Korinther in diesem Sinne bestochen haben sollen" [Medea's infanticide sprung from the fantasy of the poet Euripides, who supposedly was bribed by Corinthians in this way] (11). Deliberate filicide is absent from the Medea and Argonaut stories of both Eumelos of Corinth (eighth century BCE) and Apollonius of Rhodes (third century BCE) so, even in ancient Greece, this aspect of the story was far from fixed. Haas describes Euripides's decision to make Medea a child-murderess as one that is imbued with self-interest. He shamelessly panders to the Corinthians, the parties who in other adaptations are actually responsible for this violence, at the expense of this innocent woman. By blurring the boundary between fact and fiction in an effort to save the *real* Medea from Euripides's misinformation campaign, Haas's work initiates a series of Medea stories in the German context, all of which seek to redeem the protagonist from slanderous lies. The two most prominent examples being Dagmar Nick's *Medea, Ein Monolog* (Medea: A Monologue) (1988) and Christa Wolf's *Medea. Stimmen* (*Medea: A Modern Retelling*) (1996, 1998), which I will discuss in the next chapter.

Salvaging Medea's reputation by turning her filicide into a more relatable abortion is supposed to teach us something about the role of women in Haas's contemporary world. Haas describes how discovering Euripides's alteration of the story freed her from feeling forced to reckon with the moral issues surrounding Medea's filicide. Instead, Haas "versuchte ihn vielmehr aus dem Charakter der Medea und der Sicht einer heutigen Frau begreifbar darzustellen" [tried to present it [Medea's filicide] through Medea's character in order to make it understandable from a contemporary woman's perspective] (11). Haas goes on to say that Medea is "bis heute parabelhaft für eine mögliche weibliche Struktur" [still today parable-like for a possible structure of femininity] (12). The story of Medea, as retold by Haas, should provide us with an understanding of what it means to be a woman in an androcentric world. Why does Medea specifically suit this purpose so well? Haas answers this question by focusing on Medea's contradictions as the character's primary didactic and sympathy-inducing feature. Medea contains "Menschliches und Unmenschliches, Kraft und Zerstörung, Lieb und Haß" [human and inhuman, strength and destruction, love and hate] (Haas 12). She is a modern woman, struggling to contain her multitudes in a world that cannot handle her complexity.

Although *Freispruch für Medea* is not a theatrical work, Haas draws on techniques of the Brechtian theater in order to further instruct her audience about contemporary gender roles and reproductive politics. Messerschmidt and Peters describe Haas's (and later Wolf's) efforts to make Medea more realistic and contemporary as a *Verfremdungseffekt* [alienation effect] that "zerstört die Illusion der bloßen Nachahmung des antiken Kontextes" [destroys the illusion of a mere imitation of the ancient context] (531). Defamiliarizing the familiar myth of Medea serves Haas's desire to create a Medea who is a comprehensible and sympathetic representation of contemporary womanhood. Aesthetically, both Haas and Bertolt Brecht share an interest in making things that we think we know appear foreign to us in the service of didactic goals. Setting her Medea story in the ancient world while changing the narrative so that Medea has an abortion is just one example of how Haas works to alienate her readers from what they think they already know about Medea.

Haas also takes more specific techniques from Brecht and adapts them to her own context and purpose. For example, one technique of the Brechtian theater was to introduce the highlights of the plot through scene titles or so-called epic banners before viewers had the opportunity to see the events in question acted out on stage. The goal behind this staging technique was to allow the audience to focus on the (political) messages being communicated, rather than any emotion-inducing plot twists. In other words, if you know what will happen in advance, you can concentrate instead on why it is happening. The audience can focus on the social conditions and structural inequities underpinning the actions depicted on stage. Haas employs a similar technique in *Freispruch für Medea* when she provides short descriptions of the action to come, both throughout the text itself and within the table of contents (itself a somewhat didactic paratextual element). Attentive readers will already know before they read what is going to happen in terms of the plot, and so the details of exactly how the described events take place are what they experience through the process of reading the full novel.

Haas uses these epic banners to, as David Barnett also notes of Brecht, emphasize "the process, rather than the outcome" (73). Some of Haas's plot descriptions are rather matter of fact, for example, "wie Medeas Halbbruder Apsyrtos getötet wird" [how Medea's half-brother Apsyrtos is killed] (70). The death of Medea's brother is not as important as the role that Medea plays in his death. The passive voice in the chapter introduction preserves the mystery of Medea's exact role in the murder until we read the scene and discover that it is actually Jason who deals Apsyrtos this fatal blow, thereby protecting the couple's escape from Colchis with the Golden Fleece. The death of Medea's brother is fairly insignificant in and of itself and, as in most Medea stories, we are only introduced to the brother at the time of his death. What matters is the aftermath and the guilt that Medea feels, or at times does not feel, for contributing to his demise. The reader must decide whether they continue to sympathize with Medea or not, as she expresses simultaneous grief and relief. This contradiction is apparent when the narrator describes how "Medea war ganz umklammert vom Schmerz. Schuld spürte sie nicht; vielmehr Verwirrung und Staunen, daß sie es hatte tun müssen" [Medea was clutched by pain. She felt no guilt; but more so confusion and astonishment that she had had to do it] (Haas 71–72). The why and how of Apsyrtos's murder is far more interesting and complex than the act itself. Knowing in advance that Apsyrtos will die gives readers ample opportunity to wonder about Medea's reaction and to critically examine her complicated mix of emotions after his death.

By summarizing the plot before it happens, Haas instructively guides her reader toward the important gaps in knowledge for which they should be reading. She alerts us to moments of ambiguity, thereby drawing our attention to how these tensions are or are not resolved in the novel and, by extension, in contemporary life. One of the most controversial and opaque lines from these chapter introductions surrounds the death of Medea's unborn child. In a highly euphemistic description, Haas characterizes Medea's impending abortion as "wie Medea sich gegen das Kind entscheidet" [how Medea decides against the child] (140). While I will return to the details of this scene and its broader implications later in this chapter, for the purpose of further examining the role of these plot summaries, I want to highlight how this language emphasizes Medea as an agent, capable of making decisions about her life, body, and pregnancy. Whatever exactly happens with the fetus inside of her, the chapter introduction describes Medea as in control of this process, making decisions that affect the outcome. Particularly in the context of the United States of America, using language of *choice* to talk about political positions that favor the loosening of abortion restrictions has become a common rhetorical device. It is likely intentional that Haas employs similar language here. When she presents the abortion as a decision, Haas implies that Medea has a choice, and by extension encourages her readers to demand that same ownership over their own bodies. When explicating the emotional work performed by words, Judith Butler talks about the censorship of the word "abortion" itself because "the utterance is understood not merely to offend a set of sensibilities, but to constitute an injury, as if the word performed the act, and the injured party were the defenseless 'unborn'" (*Excitable Speech* 21). Haas deliberately never mentions the word "abortion" in her novel, instead giving preference to the language of decision. Attempting to distance herself from the potentially injurious language of abortion, Medea decides against the child, rather than for an abortion. However, this language still centers around what happens to the fetus, and thereby gives in to the injurious nature of the word "abortion" as defined by Butler. In this initial plot summary, Haas tries to focus solely on Medea's decision-making power. Haas desperately wants her readers to understand and believe that if Medea has enough control to decide against having a child, then by extension, so do they. However, from the standpoint of feminist rhetoric on abortion, Haas's success in reclaiming Medea's pregnant body is incomplete because Haas's language ultimately fails to pull focus away from the fetal body and toward the pregnant body.

In spite of Haas's articulation of her redemptive project in the foreword, Medea is not so easily redeemed, even putting aside the question of her filicide. Haas's Medea is ultimately more of a cautionary tale than a role model for her contemporary audience. Though not a child-murderess, Medea's violent actions in *Freispruch für Medea* make her far from innocent. She is still murderous, playing a role in the deaths of at least three people. Much like the contradictions inherent in the character herself, Haas cannot always maintain consistency in her depiction of Medea. The figure continuously elides any of the straightforward political aims for which Haas tries to employ her and in this regard, she is more human and realistic than many of the Medeas before her. Despite Haas's best efforts, Medea escapes the labels of both victim and perpetrator, landing somewhere else instead. Haas sees this as a part of her educational project, but the contradictions inherent in her Medea character make it unclear exactly how we are supposed to read this Medea in terms of her potential to educate contemporary readers. Is she a model for how women are or an aspirational figure depicting how they should be? In my reading of the text, the answer is both.

A Witch's Body

> Three nights must pass before the moon's horns close
>
> into a circle; now when it is complete,
>
> and in its fullness gazes down on earth,

> she sets out walking barefoot from her house,
> with garments loosened and with unbound hair
> cascading down her back [...] (Ovid 230–231)

The figure that best captures the ambiguity of the female body depicted in *Freispruch für Medea* is the witch. The above passage, which reads like a more contemporary depiction of witchcraft, is from Ovid's *Metamorphoses* (around 8 CE). Medea prepares to perform a spell for restoring youth, and in so doing her vibrant body is emphasized. Medea glows in the light of the moon, also a reference to Hecate, the goddess of witchcraft, who shares an intimate, if not familial relation to Medea. In her own version of this myth, Anna Seghers has Jason articulate the transformative power of Medea's magical development saying, "aus der kindlichen, beerenäugigen Zauberin war eine erwachsene Hexe geworden" [out of the childish berry-eyed enchantress there emerged an adult witch] (Seghers 264). This short story from 1948 predates Haas's work, and yet Jason's statement cuts to the core of one of the central conflicts explicated by Haas's novel. In the eyes of Jason, Medea is either a good witch, when she uses her powers for his benefit, or a bad witch, when she becomes too powerful. Medea does not actually change, but Jason's perception of her power certainly does and his feelings alter in ways that reflect perceptions of witches from far earlier contexts.

In her analysis of early modern witch iconography, Lyndal Roper describes the ambiguity of the witch's body when she writes that the witch "permitted a host of complex emotional responses: fear, loathing, dread, but also allure and fascination" (19). Witches are terrifying and simultaneously attractive. This tension is evident in Haas's portrayal of the magical, sexualized rituals led by Medea. While imbuing women with some degree of power, these portrayals, like the figure of the witch, are also fed by male fantasies and stereotypes. As Sigrid Brauner articulates in her own work on witches,

> we have no evidence that women practiced witchcraft in order to satisfy sexual urges, or that women felt weaker than men and therefore turned to sorcery. Such views are based on male fantasies about female sexuality and the male projection of women as weak. (Brauner 21)

The danger of staging Medea's magical abilities and her body as a means of attempted emancipation is that Haas's Medea falls into the same bind faced by the witch according to Brauner. The magical acts of her body, especially those that fly in the face of gendered norms, set her free and are also easily co-opted by a male gaze that seeks to sexualize her.

For Haas's Medea, becoming a woman means discovering the ability to use plants to perform magic. As a young person, Medea uses the symbolic *Kolcherblumen*, the flowers of her homeland, to heal her sick father. The narrator describes this moment as Medea's "Abschied der Kinderzeit" [farewell from childhood] (43). When he overcomes his illness thanks to her tireless physical labor, Aietes repays his daughter by infantilizing her saying: "Schaut euch die kleine Hexe an! Sie hat mich gesund gemacht, mein Kind, mein Mädchen [...] Ja, du bist eine Hexe, und wie süß und wild du bist" [Look at the tiny witch! She made me healthy, my child, my little girl [...] Yes, you are a witch, and how sweet and wild you are] (47). Aietes has not yet noticed his daughter's transition to womanhood. Even though what Medea has done saves his life, he is quick to diminish her role and her power in order to preserve his authority. Just as Jason will eventually feel embarrassed by Medea's assistance, her father refuses to acknowledge the true extent of her role in his recovery. Unfortunately for him, underestimating Medea is always a critical error with often fatal consequences. In part because of her father's inability to take her seriously, Medea subsequently uses her newfound powers to help Jason acquire and then abscond with the Golden Fleece. After this betrayal, Aietes is no longer laughing about his daughter's cute little tricks.

Unlike Medea's father who jests about Medea's magical abilities, Jason uses them as a means for enhancing his own fame and heroism. At first, Jason enjoys showing off his new bride in Greece, because "Medea war die Schönste und Fremdeste des Landes zugleich" [Medea was simultaneously the most beautiful and the most foreign in the land] (Haas 101). This combination of beauty and of exotic foreignness makes Medea a prize fit for Jason's kingly image of himself. Even having sex with Medea becomes a heroic conquest. As the narrator remarks, from Jason's perspective: "der sexuelle Tanz mit der Hexenfrau krönte ihn zum tollsten und größten aller Männer" [the sexual dance with the witchy woman crowned him the best and the greatest of all men] (105). When Haas describes Medea as a witch figure, it also means that Jason can problematically affirm his masculinity and power through his control over her body. The danger represented by Medea's witchy body transforms her love into a prize to be won through heroic conquest.

Medea's body is also volatile, seductive, and capable of fatal deceit. One of the most striking examples of this is when Medea throws her body at the problem of getting revenge for Jason against King Pelias, the uncle who stole Jason's rightful throne. Medea experiences her need to help Jason as a physical transformation: "Ihre Haut leuchtete und gab ihrem Körper die Härte und Kraft, mit der sie seinen Wunsch nach Rache in die Tat umzusetzen sicher war" [her skin glowed and gave her body the toughness and strength with which she was sure to turn his wish for revenge into action] (Haas 83). Medea's plan also involves the beauty and the bodies of numerous other women. First, she seduces Pelias by leading a procession of half-naked women up to his court. As a part of this "erotisches Spiel" [erotic game], the women sway their breasts with their hands and shake their butts (88). Medea promises to restore Pelias's youth, a feat of magic that she performs first on a ram and that she will eventually perform on Jason. Medea then hypnotizes Pelias's daughters, and thereby persuades them to murder their own father: "sie zerteilten den Vater, wie es vorher mit dem alten Widder geschehen war, und warfen die Körperteile in den gleichen brodelnden Kessel" [they cleaved their father apart, as they did earlier with the old ram and threw the body parts into the same bubbling pot] (92). Pelias's daughters commit this gruesome patricide under Medea's magical influence, a magic that is driven by her seductive female body and which results in the absolute destruction of male bodies, both human and animal.

In addition to avenging Jason, Medea's actions here are themselves exploitative. She uses Pelias's daughters in a way that is similar to how Jason uses her. While her actions serve as a warning about the power and the potential for violence lurking within female bodies, she accomplishes this task on patriarchal terms. What starts out as a seduction, as something that pretends to be designed for Pelias's pleasure, ultimately becomes his brutal undoing as his own entranced daughters literally rip him apart. Pelias learns a fatal lesson about the dangers of the female body. But Medea's actions also lack any feminist sympathy that she might feel for Pelias's daughters, who she has tricked into performing this gruesome act. Haas provides no indication of how *they* are supposed to come to terms with what their bodies have been convinced to do as a result of Medea's magical intervention. Pelias's daughters are simply added casualties of Medea's murderous intentions and seductive, witchy body.

While Medea's plan certainly is effective, it is important to remember the ways in which she is also limited in terms of her ability to exercise power through her body, particularly in terms of how that power is instrumentalized for the service of men. The fact that Medea needs to use her sexuality in order to achieve her goals is certainly problematic from a feminist standpoint. As Kevin J. Wetmore Jr. argues "while her sexuality can be a form of power (and it is often represented as such), it is also a means to reduce her to a source of pleasure for men" (9). And it is not only the late King Pelias's pleasure that I am talking about here, but also Jason's pleasure in using Medea and her magic to help him conquer his enemies. Christoph Steskal further writes that the problem with Jason, and by extension Greek/Western white men, is "die zweckrationale und libidinöse Instrumentalisierung der Frau durch den Mann" [the purely rational and libidinous instrumentalization of women by men] (280). The central problem that Medea must confront in Haas's novel is not Jason's betrayal of their marriage through his engagement to Kreusa, but rather the ways in which he has exploited Medea's power and used her body for his own ends. This refiguration transforms Medea from a jealous woman scorned into a woman who has been deliberately used and then discarded. By reframing Medea's situation in this way, Haas presents us with a Medea whose violent actions are not driven by emotional overreaction, but rather by the understanding that she has been duped into using her power to help an undeserving oppressor. If Medea's power must be used in the service of a man (and it seems that there is no alternative), she has chosen poorly in the exploitative Jason.

Instead of holding Jason accountable, Steskal places blame on the female characters in the novel for willingly participating in this system in which their bodies are used for men's pleasure and political gains. Steskal cites a "Mangel an weiblicher Solidarität" [dearth of female solidarity] as one of the political issues that Haas brings to the fore (287). As evidence for this, Steskal cites the actions of Jason's mistress and Kreusa as two women who fail to join in solidarity with Medea. While I agree that not enough attention has been paid to other women in the Medea story (likely because Medea herself is such an imposing figure), it is clear in *Freispruch für Medea* that the figures Steskal cites to support his claims are only half of the story. While there are moments (such as King Pelias's murder) where solidarity between women is woefully lacking, Medea is also frequently capable of summoning vast crowds of women (or a coven, if one wants to stick to the witch metaphor) for help when necessary. For instance, when the city of Corinth faces a famine, Medea rallies the women to an ecstatic, corporeal "prayer" at the temple of Demeter in an effort to end the community's suffering.

The gathering at the temple of Demeter turns into a celebration of the female body and sexual pleasure. The bodies of the assembled women walk a thin line between birth and death. They are full of both life-giving and life-taking power: "Ihre Körper zogen sie von einem Ufer zum anderen: Geburt und Tod, Tod und Geburt, Anfang und Ende, Ende und Anfang" [Their bodies pulled them from one shore to another: Birth and Death, Death and Birth, Beginning and End, End and Beginning] (Haas 113). These ebbs and flows culminate in an image of earth and blood: "Der Kreislauf der Zeit, umrankt von Lust und Schmerz, von Blut und schwarzer Erde" [The circulation of time, entwined with Desire and Pain, with blood and dark earth] (113). The female bodies assembled by Medea are notable for their fluidity and simultaneously, like witches, for their connection to nature and to the earth. The narrator brings these stereotypical connections between women and blood or women and Mother Earth to a climax as the activity at the temple escalates into a wild display of female sexual pleasure. The narrator vividly describes the scene, saying:

> Sie fingerten an den modellierten weiblichen Geschlechtsorganen, kicherten grell und stachelten einander mit scharfen Reden an. Sie pflanzten die Phalli in den Boden und bespritzten sie mit Urin und Speichel. Menstruationsblut tropfte auf den Boden. (Haas 115)

> [They fingered the models of female sex organs, chuckled garishly and incited each other with spicy speeches. They planted the phalli in the ground and sprinkled them with urine and saliva. Menstrual blood dripped onto the ground.]

This ritual plays out like a witches' sabbath as the women indulge in a variety of sexualized activities normally forbidden to them. Roper articulates the effects of equally graphic depictions of witches arguing that "such writing is certainly designed to shock and appall, and the savoring of vivid details suggests it is also a part of the text's attraction" (31). Haas replicates these witch tropes in this scene, which deliberately draws attention to the women's bodies and their gender-bending activities. The women at the temple fertilize phalluses, symbols of masculinity, by planting them in the ground like flowers and covering them with their own bodily fluids. In a provocative role reversal, fertilization comes from female, rather than male bodies, thereby created a scenario in which women have a monopoly on reproductive power.

The flowing bodily fluids of the women also connect them to associations between femininity and liquids, which permeated late twentieth-century feminist discourses. One prime example is French feminist theorist Luce Irigaray's answer to the German philosopher Friedrich Nietzsche, *Marine Lover* (1991). Although Haas wrote her Medea novel several years before this theoretical work, Irigaray's citation of the myth of Odysseus and the Sirens and her use of the sea as a metaphor for dangerous female power, resonates with the scene at Demeter's temple. Irigaray writes:

> No rapture, no peril is greater than the sea. [...] Even the most intrepid tie themselves to the mast, for fear of succumbing to the spell of the undauntable one. And they want to drive their prows over her. But her depths are never ploughed by their blades. Which barely cleave the crest of her waves. (*Marine Lover* 47–48)

Irigaray's ocean metaphor generates an understanding of femininity as deeply complex and unable to be truly known or experienced by men. The fact that Jason is also the captain of a ship is no coincidence. The danger of watery seduction is something he has seen firsthand. Perhaps the most symbolic female waters, those of the amniotic fluid in the womb, represent an obstacle for men to overcome. Men without wombs grow to disregard the reproductive power to which only people with wombs have access. Irigaray remarks, "And isn't it by forgetting the first waters that you achieve immersion in your abysses and the giddy flight of one who wings far away" (*Marine Lover* 38). The notion that men want to fly while women want to flow plays itself out in Haas's Medea story as Jason seeks greater and greater heights of wealth and of power, while Medea and the other women use their liquid bodies to tap into the ebbs and flows of the world, to drift between life and death.

By letting their blood drip freely, the women at the temple also resist taboos surrounding menstruation, which in a variety of cultures and religious traditions labels women as "unclean." Menstrual blood defies the typical connotations of flowing blood as having to do with illness or injury. Instead, this moving blood represents reproductive potential, albeit unrealized potential in that menstrual blood appears only when fertilization has not occurred. In addition to celebrating their bodies, these women simultaneously reify negative understandings of menstrual blood because their freedom to flow only happens within the confines of this specific, emergency-driven ritual. They are still not free to use their bodies wherever and whenever they choose. Medea and her female cohort are just as horrifying and titillating as the witches documented by Brauner and Roper. The women at the temple are immersed with all of their senses in these excretions as the narrator describes how "die Luft roch nach Ausdünstungen der Frauen" [the air reeked from the vapors of the women] (Haas 115). In an effort to save their city from famine, these women release the life-giving powers of their bodies as expressed through their bodily fluids. The physical signs of their bodies are all-consuming and impossible to ignore. At the temple (and only at the temple) female bodies move exuberantly and without shame, convinced that only they are capable of bringing the community back to life.

Steskal calls the Demeter procession a "feministischer Demonstrationsmarsch mit dem Medea versucht, den griechischen Frauen Selbstbewußtsein zu vermitteln" [a feminist demonstration march with which Medea attempts to imbue the Greek women with self-confidence] (286). These women are certainly not shy or demure, but their freedom and power is limited to the context of the temple. Steskal fails to acknowledge that these women are not really capable of marching through just any streets with their display of female bodily power and sexuality. These women cannot exist in this emancipated way in any other space. As the narrator remarks, "Die Frauen und Medea, die neue Griechin, lebten von dieser Welt der Männer und Jason ausgeschlossen" [the women and Medea, the new Greek, lived shut out from this world of the men and Jason] (Haas 94). Ultimately, this mission to throw the female body at the problem of the famine fails to produce lasting social change.

While it may seem empowering for women to see themselves portrayed in all of their liquid glory, Haas ultimately cannot deliver to her readers a female power that is not in the service of, or organized around, masculine terms and desires. Medea's life-giving powers are ultimately negated and overlooked because they do not fall into a heteronormative narrative of motherhood and reproduction. Despite all of the drama at the temple (and presumably a large mess after all of those free-flowing fluids), the action that actually ends the famine is Medea buying and growing plants from her native land, thereby generating additional food sources. The corporeal female magic on display at Demeter's temple does not actually work to end the food emergency. In fact, only practical, non-spectacle driven solutions are effective in solving the problems of the community. Yet, Haas proves that it does not necessarily matter how the famine really ends because people will believe what aligns with their gendered understanding of the world. The narrator tells us that the women of Corinth attribute the end of the famine to Medea's "hingebungsvollste Opfer" [devoted sacrifice] to Demeter and to her husband, while the men comment that Medea will be rewarded with a pregnancy (Haas 116–117). The narrator then undermines these attributions of helpfulness and of success remarking, "Die Griechen aber meinten Demeter, wenn sie Medea sagten" [but the Greeks meant Demeter, when they said Medea] (117). Even when they verbally give Medea some credit, the Greeks do not really grant her the respect she deserves for ending the famine. Medea's ingenuity in buying the plants is coded as masculine in that it is practical, logical, and not sexual or provocative. Therefore, it is impossible for the Greeks to fully acknowledge it as the work of Medea. In contrast, her wifely sacrifice can be acknowledged, but its results are the "reward" of her pregnancy, not public recognition for civic assistance. Medea should receive credit for the vitality of the plants that she nurtures, but instead she only is given credit for the eventual vitality of her womb. Though Medea later decides against her child, the plants she grows prove that she is not devoid of life-giving energy and capabilities. However, these nurturing powers are overlooked because they do not initially take the expected form, namely motherhood.

Medea as Colonial Subject

Medea's identity as a colonial subject also plays a significant role in terms of her position as an instigator of magical, sexually explicit displays. Anette Dietrich writes that during the German colonial period "ungezügelte Sexualität galt im bürgerlischen Selbstverständnis als Bedrohung der modernen Zivilisation, und diese wurde auf Schwarze projiziert und pathologisiert, insbesondere Schwarze weibliche Sexualität" [uninhibited sexuality was seen within the bourgeois self-understanding as a threat to modern civilization and this threat was projected and pathologized onto Blackness, especially Black female sexuality] (365). With this in mind, Medea's role as a leader of taboo sexual displays reveals Haas's entrenchment in the sexualization of Black women. In her analysis of Black femmes in cinema, Kara Keeling articulates the importance of constructions of race within the political project of humanizing and emancipating the female body. In her description of the Ethiopian film *Sankofa* (1993) Keeling writes:

> To the extent that the perception of the female body commonly carries a notion of femininity in the sense of passivity or receptivity to sensations from the outside or in the sense of being an object for desire, the female body poses a series of difficulties for any attempt to be recognized as human. (Keeling 64)

Haas's Medea story proves to be well aware of such struggles as the women at Demeter's temple seek to exaggerate, and thereby to reach the limits of their corporeal powers. However, while Haas seems cognizant of the issues that women face to be recognized as fully human, she remains blind to the ways in which constructions of race further confound this question for Black women. Haas fails to understand, as Keeling writes, that "the notions of femininity and genital sexuality that commonly inhere in perceptions that posit a 'black female body' are Western conceptions deposited in common sense as part of the colonial mission" (64). While Haas's Medea certainly channels the ambiguous witch, independent and free, yet driven by male sexual fantasy, she is also a colonial stereotype of the Black woman. In trying to make her Medea more relatable, Haas problematically relies on colonial rhetoric that was used to exclude Black Germans from equal participation in the emancipatory projects of the New Women's Movement in West Germany.

Haas exoticizes Medea to highlight her position as an outsider within Greek society. This racist characterization ultimately serves to unravel any progressive work done in the service of bodily autonomy for women through other aspects of this text. Barbara Feichtinger writes that "das Ungleichgewicht der Geschlechter, das Medea bereits durch den Vater erfahren mußte, wird durch das Ungleichgewicht zwischen den Kulturen tragisch verstärkt" [the imbalance of the sexes, that Medea already had to endure from her father, is reinforced through the imbalance between the cultures] (217). By turning Medea into an exotic racialized Other, Haas fails at her own project of emancipating all women's bodies from male imperialist interests. Florvil writes that one of the most prominent barriers faced by Black Germans is the failure of white Germans to recognize them as both Black and German saying, "in essence, they are always arriving, considered to be from somewhere else, nonexistent as Germans" (180). This mirrors Medea's experience in that she is consistently cast out of all of the places she tries to call home, even when she has a direct familial claim to them. For example, her outsider status also gets her and her son kicked out of Athens. In contrast with Medea's son by Aigeus, Medos, the newly returned Theseus is a more desirable heir for Aigeus because he is "ein ganzer Grieche, ein Vollblut" [a full Greek, a pure bred] (186). Even when she returns to her homeland of Colchis, Medea feels unwelcome when she remarks, "Hier fühlte ich mich so griechisch, und in Griechenland war ich eine Kolcherin!" [here I felt so Greek and in Greece I was a Colchian!] (199). Similar to the experiences of Black Germans, Haas's Medea is excluded from the national imaginary of the country she calls home.

The connection that Haas draws between Medea and nature also has racist implications because of the way she uses this bond to stereotype Medea as an uncivilized colonial subject. Haas begins her Medea novel with a quotation about the force of love taken from Hans Henny Jahnn, who wrote his own racialized Medea adaptation in 1926. In Jahnn's version of the story, Medea is explicitly African with one light-skinned and one dark-skinned son. The two sons compete for Jason's affection and eventually Jason steals Kreusa out from under one of them. Sometimes offensively performed with Medea in blackface, Jahnn's Medea understands her own marginalization as connected to her skin tone, saying to Jason, "Barbarenfrau schimpfst Du auf meine dunkle Farbe" [barbarian woman, you rant against my dark color] (16). Jahnn's Medea later faces explicit racism, especially at the hands of Creon. After Medea plucks out the eyes of the servant who brings her the news of Jason's engagement, Creon rants angrily, "du bist ein Tier! Ungriechische Barbarin. Wie Deine Haut so schwarz ist auch Dein Tun" [you are an animal! Un-Greek barbarian. Just like your skin, so black are your deeds] (Jahnn 30). Associations between Medea and the natural world, the term "barbarian" itself, and Medea's connection to metaphorical (if not literal) darkness, are all present in Haas's novel.

The map that Haas includes in the front of her novel reminds her readers that the location of ancient Colchis is on the Black Sea, in present day Georgia. Medea is quite literally Caucasian, a term that has become synonymous with whiteness. However, it is easy to be confused about the topic of Medea's racial identity because the Ancient Greeks had different understandings of race in mind when, in other primary sources, they described the Colchians as darker-skinned descendants of the Egyptians with "wooly hair" (Wetmore 4). Geography and ancient understandings of race aside, the depiction of Medea as a Woman of Color can most accurately be thought of as a translation of her role as an outsider into more contemporary terms. In her depiction of Medea, Haas builds on the work of authors such as Jahnn and repeatedly associates Medea with Blackness and colonial subjects, contrasting her with the white, Greek, imperialist, Jason. By engaging uncritically with this colonial language, Haas normalizes white supremacy and fails to acknowledge the culturally constructed nature of racial categories.

By citing Jahnn, Haas also invokes a history of racist characterizations of Medea in the German-speaking context. Heike Bartel traces a trajectory from Franz Grillparzer's Medea (1821), who is white-skinned but dabbles in so-called black magic, to Paul Heyse's biracial Medea-figure named Wally (1898), to Jahnn's explicitly Black Medea (1926) who is "much less an individual human being than an embodiment of uncomplicated female sexuality" (Bartel, "Medea Called Wally" 63). This trajectory points to a central problem in terms of how the Medea story has been racialized, namely that making Medea a Black woman all too often goes hand in hand with removing Medea's complexity as a human being. When Medea is associated with Blackness, in the German context at least, she loses her agency and her decision-making is oversimplified to one single cause, namely her race. Bartel writes of Heyse's biracial Medea that "she is miles away from the strong, threatening classical Medea, and her breakdown is presented as almost biologically predetermined through the conflict of her differing 'Blut'" ("Medea Called Wally" 70). In other words, Black Medeas can be used to provide an easy way out of the problem of justifying Medea's infanticide and violence. Her position as a Black woman, according to these German authors, makes these horrendous crimes inevitable. Instead of a Medea forced into impossible choices or driven by a multitude of complex factors, Black Medeas as conceived by white German authors, are racial Others, who cannot escape the violence for which their skin color makes them destined. Unfortunately, *Freispruch für Medea* continues in this tradition by using racialized, exoticizing, and sexualized language to describe its titular figure.

In her foreword to the novel, Haas deems Medea an "Ausländerin aus dem Osten" [foreign woman from the East] (11) and her language describing Medea only gets more Orientalist in the body of the novel itself. Jason's first encounter with the Colchians is exoticized and sexualized. Medea comes from the "schwarzen Land Georgien" [black nation of Georgia] full of "schwarzen Barbaren" [Black barbarians] (52). In contrast, the Greeks are described as having a "Haltung der Verneinung" [a withholding stance] (53) that is disrupted by arousal and excitement (the German word used is *Erregung*) upon encountering these foreigners. The men and women of Colchis are intrigued by Jason and his crew when they first arrive, crowding around them and touching their clothing and bodies. In an act that foreshadows the provocative excretion of female bodily fluids at Demeter's temple, one woman goes so far as to spray Jason with her breast milk (55), an act that is simultaneously naïve and sexual. This description is overwhelmed by colonialist tropes of half-naked natives encountering the *civilized* Greeks for the first time and sets the stage for reading the stealing of the Golden Fleece as an act of imperialist conquest. Significantly, Medea and the other members of the Colchian royal family defer to the supposed cultural superiority of the Greeks by making an effort to dress and to behave like them. The Colchians throw an elaborate party to welcome their guests, and this hospitality demonstrates a greatness of moral character. They offer this friendship, even though they already know that Jason's sole purpose in coming to Colchis is to collect the treasured Golden Fleece for himself. As in many instances to come, it will not be Jason's cunning or strength, but rather Medea's love for Jason and her sorcery that determines how the rest of the encounter between these two cultures plays out.

When Medea runs away with Jason, the language used by the narrator to describe her continues to highlight her racialized difference from the Greeks among whom she now lives. The narrator attributes Medea's difference to a cultural distinction between East and West. They describe Medea's journey as follows: "Der Westen, der glorreiche auch damals, war zwar noch nicht greifbar, aber näher schon als eben noch am finsteren Ort der an Bord genommenen schwarzen Barbarin" [The West, which was also glorious back then, was not yet graspable, but nearer still than the dark place for the Black barbarian, who was brought onboard] (Haas 68). The narrator describes Medea's desire to move to the West in colonial terms as a step out of the "darkness" of her homeland. This contrast between light and dark has long been a staple of the Medea material. As Inge Stephan writes, since the plays of Euripides and Seneca "die Barbarin Medea [...] führt zu Metaphorisierungen, die auf den Gegensätzen zwischen 'hell' und 'dunkel' basieren" [the barbarian Medea [...] leads to a metaphorization that is based on the opposition between "light" and "dark"] (50). The racist literalization of this classical metaphor is a translation of the mythological material that reveals the biases of Haas's own culture. When Medea leaves her home behind, her (Black) body is meant to be used in the service of the white Greeks. This is the cost of entering into "civilization." For instance, the narrator describes her as "das barbarische Mittel der zivilisierten Griechen" [the barbaric instrument of the civilized Greeks] (Haas 79). Medea is there to literally do Jason's dirty work.

The narrator later doubles down on this image of Medea as enslaved or captured, describing how "Jason hatte das dunkle Mädchen aus dem fernen Land geholt und hielt es wie sein exotisches Eigentum in dem süßen Gefängnis" [Jason had brought this dark girl from a distant land and held her like an exotic possession in a sweet prison] (Haas 99). By framing Medea's support of Jason as a price she pays for being allowed to enter the supposedly superior Greek society, *Freispruch für Medea* strips Medea of her complexity and decision-making power. Steskal argues:

> Der im Roman von Medea in Korinther erfahrene Zwang, ihr exotisches Äußeres dem männlich vorgegebenen weiblichen Schönheitsideal Griechenlands anzupassen [...], spiegelt dabei den Assimilationsdruck der abendländischen Zivilisation gegenüber anderen Kulturen wider. (Steskal 281)
>
> [In the novel, the coercion that Medea feels in Corinth to align her exotic appearance with the female beauty ideals determined by Greek men mirrors the pressure for assimilation of occidental civilizations into other cultures.]

As we have seen, Medea makes a number of foolish decisions out of love—she murders for Jason, restores his youth, and changes her own appearance and attitude to please him. However, the racialization of Medea problematically connects those decisions to a long history of colonial oppression, implying that Medea's racial identity makes it impossible for her to have acted otherwise. Her culture is simply too *primitive* to have educated her properly, or to have given her the tools to be anything but a slave to Jason's will. The pressures to assimilate into the presumed superior Greek culture are simply too great, and yet Medea's status as a racialized Other means that she is also doomed to failure in her efforts to become a *true* Greek.

In addition to having a negatively connotated racial identity forced upon her, Haas's Medea parrots this racist language in her own descriptions of her unborn child. There is no way out of this racist rhetoric since it is also adopted by the protagonist herself. Ultimately, Medea comes to believe the negative information she has been fed about herself. Therefore, her abortion, while harming Jason, is also uncomfortably self-negating. In a moment of free indirect discourse, she asks herself:

> Würde aber Jason seinen Sohn beschützen, ihn stark werden lassen, bis er als kolchischer Grieche, als Mischling, als Halbblut, als Besitze, als Ausländerkind und als Barbar, das einmalige Wesen aus Ost und West, von Medea und Jason, der neue Grieche geworden wäre, der die Kraft hätte, in dieser Welt so zu bestehen? (Haas 142)
>
> [But would Jason protect his son, let him grow strong until he as a Colchian Greek, as a mixed-breed, as a half-blood, as a possession, as a foreign child, and as a barbarian, a unique being of both East and West, from Medea and Jason, would become the new Greek, who would have the strength to persist in this world?]

Haas portrays Medea's difference as something that makes her inescapably foreign and, therefore, incapable of eliciting any emotion in others besides sexual desire or fear. This ultimately works against Haas's own feminist liberation project. In the introduction to his collection of non-German Black Medea adaptations, Wetmore argues that "Modern Medeas, and especially black Medeas, do not seek assimilation; they seek their own dignity, identity, and justice in a society that wants to withhold all three from them" (10). Wetmore's assessment demonstrates another path that Haas's Medea might have taken, if given the opportunity. The problem is that Haas fails to take advantage of this possibility, instead portraying Medea as completely accepting of, and even an active participant in, the racist and sexist systems that try to limit her. Channeling Franz Fanon, Keeling writes that "the black's explosion is a violent (re)action that shatters the cycle of anticipation, yet conserves colonial reality's foundational violence by reinstating its temporal structure" (36). Haas's novel takes this cyclical violence a step further in that neither Medea's violence, nor her life-giving power, stops colonial violence from reasserting itself into Medea's life. There is no place for a Black woman in Greece and consequently, *Freispruch für Medea* provides no solution that would give all women permanent access to the kind of bodily autonomy experienced fleetingly at Demeter's temple or during Medea's abortion.

Medea's Abortion

Finally, I want to turn to what is the central (and most physically visceral) moment in almost all Medea stories, the scene in which Medea's children (or in this case future children) are killed. Medea's abortion is *Freispruch für Medea*'s most significant example of the female body as a powerful life-giving and life-taking force. Medea's abortion also returns us to the image of the witch. As Roper writes, witches often represent a threat to motherhood "because she embodies the envious woman who devours children and destroys fertility" (17). This characterization of the witch offers a route toward cannibalism that Haas's Medea does not follow. However, the point about the witch as a symbol of anxieties surrounding motherhood is well taken in the example of Medea's abortion. The relationship between Haas's Medea and Jason begins to disintegrate, not when he decides to marry Creon's daughter, but when she restores his youth. During Medea's pregnancy, Jason decides to leave her, thereby reframing the situation as an abortion rather than a filicide. As per the *Freispruch* [acquittal] referenced by Haas's title, Steskal argues that this abortion is the deed from which Medea must be redeemed, writing, "drittens wird der Kindesmord abgemildert zur Abtreibung des von Jason gezeugten Fötus, wodurch Medeas 'Schuld' von der sie durch die Romanhandlung 'freigesprochen' werden soll, gemindert wird" [thirdly, the filicide is attenuated to an abortion of the fetus fathered by Jason, through which Medea's "guilt," from which she should be "acquitted" by the novel's plot, is lessened.] (278). I argue instead that within the context in which Haas was writing, the shift from filicide to abortion is far from a milder take on the issues of bodily autonomy and of reproductive justice.

By changing the filicide of the Medea story into an abortion, Haas continues her project of making Medea more real and relatable to her contemporaries. Instead of the horrific crime of child murder, Medea's abortion (whether one is in favor of legal abortion or not) is still a far more prevalent and normalized act. When the details of the abortion scene are closely examined, it becomes clear that not just the fact of Medea's abortion, but also how it takes place is crucially important. Brauner notes that witch trials in German-speaking Europe were often precipitated by restrictions on midwifery, explaining that in the early modern period

> midwives were no longer allowed to form guilds. Instead, they were required to report to the municipal physician, and to notify the authorities when clients had abortions, used birth control, or gave birth to illegitimate children. Midwives suspected of non-compliance were sometimes accused of witchcraft. (Brauner 17)

This situation mirrors the one faced by Haas and her contemporaries as abortion was legalized in West Germany. Medea's abortion harkens back to several key aspects of the German abortion debate, especially the misrepresentation of back-alley abortionists and the subsequent medicalization of the procedure. When carefully reading the scene of Medea's abortion, one does not get the sense that this is the deed for which Medea needs to be acquitted. Instead, her abortion is depicted as the necessary consequence of her breakup with Jason, one which she enacts through a method that calls to mind a time when abortions were officially illegal, but also common non-medical procedures performed by women in their homes. If Medea feels the need to be acquitted for anything, it is not her abortion, but rather her poor judgment in letting love blind her to Jason's abuses.

After restoring his youth, Medea regrets the war-hungry husband she has created and Jason comes to resent his wife because of her role in bringing about his accomplishments and successes. After Medea announces her pregnancy, Jason goes to war to take advantage of his new youthful body and to create a better future for his son by expanding his own political power. In response to Jason's glory-hungry aggression Medea expresses regret for her decision to restore Jason's youth lamenting: "Ich habe das Beste gewollt und das Schlimmste bewirkt" [I wanted the best and caused the worst] (Haas 138). Shortly thereafter, the pregnant Medea moves out of Jason's palace and into her own house on the outskirts of town. In *Freispruch für Medea* it is actually Medea who first decides to leave Jason's house, not the other way around (although Jason has earlier taken a mistress). When Jason finally comes to visit Medea in order to tell her about his engagement to Kreusa, he describes feeling emasculated by the assistance that Medea and her magic have provided him over the years saying: "Ich will endlich ohne dich Jason sein" [I want to finally be Jason without you] (146). Jason is fine with Medea using her powers to his advantage in the moment, but afterward dislikes the way her interventions cause him (and perhaps more importantly the people around him) to doubt that he has actually earned his achievements. Medea and Jason both regret her assistance, but for starkly different reasons.

Due to the plot descriptions that structure this story, the reader is already aware that Medea is not going to carry her child to term. This allows our focus to be on how Medea responds to Jason's engagement and what exactly precipitates the death of the fetus in her womb. Even though Medea has already essentially left him, she gets very emotional when Jason finally visits her to tell her the news of his engagement: "Sie weinte. Ein Kind. Sie kroch auf den Knien zu ihm und umklammerte seine Beine. Sprachlos. Der Schmerz tötet das Wort" [She cried. A child. She crawled on her knees to him and clasped her arms around his legs. Wordless. The pain killed any words] (145). In this scene, Haas literalizes the way that Medea has been behaving this entire time, supplicating herself before Jason and throwing her body at him and his problems. Medea's grief over her lost love quickly transitions into anger and despair. As she undergoes this emotional shift away from subservience, the narrator articulates a connection between the similarly illogical driving forces of both love and murder, explaining that "Liebe und Töten ist ohne Bewußtsein, ohne Logik, ohne Schuld, verlangt keine Kraft, keinen Mut. Wer lieben kann, kann auch töten" [love and killing are without consciousness, without logic, without guilt, demanding no strength, no courage. Whoever can love, can also kill] (147). Through Medea, Haas equates extreme emotional states with one another. Love becomes similar to murderous rage through the excessive, illogical emotions that drive it. However, as a twenty-first-century reader, I wonder whether or not such an equation plays into stereotypes about hysterical women as capable of any and all emotional excesses. Is Medea dangerous because she is emotional and because her love for Jason inevitably triggers extreme rage? Or, is she dangerous because she finally understands exactly what has been going on, that she has sacrificed her body and all of her gifts and talents for a man who is all too willing to ditch her when a better deal comes along? Haas seems to want to have it both ways, presenting us with a Medea who is both blinded by love, and yet also made aware of how she has been used. If Medea feels guilty about anything, it is allowing herself to be manipulated by Jason.

As she reflects on what action to take, Medea conceives of the fetus inside of her as a combination of her and of Jason, thereby equating the fetus's eventual death with the death of their relationship. In other words, the fetus cannot live because it represents a unity between Medea and Jason that no longer exists. In a powerful moment of connection with her unborn child, Medea describes their joined heartbeats: "Nur ein Herz, sein Herz. Mein Herz und dein Herz. Sie schlagen. Hörst du es mein Kind? Wir schlagen" [Only a heart, his heart. My heart and your heart. They are beating. Do you hear it my child? We are beating] (Haas 151). As in numerous adaptations of the Medea story, moments such as this emphasize the fact that when Medea kills her children, she is also killing a part of herself—in this case the part of herself that was blindly and desperately loyal to Jason. Medea's primary concern is that her fetus is both a "Klein-Jason [and a] Klein-Medea" [little-Jason [and a] little Medea] (151). If she wants to completely get rid of Jason's influence, she will also have to excise a piece of herself. As Steskal argues, in this somewhat queer moment, Medea accepts "die Unmöglichkeit der Liebe zwischen Mann und Frau" [the impossibility of love between man and woman] (289). Since their union is an unequal and exploitative partnership, the only option is to get rid of all traces of it, including the fetus currently residing in Medea's womb. The issue for Medea is not so much the fetus itself, but what the fetus represents in terms of the gendered inequality that exists in Medea and Jason's now decimated relationship.

Haas's Medea is not a straightforward child-murderer, her abortion allowing her to evade some responsibility for what has become Medea's signature deed. That being said, the end result is the same, Jason will have no offspring, whether through Medea or Kreusa, who, as in most versions of the story, Medea also murders. The decision to stage Medea's revenge as an abortion also brings to mind the contentious politics surrounding abortion rights in West Germany that came to a peak about a decade before Haas's writing. Getting rid of the infamous §218, a prohibition on any and all abortion, was one of the major rallying cries of West German feminist movements in the 1970s. From the 1971 article in *Stern* magazine, in which

374 German women declared: "wir haben abgetrieben!" [we had an abortion!], to numerous street theatricals and protest actions performed by feminist activists,[1] to a much-disputed 1974 depiction of an abortion on the Norddeutscher Rundfunk (NDR) news show *Panorama*,[2] abortion rights became one of the most visible feminist causes in West Germany (Marx Ferree 63–64). Of the *Stern* article Myra Marx Ferree writes: "This self-incrimination campaign highlighted the hypocrisy of selective prosecution and women's actual need to resort to abortion even when illegal" (63). In many ways, this situation mirrors the situation that the title of Haas's novel imagines for Medea, one in which she is forced to seek acquittal for actions that, according to feminists at least, should be perfectly legal and acceptable. By 1976, a compromise was struck to allow abortion within the first trimester after counseling and a three-day waiting period. This law was revisited and relaxed slightly post-Reunification, but at the time of Haas's writing, the 1976 law represented the official West German position on abortion, a position that required women to enter into a medicalized process controlled by (mostly male) doctors in order to legally

1 In archives such as the Frauenforschungs-, -bildungs-und Informationszentrum [Center for Women's Research, Education and Information] (FFBIZ) in Berlin and the Archiv der deutschen Frauenbewegung [Archive of the German Women's Movement] in Kassel, one finds numerous scripts or accounts of these street theatricals and protest actions. Some resemble more traditional theater such as the play "Das Schicksal von zwei Frauen" [The Fate of Two Women] performed in 1974 by the 218 Gruppe Frauenzentrum, Frankfurt. (FFBIZ, "Dokumentation einer Aktionswoche" [Documentation of a Protest Week] A Rep. 400 BRD 14.3.15 1974). Others were more directly confrontational, such as the event described in this headline from April 16, 1974 in the *Süddeutsche Zeitung*: "Vier Kirchen von Schmierern geschändet: Dom, Alter Peter, Heiliggeist und Theatinerkirche mit Anti-218-Parolen beschmiert" [Four Churches Defiled with Graffiti: the cathedral, Alter Peter, Heiliggeist and the Theatinerkirche were besmeared with anti-218 slogans] (FFBIZ A Rep. 400 BRD 14.3.15 1974).

2 The program was scheduled to air and then was pulled at the last minute in an act of censorship. The documentary was eventually aired on March 15, 1974 along with a segment entitled "Was darf das Fernsehen?" [What is allowed on television?] that entailed a live debate between prominent feminists including Alice Schwarzer, television executives, and medical doctors lasting nearly twice as long as the original depiction of the abortion process.

receive reproductive healthcare. Medea, however, has her abortion outside of such a medically sanctioned setting. Through her abortion, Medea eliminates all trace of the union between her body and Jason's body, and she does so on her own terms.

Medea's abortion is notably an all-female affair that takes place at home and without the presence of medical professionals. By aborting the fetus, she (at least temporarily given her later travel to Athens) returns to an all-female way of being in the world, one that is connected to nature, rather than to male power and/or to politics. While Medea is experiencing the emotional distress described above, her companion and nurse Viviane brings her a cup of tea saying: "Ich bringe dir den starken Tee. Trink ihn schnell. Das Mutterkorn hat überwintert. Es ist aufgelöst" [I am bringing you the strong tea. Drink it fast. The ergot was hibernating. It is dissolved] (Haas 154). Viviane brings the tea, announcing that it contains poison (ergot is a fungal disease of grain that can be fatal to humans). Interestingly, the German word for the poison dissolved in the tea contains the word for mother (*Mutter*), so it is as if Medea's potential motherhood itself is the actual source of the poison in her life. Medea drinks the tea, knowing that it is poisonous, but it is Viviane who prepares it and encourages her to drink, thereby giving the women shared agency and responsibility for the resulting miscarriage. After she drinks the tea, Medea tries to direct the poison to her womb: "Der Parasit stürzte in ihren Körper und trieb sich durch ihn hindurch. Er ließ keine Windungen aus. Medea lag mit gespreizten Beinen und Armen, daß das Gift sich schnell den Weg suchen sollte" [The parasite rushed into and drifted through her body. It left no turn untouched. Medea lied with splayed legs and arms so that the poison could quickly find the way] (154). Medea is both in control of the poison and at its mercy as it courses through her entire body. Haas is very careful to avoid giving Medea clear and complete control over the process of losing her unborn child. Medea makes a choice to drink the abortifacient tea, but she cannot completely control the poison once it enters her. Nature plays just as much a role in this abortion as Medea or Viviane, reclaiming Medea's body and rejecting the fetus as a symbolic masculine invasion.

As we have seen in many other moments of potential feminist empowerment in this text, Medea's abortion is complicated by questions of responsibility and of agency. In the final moments of the abortion, Medea is not an active agent at all. The narrator describes how: "ihr Bauch rollte und wellte sich im äußersten Schmerz. Er zog sich zusammen und flog auseinander. Ihr Kopf klirrte. Sie schrie. Viviane öffnete den Weg. Das Kind stürzte heraus" [her stomach rolled and undulated in searing pain. It contracted and flew apart. Her head rattled. She screamed. Viviane opened the path. The child tumbled out] (155). Medea's body parts (her stomach and her head) move but she, as a complete subject, does not. Only Viviane and Medea's now-dead fetus are portrayed as active in this scene. Who is ultimately responsible for this abortion? Is it Jason's fault for causing Medea's emotional distress? Is it Viviane's fault for supplying the tea and preparing the way for the child to exit Medea's body? Is it Medea's fault for knowingly drinking the poison? Haas's text suggests that all of these explanations are true to some degree. Steskal describes Medea's abortion as something that appears "nicht nur als Racheakt gegenüber Jason, sondern auch als feministische, anti-patriarchale Sabotage" [not only as an act of revenge against Jason, but also as a feminist, anti-patriarchal sabotage] (288), but does not go into detail about what this actually means. What feminist point is Haas making by having her Medea undergo an abortion-by-tea, particularly in light of all of the other life-giving and life-taking liquids in this novel? Who or what is she sabotaging by excising any and all remnants of Jason from her body in this manner? I contend that Haas uses her Medea to confront the medicalization of the abortion process by making Medea's abortion one that is driven by nature and by female solidarity, rather than by doctors or medical boards.

Writing nearly a decade after the dust had settled (legally at least) on the abortion question in West Germany, Haas's Medea has a kind of back-alley-style abortion, without naming it as such. By portraying the death of Medea's unborn child in this ambiguous manner, Haas harkens back to an even earlier era of contested abortion rights, namely the Weimar Republic, during which sensational news stories about botched abortions performed by women in their homes abounded. One potential feminist critique of the loosening of abortion restrictions, particularly in West Germany with its requirement for state-sponsored counseling, was that relaxing the laws actually shifted the power to end pregnancies into the hands of doctors who were primarily male at that time, and away from the realm of women and the home. In her extremely informative look at the abortion debate in Weimar Germany, Cornelie Usborne describes the "demonization of the 'back-street abortionist' [as a] useful strategy by doctors of the time in their campaign to medicalize birth control and abortion" (15), arguing that depictions of abortions in newspapers, in novels, and in the theater, often exaggerated the dangers of such procedures. The abortion in *Freispruch für Medea* is predicated on a feminine knowledge of the natural world, rather than a medicalized process involving academic science or male doctors. As Usborne articulates, an abortion such as the one initiated in *Freispruch für Medea*, was often preferable to women for a number of reasons including "cost, safety record, methods employed and probably most importantly of all, a common cultural approach rooted in class and gender similarities" (24). In part because of this history, the discourse on abortion in Germany never adopted the language of leaving such decisions to "a woman and her doctor" that flourished in the United States. Instead, "on the whole, German doctors were framed as opponents of women's self-determination [and] the anti-218 groups staged street tribunals in which doctors were 'brought up on charges' of hostility toward women" (Marx Ferree 63). Haas's depiction of Medea's abortion highlights German feminist concerns about the potential for women to actually lose even more control over their bodies through legal abortion. There are no men present for Medea's abortion and she is helped only by Viviane. Though Haas sets out to create a Medea for her contemporary world, Hass's Medea has a strikingly old-school abortion, one that rejects a birth control model that is male and medicalized in favor of one that reinforces solidarity between women and a (feminine) knowledge of nature.

A Gay Jason?

Haas's fascination with the Medea material continued far beyond her first engagement with this story. After the novel *Freispruch für Medea*, she went on to write the libretti for four Medea-based operatic works in collaboration with composer Rolf Liebermann. The first of these was a concert for a soprano and a female chorus (a format that harkens back to the earliest days of the *Melodram*), titled *Medea Monolog* (Medea Monologue). This work was then expanded into an opera of increasing length, originally titled *Freispruch für Medea* at its debut in Hamburg in 1995, but eventually titled just *Medea* for its final two iterations, which opened in Bern in 2001 and Paris in 2002 (both opening shortly after Liebermann's death in 1999). These operatic works are significant because they add a rather unique plot twist to the Medea story. In all three of the longer operas, Jason leaves Medea not for King Creon's daughter, but for a young male priest of Apollo also named Kreon. Haas's personal website describes Jason's turn to the love of another man as driven by "seine Angst vor der starken und fremden Natur der Frau, vor Medea" [his fear of the strong and foreign nature of woman, of Medea] (Haas, "Text für Kompositionen"). This comment, which invokes Freud's description of the "dark continent" of the sexual life of women in *Die Frage der Laienanalyse* (*The Question of Lay Analysis*) (1926; 1950), reiterates just how fascinatingly foreign the figure of Medea is, especially in Haas's conception of her. Medea is so out there that her foreignness actually turns her husband gay. This gesture of Jason turning against women is not completely unprecedented in the Medea material. Even Euripides's Jason says in frustration that "mortals ought to beget children from some other source, and there should be no female sex. Then mankind would have no trouble" (333). Haas pushes these feelings on the part of Jason to their breaking point. Steskal also makes note of this dynamic, writing that Jason's turn to a gay lover is a "völliger Loslösung von jeglichen emotionalen und auch biologischen Bindung an die Frau" [complete disentanglement from any kind of emotional or biological connection to women] (282). Dubious ideas about sexuality as a choice aside, Medea is a figure who once again proves to be incommensurate with traditional, patriarchal family structures. Her queerness begets queerness, albeit misogynistic queerness, in her husband. Medea might be celebrated by feminists for this queerness, were it not for the fact that, if she can even be considered successfully emancipated from male control at all, Haas's Medea definitely pulls the metaphorical ladder up behind her. In other words, Haas's representation of Medea, while potentially empowering for some women, also reinforces the oppression of other women. As much as she creates a Medea who defies androcentrism by finding some semblance of strength and power through the liquid flows of her magical female body, Haas also creates a Medea whose racialized difference positions her as a dehumanized colonial subject.

By making Medea's body an exotic body—a dark continent, a foreign nature—Haas makes a metaphor out of the real experiences of Black German women, thereby erasing them. Forces of difference, both metaphoric and actual, underscore the representation of Medea in Haas's novel. As a result, we become like Jason in these operas, so confounded by her foreignness, so distanced by her difference, that we cannot carry on as before. In a missed opportunity, readers are forcibly pushed away from the figure that Haas claims to be at pains to help us understand. While feminism tends to call for a reordering, for a changed understanding of the world, Haas's Medea story fails to anticipate that this new world will have to recognize all women, including Black women, as full human beings in order to truly initiate structural change. As Dietrich describes, "Die Konstruktionen von Weißsein sind brüchig und nicht naturgegeben. Sie müssen daher immer wieder performative hergestellt und abgesichert werden" [the constructions of whiteness are fragile and not naturally inevitable. They must therefore always be repeatedly and performatively produced and confirmed] (371). Haas's novel is an example of a text that is deeply invested in this reification of whiteness, despite its feminist emancipatory aims and argument in favor of reproductive rights. Thankfully, *Freispruch für Medea* is not the final word, but merely an early example of Medea adaptions by German women in the late twentieth century. Despite its shortcomings, which I have enumerated in detail here, it is important not to forget Haas's novel because of the ways in which it highlights the stakes of West German feminist debates about reproductive justice and begins to imagine the Medea story as one with the potential to communicate feminist principles and ideas to a contemporary audience.

Conclusion

As one of the few scholars to pay any detailed attention to *Freispruch für Medea*, Steskal disparages its literary merits saying that its aesthetic quality falls short in comparison to other mythological adaptations (277). This claim appears to be based on the book's explicit and unapologetic feminist themes. Steskal writes that Haas makes obvious the "zivilisations- und patriarchatskritische Aktualisierungspotential des Mythos" [potential for criticism of civilization and patriarchy through the modernization of the myth] (277), which authors of other adaptations arguably approach with greater subtlety. Insofar as Haas does not shy away from vivid and explicit descriptions of Medea's body, I can agree that *Freispruch für Medea* is designed for dramatic provocation, rather than for calm contemplation. Nevertheless, I argue that the boldness of Haas's text is exactly what makes it worth reexamining in the twenty-first century. The explicitly political nature of this novel highlights both a history of legal efforts to control reproduction and the grounding of West German feminism in white supremacy.

The scholar Yixu Lü is far more friendly to Haas's overall goals, but still feels that the novel falls short because "Problematisch bleibt bei den feministischen Aktualisierungen einzig das Wahrheitspathos" [solely the pathos of truth remains problematic in this feminist update] (*Medea* 237). As we will see in the next chapter with Wolf and Nick's Medea stories, writing a realistic Medea does not mean writing a happy Medea, in fact quite the opposite. Lü goes on to argue that in *Freispruch für Medea*, Haas portrays "die Autonomie der Frau als prinzipiell unerreichbares Ziel" [the autonomy of women as in principle an unattainable goal] (242). While I agree that Haas does not provide her readers with much hope for feminist emancipation, I would counter that Medea's abortion remains an action of autonomy that Medea undertakes outside of a patriarchal medical structure, however incomplete and temporary its liberatory effects. In this chapter, I highlighted previously overlooked complexities in the novel's portrayal of gender, of the body, and of colonial subjectivity, complexities which pave the way for numerous subsequent Medea adaptations by women authors in the German context. *Freispruch für Medea* ultimately serves as a primer for the terms of the debates surrounding bodily autonomy and reproductive rights in the German New Women's Movement, while also revealing the erasure of Black women and Women of Color who were, and often still are, missing from the discourses of white (West) German feminism.

CHAPTER 2

Can Medea Speak? Voice and Victimhood in Medea Stories by Dagmar Nick and Christa Wolf

ἔρχεται τιμὰ γυναικείῳ γένει·

οὐκέτι δυσκέλαδος φάμα γυναῖκας ἕξει.

—Euripides 320

[Honor is coming to the female sex: no more will women be maligned by slanderous rumor.]

—Euripides 321

In this line from Euripides's *Medea*, the female chorus responds to the titular character's plan for revenge. They describe a world that has been turned upside down by the deceitful ways of men, thereby creating space for women to step into this vacuum of nobility and civic virtue. Despite Medea's pessimism, the chorus suggests that in a world of shifting morality, women could claim a more positive reputation for themselves. One question, as it relates to Euripides's play, becomes whether Medea takes advantage of or squanders this opportunity when she exacts her revenge. Put another way, should Medea have tried to seek justice through more conventional, less bloody channels?

German authors Dagmar Nick and Christa Wolf weigh in on this debate by turning Medea's violent deeds into examples of the "slanderous rumors" referenced by Euripides's chorus. In her 1988 novella *Medea, ein Monolog* (Medea: A Monologue), Dagmar Nick became the first German-language author to depart completely from the idea that Medea was responsible for the deaths of her children, King Creon, and his daughter. Christa Wolf later adopts a similar tactic, depicting a Medea in her 1996 novel *Medea. Stimmen* (*Medea. A Modern Retelling*)[1] who actually has nothing to do with the violence that became central to Medea's portrayal after Euripides. In their efforts to reassign guilt for the murders often attributed to Medea, both Nick and Wolf write prose adaptations of the myth using first-person narration. As if delivering theatrical monologues, Nick's and Wolf's characters express their thoughts and feelings directly to readers. By using their authorial voices to allow Medea to *speak* for herself, Nick and Wolf engage in a literary project of redemption for a female character who has been willfully and deliberately scapegoated and slandered. Wolf and Nick stage scenarios in which they, as authors, save Medea from the slanderous rumors that Euripides's chorus wants to believe are a thing of the past. Even though the chorus announces a new day for women, female authors such as Nick and Wolf argue in their Medea adaptations, that not much has changed since 431 BCE. Because of Euripides (and other male storytellers over the centuries), Wolf and Nick contend that we are still waiting for the end of misogyny and of scapegoating as a means of maintaining political power. For Nick and Wolf, the story of Medea ultimately demonstrates that Euripides's chorus is wrong. There is no honor coming to women because they are kept voiceless through the inheritance of cycles of violence and of victimhood.

Bringing Wolf's fairly canonical work together with Nick's lesser-known adaptation allows us to imagine a trajectory for this, now innocent, Medea beyond the tradition initiated by Euripides. Although written after Nick's text was published, the plot of Wolf's *Medea Stimmen* reads as a prequel to Nick's *Medea. Ein Monolog.* In combination, these texts help the reader imagine not only what happens in Corinth, but what comes after. My primary focus in what follows will be Wolf's *Medea. Stimmen* because its plot includes more of the traditional elements of the Medea story, making it more comparable to the other texts I discuss in this book. Significantly, in both Nick and Wolf's retellings there is no dramatic chariot departure, no escape to the court of Agieus. Instead, an innocent Medea must face the brutality of her society and her own infamy. This introspection, while

1 All the translations of this novel will be taken from: Christa Wolf, *Medea. A Modern Retelling*, translated by John Cullen (Doubleday, 1998).

sometimes occurring in other adaptations, takes on a different valence in both of these German works, written on either side of the *Wende*. By placing greater importance on how Medea will be remembered, rather than on what she actually does or does not do, Nick and Wolf also seek to reconcile the history of East Germany with the united future of the Federal Republic.

In a period during which the specter of Stasi surveillance loomed large, Wolf's and Nick's Medea stories confront the systemic process of censorship. For example, Wolf uses *Medea. Stimmen* to contemplate her role as a writer from the German Democratic Republic (GDR), who was accused of not doing enough to stand against an authoritarian socialist government. The period around German Reunification was one of the more difficult of Wolf's life. She saw her dreams of a reformed socialist state disappear and was publicly defamed in the infamous *deutsch-deutscher Literaturstreit* [German-German Literature Debate] of the 1990s. Instead of freedom, for authors such as Wolf the *Wende* brought with it a media campaign that, as they perceived it, "aimed to put an end to critical, political literature in unified Germany" (Klocke and Hosek 24). As her first book published after Reunification, *Medea. Stimmen* has traditionally been read as "a critique of patriarchy, war and the logics of possession [...as well as] an indirect reproach of the West German media that had projected an exceedingly unfavorable image of Wolf" (Klocke and Hosek 26). Wolf's frustration at being unable to speak for herself in the political landscape of unified Germany ultimately leads her to the figure of Medea, a perennial outsider.

Both Nick and Wolf structure their Medea stories around the process of giving voice to the otherwise silenced. The question of who is able to speak was also a critical one for feminist and postcolonial theorists during the late twentieth century. Inge Stephan links Medea, feminist theory, and postcolonial theory when she writes: "Für die Frauenbewegung nach 1968 avanciert sie [Medea] zur Ikone der Emanzipation, und für die postkolonialen Bewegung der Gegenwart wird sie zum Vorbild im Befreiungskampf" [For the women's movement after 1968, she [Medea] ascends to an icon of emancipation and for the postcolonial movement of today she becomes a role model in the fight for freedom] (73; my translation).[2] While I agree with the connection Stephan draws between Medea and these two related discourses, her characterization of Medea as a positive example does not resonate with Wolf's or Nick's portrayals. Instead, their Medea stories depict insurmountable challenges in the struggle to give voice to those who have been marginalized. Even the phrase "giving voice" itself implies a top-down model in which those in charge generously gift speech to others, rather than placing the onus on those with power to actually listen to how historically excluded people already speak. Wolf and Nick's pessimism about achieving feminist emancipation or freedom derives from these hierarchies of communicability.

Two theorists who also directly confront this dilemma are Luce Irigaray and Gayatri Chakravorty Spivak. In 1981, French feminist theorist Irigaray published an imaginative essay about mother-daughter relationships, "And the One Doesn't Stir Without the Other." Irigaray frames the inability of women to be seen and heard through the perspective of a daughter who explicates the distance that androcentrism has forced between her and her mother. Shortly thereafter, in 1988, Indian postcolonial theorist Spivak published the well-known essay "Can the Subaltern Speak?" in which she interrogates the silencing of non-Western, non-hegemonic perspectives. Both essays, written slightly before Wolf's and Nick's fictional works, ask questions about finding one's voice in the face of a lack of agency and of unacknowledged subjectivity. For Irigaray, voicelessness is gendered female and for Spivak the person denied a voice is the subaltern, colonial subject. Both accentuate how the problem of voicelessness is exacerbated by the fact that in order to be comprehensible, speech must frequently adopt the terms of the oppressors, be they men, or representatives of the imperialist West. Spivak, in particular, critiques the way that Western intellectuals claim to be able to speak for others without positioning themselves in relationship to various power structures. The unmarked voice of the intellectual contrasts with the non-hegemonic voices of those they seek to represent.

2 Please note that even though I am using a translation for the quotations from Christa Wolf's *Medea. Stimmen* (1996) (Suhrkamp Verlag, 2008) and Irigaray, all other translations in this chapter are my own.

Wolf and Nick argue for the liberation of non-hegemonic voices by blaming powerful men (Jason, King Creon, etc.) for the violence often attributed to Medea. However, by trying to give new voice to a supposedly maligned and misunderstood Medea, Wolf's and Nick's adaptations also fall victim to the paradox of voice and of voicelessness as identified by Irigaray and Spivak. Positioning Medea as the perfect victim of masculine power directly precludes the possibility that she will be heard. That being said, I believe that by reading all four of these texts together, we can gain a deeper understanding of the meaning of speech and the voice within feminist literary and intellectual history.

Wolf and Nick try to let the oppressed speak, but ultimately fall short of writing the Medea myth outside of the reification of an unnamed Western subject as defined by Spivak. While they succeed in articulating and in expanding our understanding of the interplay between gender and narrative, Wolf and Nick ultimately depart significantly from Spivak's crucial postcolonial interventions. Wolf and Nick use first-person narrative modes that evoke Medea's theatrical past to mimic, rather than to enact, the process of allowing the subaltern, the victimized, and the misunderstood, to speak for themselves. The authorial control they exert over these texts and their reliance on their own role as superior knowledge producers limits their ability to truly escape the authoritarianism they set out to critique. Through the combination of the works of Wolf, Nick, Irigaray, and Spivak, I analyze how this late twentieth-century feminist emphasis on voicelessness shapes German Medea stories and interrogates the paradox that assigning someone to the category of the voiceless also means assigning them to the category of victim. Without a way to think outside of these binaries, gendered or otherwise, there is little hope for feminist politics to fully address structural inequalities.

(Re)presenting the Medea Story

Recovering the reputation of maligned women is at the foundation of Wolf's project in *Medea. Stimmen.* In her 1968 essay "Lesen und Schreiben" [Reading and Writing], Wolf outlines her understanding of the relationship between prose author, reader, and the broader culture, by articulating a place for literature in a world increasingly defined by technology and the natural sciences. In an interview with Hans Kaufmann about this essay, Wolf elaborates that what she terms "Subjektive Authentizität" [subjective authenticity] is a way of writing that acknowledges how "für 'gegeben' angenommene Objekte werden auflösbar und offenbaren die in ihnen vergegenständlichten gesellschaftlichen Beziehungen" (Kaufman 95) ["things formally taken as 'given' start to dissolve, revealing the reified social relations they contain" (Wolf "Subjective Authenticity" 60)]. According to Wolf, what separates writers from scientists is that writers are responsible for the context of their own subjective experience and how it influences the text. Not only that, but a writer's experience "vermittelt zwischen der objektiven Realität und dem Subjekt Author" (Kaufmann 97) ["mediates between objective reality and the authorial subject" (Wolf "Subjective Authenticity" 61)]. In *Medea. Stimmen* Wolf expands her aesthetics of subjective authenticity through the inclusion of multiple first-person narrators. However, the truth claims made by Wolf's narrative voice also work against this aesthetic ideal.

Wolf uses the narrative technique of monologue, to create the illusion of a real, historical Medea whose thoughts and desires can be transmitted to the reader. Then Wolf encourages her readers to join her on the journey to recover this *authentic* Medea. To give her readers access to this revised Medea story, Wolf channels a series of voices (the *Stimmen* of the title) from fictional eyewitnesses to these events. The body of her text is made up of a series of monologues from six different characters, including both recognizable figures from the classical Medea story, such as Medea, Jason, and Glauke (Glauce), as well as figures which Wolf invents for the purposes of her own project, including: Agameda, a former student of Medea's; Akamas, the head astronomer of Corinth and Medea's enemy; as well as Leukon, another astronomer in Corinth and Medea's ally. By telling Medea's story with this series of voices, rather than through just one unified narrative voice, Wolf provides readers a more complete picture of these events. When more voices are added, the classical plot of the Medea story ruptures and readers encounter it as if for the first time.

While this effort to provide readers with multiple perspectives aligns with feminist distrust of a singular speaking subject, Wolf's narration fails to truly become polyvocal. Although each character is set up to have their own independent voice, it is abundantly clear that the text is still centered around and driven by Medea. Wolf gives Medea four monologues, while the other characters are granted no more than two. Most of the characters also maintain an interior monologue, talking about themselves in the first person. In addition to this introspection, Medea's voice addresses other figures, most notably her mother and her dead brother. Through the ability of Medea, and Medea alone, to address others, including the dead, Wolf liberates and strengthens Medea's voice, privileging it above the voices of the other characters. Even though none of these figures ever directly speak back to her, by refusing to exist in isolation, Medea's voice aggressively breaks out of the confines of interior monologue.

Spivak provides an explanation for the challenges faced by Wolf in her incomplete effort to create a non-hierarchical and polyvocal Medea story. Spivak writes that part of the colonial project "is also the asymmetrical obliteration of the trace of that Other in its precarious Subject-ivity" (281). The voice of Wolf's Medea is a strange combination of the Other and the Subject in that her voice is the one that must be recovered, and, at the same time, it is the voice that consumes and seeks to negate the voices of the other characters. In their exploration of the 1982 lectures that coincided with Wolf's best-known mythological adaptation, *Kassandra*, Thomas Beebee and Beverly Weber write that in terms of late twentieth-century feminist politics "the task of ending silence is also an important part of a woman's choice to speak" (272). The question in *Medea. Stimmen* becomes, can multiple women break their silence, or does one woman's speech necessarily come at the expense of another woman's? Although it is an example of subjective authenticity, *Medea. Stimmen* fails to critique what Spivak calls "subjective sovereignty," that is, the notion that there is one dominant perspective that supersedes all others. Just as Spivak puts pressure on the idea of the unbiased intellectual voice, Wolf tries to reject the notion of the unbiased narrator in much of her work. However, in *Medea. Stimmen* she struggles to avoid such truth claims. Spivak cautions against mere pluralization as a solution to the problem of subjective sovereignty, writing that "the theory of pluralized 'subject-effects' gives an illusion of undermining subjective sovereignty while often providing a cover for the subject of knowledge" (271) and that "the much-publicized critique of the sovereign subject thus actually inaugurates a Subject" (272). Wolf's novel allows us to see this process in action.

While Wolf's text purports to capture reality through a multitude of perspectives, it is actually the singular perspective of Wolf's Medea, and even more accurately, Wolf herself, as a misunderstood GDR author, that is reified. In other words, Wolf becomes like the Western intellectual that Spivak critiques for failing to account for their own positionality when endeavoring to speak for subaltern subjects. Wolf's readiness to equate herself and other white East Germans with asylum seekers, especially ethnic minorities who were attacked after Reunification, is a problematic conflation of difference. As Beverly Weber so eloquently puts it "race haunts Wolf's texts rather ambiguously. It erupts, at times more visibly than other, to disappear again amidst a humanism that emphasizes sameness in the face of violence" (164–165). Caroline Summers expands on this correlation between Wolf and the subaltern by applying the term to Wolf's reception in English translation. Summers elaborates on the meaning of subjectively authentic prose, saying that "the narrator is a visible practitioner of memory and narration" (223). By failing to account for the positionality of the author and Medea's dominance over other, especially over other female characters, *Medea. Stimmen* fails to make its narrator truly visible. Wolf's position as author in *Medea. Stimmen* highlights the difference between being seen and heard in terms of addressing Spivak's postcolonial call to action.

Both Spivak and Wolf understand that representation is not just about who is allowed to speak, but how. In the prologue to her novel, Wolf frames her readers' experience of this text as an act of redemptive storytelling that negates the authority of previous versions of the Medea story. Wolf writes:

> Wir sprechen einen Namen aus und treten, da die Wände durchlässig sind, in ihre Zeit ein, erwünschte Begegnung, ohne zu zögern erwidert sie aus der Zeittiefe heraus unseren Blick. Kindsmörderin? Zum erstenmal dieser Zweifel. (Wolf, *Medea. Stimmen* 9)
>
> [We pronounce a name, and—since the walls are porous—we step into her time, the wished-for meeting takes place, without hesitation she returns our gaze from

> the depths of the past. A child-murderess? For the first time, this doubt.] (Wolf, *Medea*, trans. Cullen 1)

The narrator offers her readers the opportunity to accompany her on a journey through time during which they will become skeptical of even the most established plot points of the Medea story, especially Medea's filicide. It is implied that the narrator is uniquely capable of helping us access this truth. Readers are asked to consider how they would feel about a Medea, who is not a fictional character, but rather, a real woman standing in front of them and sharing her life experiences. As Yixu Lü puts it, "Wolfs 'neue' Medea soll zugleich auch die alleingültige 'Ur-Medea' sein, die bislang durch die Arbeiten männlicher Schriftsteller verschüttet und verdeckt wurde" [Wolf's "new" Medea is simultaneously also supposed to be the only valid "ur-Medea" who until now was blocked and hidden by the work of male authors] (*Medea* 234). The narrator wonders if this exercise in empathy would not force us to question everything about the ways this story has previously been told. If we acknowledge Medea's humanity, what then? Wolf's Medea learns the hard way that, as Judith Butler contends, "what I can 'be,' quite literally, is constrained in advance by a regime of truth that decides what will and will not be a recognizable form of being" (*Giving an Account* 22). While Butler speaks about this in reference to real human beings who are limited by socially constructed identity categories, Wolf wants to argue that the same is just as true, if not more so, for Medea as a mythological character. Medea is what we make her. Merely rewriting myths is typically not very jarring because we are simply substituting one fiction for another. However, by rewriting this myth as *history*, Wolf forces us to engage with questions of accuracy and justice, despite the fictional nature of her characters. Wolf pushes the readers of her Medea story outside of what Butler might call Medea's "recognizable form of being" by presenting us with a Medea who defies past descriptions of her actions, and thereby compels us to question any narratives that we inherit, especially those that have achieved mythological status.

Similar questions about the politics of representation through narrative are central to Spivak's analysis of Karl Marx. Spivak distinguishes between two types of representation in Marx—*vertreten* and *darstellen*. She argues that there are crucial differences between *vertreten*, which is representation as a kind of substitution, where one represents the group (as in, e.g., political representation), and *darstellen*, which is a rhetorical or narrative strategy (276–277). In her Medea story, Wolf combines these two forms of representation in that her narrator depicts (*darstellen*) a Medea who represents (*vertreten*) women who have been marginalized. By presenting Medea as a *real* woman, Wolf conflates these two types of representation, trying to mask her authorial position, namely her act of *darstellen*. Spivak warns us against this kind of collapse of meaning writing that "one must nevertheless insist that the colonized subaltern *subject* is irretrievably heterogeneous" (284). While Wolf makes some attempt to honor this heterogeneity through the presentation of multiple voices, the illusion of a single historical Medea falls into the trap of concealing *darstellen* in favor of *vertreten*. According to Spivak, this problem plagues the Western intellectual when they try to represent the subaltern. As a settler-scholar and a Western intellectual myself, I too am implicated in systems through which my positionality is all too easily hidden or universalized. My uneasiness with Wolf's efforts at *vertreten* without *darstellen* stem from a recognition that my own analytical efforts are limited by my specific positionality.

It is somewhat surprising that Wolf adopts the role of the Western intellectual because of her position as an East German author. Summers even presents Wolf, herself, as subaltern, at least within the context of world literature in English translation (221). As the first book published by Wolf, after it was revealed that she had served (very briefly and ineffectually) as an informant for the Stasi, numerous critics wrote about *Medea. Stimmen* as Wolf's attempt to redeem herself and to justify her past behavior. When *Medea. Stimmen* was first published in 1996, many of the book reviews in German newspapers argued that this novel was Wolf's attempt to justify her actions in the GDR (see Volker Hage's review in *der Spiegel* or Thomas Anz's review in the *Süddeutsche Zeitung*). Literary critics, including Georgina Paul, Liliana Mitrache, Peter Arnds, and Robert Pirro, also took up this line of argumentation, suggesting that this novel is actually a way for Wolf to grapple with her various struggles and disappointments after German Reunification. Helen Bridge even contends that although the novel still plumbs great psychological depths, "Wolf's reinterpretation of Medea's story might be seen as a rather desperate attempt to assert her innocence at all costs" (39). It does not take much convincing to interpret Colchis, Medea's homeland, as a stand-in for the GDR and Corinth as a representation of the capitalist West. Transforming what in Euripides is a question of cultural Otherness into a question of economic and political Otherness, Wolf's Medea describes to her mother how a capitalist Corinth "ist besessen von der Gier nach Gold" (Wolf, *Medea. Stimmen* 36) ["is obsessed with gold"] (Wolf, *Medea*, trans. Cullen 24). Contrastingly, Jason describes Colchis as "diese östlichste, fremdeste Küste" and "ein barbarisches Land" (Wolf, *Medea. Stimmen* 44) ["this easternmost and most alien coast"] and ["[a] barbarian country"] (Wolf, *Medea*, trans. Cullen 31). In stark contrast to the language I highlight in Ursula Haas's novel, by placing this imperialist rhetoric only into the mouths of Medea's enemies, Wolf critiques Jason's Western and capitalist attitudes. After German Reunification, Wolf experienced her own battle with the stories told about her and was worried about how she would be remembered because of them. With this biographical information in mind, it is not surprising that Wolf would want to use her Medea story to illuminate the power structures that create scapegoats and silence others to maintain their dominance.

Wolf completely reframes the stakes of the Medea story, focusing less on Medea's internal conflict and more on the relationship between those in power and those who are excluded from it. No longer a child-murdering sorceress, Wolf's Medea is an herbal healer who has been turned into a scapegoat by the male leaders of Corinth. Always an outsider in Corinth, Medea uncovers a terrible secret when she follows the queen down into the catacombs and discovers the bones of Iphinoe, Creon's other daughter, who he murdered to protect his hold on power. When an earthquake followed by a plague ravages Corinth, Medea's position becomes even more precarious as she tries to use her skills as a healer to help the citizens of her new home. Instead, she ends up convincing the Corinthians that the disease follows her every move. This makes it easy to blame Medea for the eventual suicide of Glauke (Creon's daughter and Jason's intended), despite the fact that Medea is the only one trying to help Glauke work through the trauma of losing her sister. Medea's betrayal by Jason is further tempered by the fact that she has already taken a lover of her own, the sculptor Oistros, before Jason even entertains the idea of marrying Glauke. The murder of Medea's children occurs as a result of the demands of a vengeful mob, who blame Medea for the plague that is ravaging the population. As a result of these plot additions, Medea's banishment becomes even more sorrowful, in that she leaves behind both her now-dead children and her lover.

Instead of violent and vengeful, Medea becomes the pitiful victim of a system that is biased against her from the start. She is victimized in terms of her position as a woman, as an outsider from the East, and even as a mother. There is nothing that she, or any of the other women in the text for that matter, can do to disrupt the male figures' quests to attain and to maintain their power. The only options women have in the worlds Wolf (and Nick) create are either to align themselves with a powerful man or to get completely stamped out by governments that silence dissent and scapegoat anyone with the audacity to question hegemonic male authority.

Maternal Inheritance

Medea's downfall is precipitated by her failure to inherit the proper abilities from her parents, which would allow her to assimilate into the Corinthian way of life. The details of Medea's maternal and paternal inheritance are critical to understanding how *Medea. Stimmen* engages with the gendered nature of storytelling, voice, and voicelessness. For Wolf's (and also Nick's) Medea, it is the skills, attitudes, and legacies that she inherits that trap her in the position of a scapegoat.

While Medea's paternal lineage is usually quite clear, her maternal heritage is often surprisingly ambiguous. In nearly all retellings of this story, Medea is the daughter of the king of Colchis, Aietes (Aeëtes). However, the identity of her mother varies between accounts. Aietes is variously described as having intimate relationships with the nymph Asterodia, the oceanid Idyia (Eidyia), and the witch-goddess Hecate (notably the daughter of Aietes's brother Perseïs). Each of these women is sometimes identified as Medea's mother. Aietes's exact lineage also varies slightly depending on which sources one reads. When Medea's extended family is brought up, it is most often to emphasize her connection with the sun god Helios, her paternal grandfather, and the nymph/sorceress Circe (Kirke), her aunt/sister, who is famous for turning men into pigs. Within this complicated lineage, Medea's paternal line is fairly explicit (Helios to Aietes to Medea), while the maternal side of things is quite muddled, with many adaptations failing to depict Medea's mother at all.

In *Medea. Stimmen*, Medea is not the only mother figure, but all mothers are equally inept in the face of male power. Medea's mother in Wolf's novel is far more present than most mothers or mother figures in other adaptations. Medea's filicide, so often regarded as an unthinkable rejection of Medea's own motherhood, becomes easier to explain if Medea does not have a maternal role model from whom to learn proper mothering. Contrastingly, when Wolf eliminates the filicide plot, it opens up space for Medea's mother to play a more significant role in Medea's childhood and education. Although Circe also makes a brief appearance, overall Wolf deemphasizes Medea's connection to magical intervention and to the gods, instead fostering an image of Medea as a natural healer, rather than as a witch or a priestess. Medea's mother is never named, and thus retains some of her mystery, but she also takes an active role in passing down a set of domestic and medicinal skills to her daughter. Although Medea's mother does her best to teach useful lessons, not all that Medea inherits from her is positive or protective.

Similarly to how Wolf channels the voice of Medea in her monologues, Irigaray channels the voice of the daughter in her essay on mother-daughter relations, "And the One Doesn't Stir Without the Other." Irigaray speaks from the perspective of a child caught between her mother and her father. The girl debates which parent she should emulate and identify with, ultimately concluding that her greatest desire is to maintain her bond with her mother in a way that is not at the expense of her mother's own subjectivity. As the title of the essay suggests, Irigaray outlines a forced competition between mother and daughter in which one of them always achieves life or subjectivity at the expense of the other, at least within their androcentric world. As in Wolf and Spivak, this is also identified as a problem of silencing, as the daughter laments, "But we have never, never spoken to each other. And such an abyss now separates us that I never leave you for whole" (Irigaray, "And the One" 67). Wolf interrogates this same problem of maternal inheritance, namely that mother and daughter are deeply and intimately connected, and yet not allowed to thrive together under a patriarchal system. However, Wolf adds a dimension of cultural specificity to this discourse, which puts some pressure on Irigaray's notion of a generalizable understanding of mother-daughter inheritance.

Unlike in Irigaray, where we are thrust into the mother-daughter relationship as it turns sour, *Medea. Stimmen* begins with the depiction of an idyllic mother-daughter relationship. In her first monologue, Medea talks directly to her mother, speaking about all the important domestic skills that she learned from her. During a fever dream, Medea describes her childhood saying, "ich ziehe das weiße Kleid an, das ich selbst gewebt und genäht habe, wie du es mir beigebracht hast" (Wolf, *Medea. Stimmen* 15) ["I'll put on the white dress I wove and sewed myself, just the way you taught me"] (Wolf, *Medea*, trans. Cullen 6). Medea also learns healing skills from her mother that, while bordering on the magical, do not cross over into this territory. For instance, she describes how her mother taught her to read palms:

> [du hast] mir meine Hände dicht vor die Augen gehalten und mir die Linien in den Handflächen gezeigt, zuerst die linke, dann die rechte, wie verschieden, du hast mich gelehrt, sie zu lesen, oft habe ich mich ihrer Botschaft entzogen. (Wolf, *Medea. Stimmen* 13)
>
> [you sat by me [...] holding my hands up in front of my eyes, and showing me the lines in my palms, first the left one, then the right, how different from one another. You taught me to read them. I've often tried to ignore their messages.] (Wolf, *Medea*, trans. Cullen 5)

This lesson in palm reading has increased symbolic significance because Medea's mother imparts this knowledge to her after Medea menstruates for the first time and subsequently becomes sick. Medea emphatically claims that her menstruation and her illness are not connected, but the actions of her mother suggest otherwise. Medea's mother imparts these skills to her daughter because she thinks that they will help her to overcome the difficulties, both physical and emotional, that come along with being a woman. Unfortunately, this effort fails because the mother, as Irigaray emphasizes, is in no position to give her daughter any true freedom.

Although her mother's intentions are good, Medea's maternal inheritance ultimately becomes just as paralyzing as mother-daughter relations are for the daughter in Irigaray's essay. Irigaray writes: "With your milk, Mother, I swallowed ice. And here I am now, my insides frozen. And I walk with even more difficulty than you do, and I move even less" ("And the One" 60). According to Irigaray, immobility and an inability to establish an independent, individual identity, are the foundations of the inheritance passed down from mother to daughter. There is no avoiding it and it is always bittersweet, just as the infant in Irigaray's essay is both nourished by and paralyzed by her mother's milk. Once Medea arrives in Corinth, her skills as a natural healer become an immediate liability. King Creon's head astronomer Akamas describes being taken aback when a very pregnant, exhausted Medea walks off of the boat in Corinth declaring that, "solange eine Frau kalte Füße hat, geht die Geburt nicht los" (Wolf, *Medea. Stimmen* 111). ["as long as a woman's feet are cold, [...] the birth can't begin"] (Wolf, *Medea*, trans. Cullen 89). Her very first words in Corinth mark Medea as a woman who knows more than she should, as a woman who knows, at least to some extent, how to take control of her own body and health. As Creon himself admits in Euripides's Medea "a hot-tempered woman—and a hot tempered man likewise—is easier to guard against than a clever woman who keeps her own counsel" (Euripides 313). For Medea, knowledge is not power, but rather a threat to power.

The anxiety surrounding Medea's medicinal skills only grows from this moment onward, culminating in her being blamed for carrying a disease that she is actually trying to cure. As Medea's ally Leukon describes,

> Medea hat in diesen Wochen mehr als jeder andere getan, die Kranken verlangen nach ihr, sie geht zu ihnen. Aber viele Korinther behaupten, sie ziehe die Krankheit hinter sich her. Sie sei es gewesen, die der Stadt die Pest gebracht habe. (Wolf, *Medea. Stimmen* 170)
>
> [Medea has done more than anyone else in these last weeks—the sick call for her, she goes to them. But many Corinthians claim that she drags the disease along in her wake. They say it was she who brought the plague upon the city.] (Wolf, *Medea*, trans. Cullen 139)

By trying to use the healing skills she inherited from her mother to help the Corinthians, Medea ends up being misunderstood and blamed for the illness. Because her knowledge sets her apart from the other women in Corinth, Medea's maternal inheritance is ultimately not empowering. Instead, it puts her in the vulnerable position of becoming an easy scapegoat for all that is going wrong. Medea's activity is incomprehensible because she, as a woman, is supposed to be immobile, to have ice in her veins (to borrow Irigaray's metaphor). Leukon describes a Medea in motion, a Medea who has temporarily broken out of the motionless and voiceless absence of female subjectivity as depicted by Irigaray. However, despite her initial success in terms of mobility, Medea ultimately remains voiceless, at least within the plot of Wolf's novel. Medea can act, but not speak for herself, at least not without Wolf's intervention. The daughter in Irigaray laments that "the more I love, the more I become captive" ("And the One" 60). The same is true for Medea in that the more she tries to help, the more she becomes a target of the men in power.

This understanding of why Medea's actions are misinterpreted by the Corinthians is further supported by Leukon's explanation for the ease with which Medea becomes a scapegoat. It is impossible for Medea to overcome her outsider status because her inability to defend herself in Corinth derives from a lack of a properly Corinthian maternal inheritance. Unlike Irigaray's essay, which aims at universality, Leukon argues that maternal inheritance is culturally contingent saying:

> Irgend etwas fehlt dieser Frau, was wir Korinther alle mit der Muttermilch einsaugen, das merken wir gar nicht mehr, erst der Vergleich mit den Kolchern und besonders mit Medea hat mich darauf gestoßen, es ist ein sechster Sinn, eine feine Witterung für die kleinsten Veränderungen der Atmosphäre um die Mächtigen, von der wir, jeder einzelne von uns, auf Leben und Tod abhängig sind. (Wolf, *Medea. Stimmen* 158)
>
> [This woman is missing something that all we Corinthians suck in with our mother's milk. We never even notice it anymore, only comparison with the Colchians, and especially with Medea, made me hit upon it. Call it a sixth sense, a fine nose for detecting the tiniest changes in the atmosphere surrounding the powerful, upon whom we, every single one of us, depend for life or death.] (Wolf, *Medea*, trans. Cullen 129–130)

Because she has a mother who was not brought up in the cultural context of Corinth, Medea lacks the same survival strategies that those native to Corinth received from their mothers, a skill, symbolically at least, transmitted through the act of breastfeeding. Although Leukon's description is not gendered in the same way as Irigaray's, Leukon does make a distinction between the cultures of Colchis and Corinth. While the metaphorical milk might always be paralyzing, it is paralyzing in culturally specific ways. Medea does not have an innate sense of how to navigate the political conditions in Corinth; therefore, her status as a cultural outsider makes her an easy target for those looking to shore up their own power. Leukon also highlights the fact that his own attunement to these power structures is the direct result of his encounter with Medea's difference. As in Spivak, hegemonic structures and voices often have the privilege of going unmarked. Leukon only recognizes the power structures of his own culture when confronted with a differing perspective. While this is productive for Leukon's own self-understanding, it fails to help Medea escape the violence that is to come.

It is critical to note that in this novel Medea is not only a daughter, but also a mother. Irigaray describes the cycle through which daughters become mothers over and over again: "We come to relearn ourselves and each other, in order to become women, and mothers, again and again" ("And the One" 67). While navigating these culturally contingent modes of maternal inheritance, Medea tries and fails to be a better mother than her own. Before she leaves Colchis, Medea's mother implores her: "werde nicht wie ich" (Wolf, *Medea. Stimmen* 35) ["don't become like me"] (Wolf, *Medea*, trans. Cullen 23). Just like the downtrodden mother in Irigaray's essay, Medea's mother wants her to live the life that she was unable to live. Irigaray's daughter-narrator describes this dynamic saying: "You wanted me to grow up, to walk, to run in order to vanquish your own infirmity" (64). In the case of Medea's mother, this infirmity is represented by her inability to protect her son from his own father. Part of Medea's reason for leaving Colchis is that she cannot make peace with the fact that her father has murdered her brother in order to retain his grip on power. I will speak more about the specifics of father-child relationships later, but for now it is most important to point out that Medea fails epically in her task to avoid becoming her mother because she is also unable to protect her own children from violence.

Medea tries hard and yet fails to be a nurturing and caring, maternal figure to almost everyone she meets. She attempts to help Creon's daughter Glauke, but cannot prevent her suicide. She tries to be a good teacher to Agameda, but her student eventually turns on her. She endeavors to protect her sons by sending them to the temple of Hera, only to leave them vulnerable to the mob that eventually stones them to death. Although she is not a murderess, Wolf's Medea still has much to answer for in terms of her effectiveness as a mother. Wolf's Medea is a mirror image of her own tragically ineffectual mother. In the words of the daughter in Irigaray "I look at myself in you, you look at yourself in me" ("And the One" 61). Creon's daughter Glauke describes how her feelings of hatred for Medea grow, despite the fact that Medea tries her absolute best to help her: "Sie [Medea] sprach von Wiedergeburt. Es waren Tage voller Hoffnung, bis sie mich im Stich ließ, wie meine Mutter mich einst im Stich gelassen hat, es war das, was sie niemals hätte tun dürfen. Ich hasse sie" (Wolf, *Medea. Stimmen* 141) ["she [Medea] spoke of rebirth. Those were days filled with hope, until she deserted me, just as my mother deserted me once, that's something she should never have dared to do. I hate her"] (Wolf, *Medea*, trans. Cullen 115). Medea is (Wolf suggests, unfairly) blamed for not being able to hold everyone around her together. In Irigaray, the daughter similarly feels simultaneously abandoned and desires to be separated from her mother saying, "for even when I was yet inside you, you kept me outside yourself" ("And the One" 66) and "I'll leave you for someone who seems more alive than you" ("And the One" 62). Being a mother for Wolf and for Irigaray means paradoxically doing both too much and too little for your children.

As in Irigaray's essay, the expectations for mothers in *Medea. Stimmen* are high, so high that they are impossible for any woman to fulfill. While we cannot live without mothers, Wolf and Irigaray both suggest that we also cannot live without hating and rejecting them for never doing enough to set us free from whatever plagues us, be it actual disease or emotional discomfort. Medea cannot be free because she cannot avoid becoming her mother and taking the place of the ineffectual parent, unable to save her children from patriarchal violence. Irigaray's narrator claims that "what I wanted from you, Mother, was this: that in giving me life, you still remain alive" (67). Wolf's Medea also wants to live in a world in which both (mother and daughter, man and woman, Colchian and Corinthian) can survive. Unfortunately, she discovers too late that culturally contingent maternal inheritances are not enough to counteract universalized and normalized paternal power structures.

Paternal Inheritance

The ineffective mothers in *Medea. Stimmen* are symptomatic of the intractable nature of male power. Unlike maternal inheritance, paternal inheritance operates similarly no matter the cultural context. Although in many respects the scholar John Pizer is correct to argue that *Medea. Stimmen* undermines ideas of pangermanism by portraying "a conflict between two groups completely alien to each other racially, religiously and geographically" (149), Colchis and Corinth, like East and West Germany, share a reliance on patriarchal power structures. Unlike maternal skills or knowledge, both Wolf and Irigaray depict paternal violence as naturalized and universal. As Christoph Steskal argues, "die latent-abgründige Gewaltbereitschaft des Menschen ist ein konstantes Thema bei Christa Wolf" [the latent, unfathomable willingness of people to commit violence is a consistent theme in Christa Wolf] (312). It does not matter where one is from, the maintenance of male power is always predicated on family-destroying violence.

Traditionally, Medea's misdeeds include betraying her father to assist Jason in capturing the Golden Fleece and, perhaps even more significantly, the murder of her brother. This act of fratricide has led scholars, including Stephan, to characterize Medea as an anti-Antigone (Stephan 32). Known for the defiant act of burying her brother against the orders of the king, Antigone does everything, including giving up her own life, to honor her brother's memory. Contrastingly, Medea kills, or has her brother killed, to protect her escape from Corinth, often chopping him up and tossing his body parts back into the sea as a distraction for her father and the pursuing Colchians. Where Antigone prioritizes the needs of the biological family (even her extremely fraught one) above the rule of law and the state, Medea destroys the family in the service of her romantic attachment to Jason. In many respects, this is the initial unforgivable act from which Medea is never able to recover. It is also one way of explaining why Medea ends up killing her children. When things do not work out with Jason, after she split from her own family to be with him, there is no way to properly atone for her behavior, other than by destroying Jason's (and by extension her) new family. In such a reading of the Medea story, there is something so deeply wrong in Medea's decision to betray or to kill her own (male) relatives that it can only be rectified through the even greater violence of filicide.

In *Medea. Stimmen*, however, Medea is not responsible for the death of her brother. This chain reaction of killing her brother and then later killing her children is not set into motion. Instead, Medea's brother is killed by their father in an effort to maintain his own political position. This human sacrifice of the brother by the father is extremely upsetting to Medea and is cited as one of the reasons that she decides to leave Colchis. Medea helps Jason in part because it goes expressly against the wishes of her abusive and violent father:

> Ich wußte, Jason wollte das Vließ. Ich wußte, der König wollte es ihm nicht geben. Warum nicht, das fragte ich nicht. Ich müsse ihm helfen, diesen Mann unschädlich zu machen, um jeden Preis. Ich sah, wie hoch er den Preis ansetzte, zu hoch für uns alle. Mir blieb nichts übrig als Verrat. (Wolf, *Medea. Stimmen* 34)
>
> [I knew that Jason wanted the Fleece. I knew that the King didn't want to give it to him. I didn't ask why not. My duty was to help Father render this man harmless, no matter what the price. I saw how high he set the price—too high for us all. The only choice left me was to betray him.] (Wolf, *Medea*, trans. Cullen 22)

Medea knows that the price of loyalty to her father is often life itself and, unlike Antigone, she wants to avoid making the ultimate sacrifice out of a sense of familial duty. Unfortunately, what she does not yet realize is that loyalty to Jason (and to the Greek society that he represents) will ultimately have similar consequences, when Jason betrays, rapes, and otherwise abuses her. Although in many versions of this myth, Medea is a priestess, responsible for performing sacrifices of animals and of humans alike, Wolf's Medea finds the idea of sacrificing herself for her father unacceptable. She refuses to end up like her brother whose bones she steals and (in a mimicry of herself in other versions of this story) throws out of the Argo as she flees. These bones, unlike the severed body parts of her brother in other adaptations, are a reminder to her father of the horrible acts of which *he* is guilty, not a marker of Medea's guilt or shame. Instead of serving as the beginning of Medea's violent crimes, the murder of her brother serves as a physical representation of a brutal and violent patriarchal system from which Medea tries unsuccessfully to escape.

By using her departure to draw attention to her father's violence, Medea, like the daughter in Irigaray, tries to assume the same level of power and control exhibited by her father. For Irigaray, the father is someone who naturally draws the attention of the daughter because of his independence. As an act of rebellion against the mother's efforts to fill her with (feminine) breast milk, Irigaray's daughter-narrator threatens to reject her mother saying:

> I'll turn to my father. I'll leave you for someone who seems more alive than you. For someone who doesn't prepare anything for me to eat. For someone who leaves me empty of him, mouth gaping on his truth. I'll follow him with my eyes, I'll listen to what he says, I'll try to walk behind him. (Irigaray "And the One" 62)

The daughter wants to follow in her father's footsteps because she recognizes that he has an energy and a power that her mother lacks. Despite her best efforts, the daughter's assigned sex prevents her from capturing any of this life-force. The problem for Medea is that she gets stuck in the middle when she tries to escape her father through her husband, exchanging one male authority figure for another. She can never wield power like her father, yet she also cannot comprehend being a woman and, as a wife, being kept from having any subjectivity at all. Spivak compares the projects of feminist theory and "subaltern historiography" writing that "the narrow epistemic violence of imperialism gives us an imperfect allegory of the general violence that is the possibility of an episteme" (287). In *Medea. Stimmen* the specific domestic violence of Medea's father, and later King Creon, serves as a similar allegory for the structural violence to which Medea, as a woman, is inevitably subjected. In failing to follow in the violent deeds of her father, Medea also fails to stand against him.

Instead of following a man, Medea follows Creon's wife Merope into the catacombs. In her efforts to discover Corinth's dark secret, Wolf's Medea walks not in the path of her father, but in the path of yet another mother who has failed to protect her child from violence. Medea describes her ability to move silently through the passages saying, "du hast mir sehr früh diese Art der Bewegung beigebracht, Mutter, die aus winzigen Nichtbewegungen besteht [...] ich brauche das in meines Vaters Palast, sagtest du, ehe ich verstand, warum" (Wolf, *Medea. Stimmen* 22) ["for you taught me how to move like that at a very early age, Mother, showed me movement made up of tiny non-movements [...] I'd need that in my father's palace, you said, before I understood why"] (Wolf, *Medea*, trans. Cullen 12–13). The ability to avoid being seen or heard, yet another of her mother's lessons, enables Medea to uncover the fact that Corinthian patriarchal power is no different from Colchian. Silence is a survival strategy, but it requires sacrificing one's personhood. As Lü articulates, Wolf makes "the community [as personified by the father] rather than the individual the centre of violence" ("Myth and Apologia" 11). Wolf's Medea is not violent, but kings as representatives of the state are always aggressive. Although she does not understand it fully at the time of the lesson, Medea soon realizes the often deadly consequences of drawing too much attention from powerful men.

Despite their shared maternal traumas, the women of Corinth do just as much policing and judging of Medea as the men. Medea's difference represents a threat to all Corinthian self-images, whether one is male or female. Medea also endeavors to distance herself from the obedient Corinthian women saying:

> Ach, Mutter. Ich bin keine junge Frau mehr, aber wild noch immer, das sagen die Korinther, für die ist eine Frau wild, wenn sie auf ihrem Kopf besteht. Die Frauen der Korinther kommen mir vor wie sorgfältig gezähmte Haustiere, sie starren mich an wie eine fremde Erscheinung. (Wolf, *Medea. Stimmen* 18)

> [Ah, Mother. I'm not a young woman anymore, but according to the Corinthians I'm still wild, as far as they're concerned a woman is wild if she has a mind of her own. The Corinthian women seem like thoroughly tamed house pets to me, they stare at me as though I'm some strange apparition.] (Wolf, *Medea*, trans. Cullen 9)

The lie that Corinth is that one "Ort auf der Welt, da kann der Mensch glücklich sein" (Wolf, *Medea. Stimmen* 16) ["place in the world where a person can be happy"] (Wolf, *Medea*, trans. Cullen 7), is threatened by Medea's very presence. As Pizer points out, it is only Medea who "perceives the commonality of the two nationalities" (154) and it is this superior vision (not unlike Kassandra, Wolf's other mythological heroine) that gets Medea into trouble. Medea sees through the facade, but cannot speak about it. Through her difference, and her efforts to break free from gendered norms, she resists becoming a reflection of male domination and instead holds a mirror up to the awful evidence of paternal violence literally buried beneath Corinth.

Medea's own response to discovering the secret of Iphinoe's death is visceral and emotional. She describes feeling the bones of the dead girl for the first time saying:

> An der Stelle, an der Merope gehockt hatte, ließ ich mich auf alle viere nieder und kroch hinüber zu der Wand, auf die die Königin gestarrt hatte, ertastete mit widerstrebenden Fingern die tiefe Einbuchtung im Stein und fand, wovor ich mich gefürchtet hatte, stieß einen Schrei aus, der in dem Höhlensystem widerhallte. (Wolf, *Medea. Stimmen* 23)
>
> [At the spot where Merope had sat, I went down on all fours and crawled across to the wall the Queen had stared at, felt with relevant fingers for the deep niche carved into the rock, found what I had feared to find, and uttered a cry that echoed in the maze of caves.] (Wolf, *Medea*, trans. Cullen 13)

Medea knows from her experience in Colchis what to expect, and yet she is still shocked and deeply affected by this (re)discovery of the brutality necessary to maintain the current power structure. After her encounter in the catacombs, Iphinoe haunts Medea's thoughts, as Medea finds this knowledge difficult to live with. As she articulates, "[Ich] kann seitdem an nichts anderes denken als an diesen schmalen kindlichen Totenschädel, diese feinknochigen Schulterblätter, diese zerbrechliche Wirbelsäule, ach. Die Stadt ist auf eine Untat gegründet" (Wolf, *Medea. Stimmen* 23). ["since then I can think of nothing but that meager, childish skull, those fine-boned shoulder blades, that brittle spinal column. Ah me. The city is founded on a monstrous deed"] (Wolf, *Medea*, trans. Cullen 13). The detail with which

Medea repeatedly remembers this scene is striking and confirms its importance as a cipher for her understanding of her own powerless position within Corinthian society.

Medea spends a great deal of time in her monologues considering the similarities between her brother's murder and the murder of Iphinoe, around both of whom a plot for a coup was hatched. In her first monologue, Medea connects her brother's bones to those of Iphinoe describing how, "Seit ich die Knöchelchen dieses Kindes betastet habe, erinnern sich meine Hände jene anderen Knöchelchen, die ich dem König, der uns verfolgte, von meinem Fluchtschiff aus zugeworfen habe, laut heulend, das weiß ich noch" (Wolf, *Medea. Stimmen* 34). ["ever since I touched that child's little bones, my hands remember those other little bones, the ones that I—loudly weeping, I still remember that—threw from my fleeing ship to the King, who was pursuing us"] (Wolf, *Medea*, trans. Cullen 22). Paul argues that both Iphinoe's death and Medea's eventual banishment from Corinth represent "die Verdrängung des Weiblichen" [the suppression of the feminine] because both women are punished for threatening to reveal the violence of patriarchal systems (231). Contrary to this reading, Medea herself feels that Iphinoe's death is more closely tied with the fate of Medea's brother, challenging Paul's notion that the system of patriarchal power only serves to hurt women. Medea even goes so far as to say that Iphinoe is actually a truer sister to her brother than Medea ever could be because of their similar fates. For example, as she once again relives the experience of touching Iphinoe's bones Medea says:

> Und Nacht für Nacht ertasten meine Fingerspitzen die feinen Knöchelchen, die ich in jener Höhle unter dem Palast fand, den schmalen Schädel, das kindliche Schulterblatt, die zerbrechliche Wirbelsäule. Iphinoe. Sie ist mehr deine Schwester, als ich es je sein konnte. Wenn ich in Tränen erwache, weiß ich nicht, habe ich um dich geweint, Bruder, oder um sie. (Wolf, *Medea. Stimmen* 99)
>
> [And night after night my fingertips touch the delicate bones I found in the cave under the palace, the thin skull, the childish shoulder blade, the brittle spine. Iphinoe. She's more your sister than I could ever be. When I awake in tears, I don't know if I've wept for you, brother, or for her.] (Wolf, *Medea*, trans. Cullen 78)

Medea's direct repetition of her own language when once again describing Iphinoe's bones is one indication of her inability to move on from this knowledge. She is caught in a loop physically, linguistically, and emotionally. These bones, these physical signs of the unspeakable sacrifices made to maintain the hegemonic hierarchy, take on a mythological quality of their own as Medea continues to repeat the telling of her encounter with them.

The similarities between these sibling deaths are so stark that Medea's emotional responses to the death of her brother and the death of Iphinoe become indistinguishable from one another. Her tears flow for both of them simultaneously because their deaths were part of the same system of paternal violence. Again, Medea repeats this sentiment using almost the same language, just like her description of the bones. A few pages after the passage above, Medea declares that "Sie hatten Korinth retten wollen. Wir hatten Kolchis retten wollen. Und ihr, dieses Mädchen Iphinoe und du, Absyrtos, ihr seid die Opfer. Sie ist mehr deine Schwester, als ich es je sein kann" (Wolf, *Medea. Stimmen* 106) ["she wanted to save Corinth. We wanted to save Colchis. And the two of you—this girl Iphinoe and you, Apsyrtus [English transliteration of Absyrtos]—you are the victims. She's more your sister than I can ever be"] (Wolf, *Medea*, trans. Cullen 83). The crime of which both Iphinoe and Apsyrtus (Medea's brother) are guilty is trying to speak out against an unjust power structure. Like Medea, they wanted to do what was right and they wanted to help people. Also like Medea, this desire ultimately proves to be their undoing. Similar to the cycles of victimization and of paralysis highlighted in Irigaray's essay, the force of these stories takes over Medea's mind and, like myth itself, keeps her trapped in their repetition. Although Medea insists that Iphinoe makes the more appropriate sister, her eventual suffering at the hands of the Corinthians and her subsequent banishment makes it clear that actually, she belongs just as much to this group of ineffectual freedom fighters as either of these dead siblings.

In Wolf's text, as in Irigaray's, the primary inheritance that is passed down from fathers to their daughters is the knowledge that their lives are an expendable resource to be used in support of masculine authority. As Jason describes when recounting his rape of Medea, the power structure in Corinth is always to some degree based on the ability to control women: "Ich habe verstanden. So ist es gemeint. Wir sollen die Weiber nehmen. Wir sollen ihren Widerstand brechen. Nur so graben wir aus, was die Natur uns verliehen hat, die alles überspülende Lust" (Wolf, *Medea. Stimmen* 208) ["I understood. That's the way it's meant to be. We should take women. We should break down their resistance. That's the only way to root out what nature has endowed us with, the vile lust that spills over everything"] (Wolf, *Medea*, trans. Cullen 171). Jason clearly, albeit somewhat reluctantly, buys into the idea that he has a natural right to control women's bodies. As Creon remarks in Seneca's "Medea," patriarchal power means that "you must endure a king's command, just or unjust" (335). Some women, like Medea, may be able to see this power structure for what it is, but seeing is not speaking. Wolf and Irigaray suggest that escaping this cycle of violence is difficult, if not impossible. If maternal inheritance fails to make Medea an effective mother, the legacy of paternal violence in both Colchis and Corinth prevents Medea from acting as an agent for change.

Medea as Perfect Victim

Feminist movements, from suffrage to #MeToo, have struggled with questions about how to best employ understandings of female victimhood in the service of their political goals. To what extent is it politically desirable to characterize women as victims, and to what extent does this victimhood discourse reinforce stereotypes about women as the *weaker sex*? Conceiving of Medea as only a victim, and not also as a perpetrator, of violence reinforces ideas of gender essentialism because such a model reifies the gender binary and fails to account for a complex array of gender identities and sexualities. As Lü quips, Wolf's Medea (just like Haas's) is easy to read as "a deliberate incarnation of trendy, feminist virtues" (Myth and Apologia 5). Wolf's Medea comes across as unrealistic to a twenty-first-century readership accustomed to antiheroines, because she is too perfect in her maternal femininity. The process of mythologization, of repeated storytelling, is also itself an essentializing gesture. German feminist Silvia Bovenschen connects silencing to myth when she articulates how, in the case of women “selbst deren Sprachlosigkeit ist noch Teil ihrer Mythologisierung” [their speechlessness itself is yet another part of their mythologization] (41). In other words, femininity is constructed through women’s speechlessness and so any attempt to give women a voice would not only be a feminist act, but also an act of demythologization. Further complicating this situation, Spivak warns about relying on the categorization of historically excluded groups in efforts to achieve emancipation. She writes that “Nor does the solution lie in the positivist inclusion of a monolithic collective of ‘women’ in the list of the oppressed whose unfractured subjectivity allows them to speak for themselves against an equally monolithic ‘same system’” (Spivak 278). This is the trap into which Wolf falls when she describes her Medea story as a more authentic retelling, while making her Medea character a pure victim of violence. If Medea is only one thing, and that thing is a victim, then her subjectivity remains problematically compromised. Put another way, Lü contends that Wolf “strands her heroine in a situation in which insight and exculpation do *not* produce a freeing of the figure from the alienation that besets her in all phases of her life” (Myth and Apologia 17). A Medea that is only a victim and not a perpetrator of violence actually reifies gendered binaries, rather than breaking them down.

In *Medea. Stimmen*, Wolf transforms her protagonist into a perfect and complete victim and therefore, a (feminine) non-subject. When Spivak warns us against the creation of a monolithic category of woman, she encourages us to counter uniformity with an acknowledgment of and respect for differences within groups, even while trying to establish political solidarity. Literary critics such as Britta Kallin and Nikolaos Ioannis Koskinas argue that, at least by the end of the text, Wolf’s Medea has become “ein autonomes Subjekt, das konsequent hinter seinen Entscheidungen steht und das Schicksal alle Frauen und das eigene durchschauen kann” [an autonomous subject, who forcefully stands behind its decisions and can look at the fate of itself and all women] (Koskinas 99; see also Kallin 46). While it is true that by the end of the novel Medea has uncovered, literally in the case of Iphinoe’s bones, some uncomfortable truths about the way that her society works, I am skeptical about how much this really implies that she has become an autonomous subject. Ultimately, Wolf's Medea remains trapped in the flattened, unnuanced categories that Spivak cautions against. For example, Mitrache writes that "Medea scheint in Wolfs Roman zu einer Opferfigur reduziert worden zu sein, eine Märtyrerin, welche die Ungerechtigkeiten, denen sie ausgesetzt ist, ohne großen Widerstand zu leisten, akzeptiert" [In Wolf's novel, Medea seems to be reduced to a victim character, a martyr, who accepts the injustices, to which she is subjected without resistance] (212). I am more inclined to agree with Mitrache's assessment of Medea as a victim twice over. First, she suffers under the masculine power structures of her world, and then she is unable to escape the binary thinking that categorizes men as perpetrators and women as victims of violence.

Wolf's Medea affirms this binary between perpetrators and victims herself, suggesting that there is no middle ground when it comes to these terms. As Medea speaks to her dead brother, she remarks that "Auf dieser Scheibe, die wir Erde nennen, gibt es nichts anderes mehr, mein lieber Bruder, als Sieger und Opfer" (Wolf, *Medea. Stimmen* 106) ["there's nothing anymore but victors and victims, my dear brother, on this disc we call earth"] (Wolf, *Medea*, trans. Cullen 84). From Medea's perspective, there is no alternative to victimhood if one is not born into a position of power. Knowledge of her fate is not enough to drive Medea toward effective action or self-advocacy. Although she may understand why she is victimized, this does not mean that she has the ability, or even the will, to change her situation. As Medea remarks in her final monologue, after she realizes that she will be blamed forever for the murder of her children, "wir sind unbelehrbar" (Wolf, *Medea. Stimmen* 224) ["we are not teachable"] (Wolf, *Medea*, trans. Cullen 186). According to the pessimistic Medea, there is nothing that we might learn to help us overcome systemic oppression.

Wolf's Medea is attacked from all sides, victimized by both men and women, and there is almost no sense of feminist solidarity among the female characters within this text. Astrid Messerschmidt and Eva Peters describe this dynamic when they write that "Christa Wolfs Patriarchatskritik ist nicht—wie in der feministischen Literatur oft anzutreffen—mit einer Apologie oder Glorifizierung einer matriarchalen Kultur verbunden" [Christa Wolf's critique of the patriarchy is not—as one often comes across in feminist literature—connected to an apologia or a glorification of matriarchal culture] (535). Wolf's Medea encounters men who sympathize with her and women who betray her. In this sense, Wolf does push back against a reductive notion of feminist politics in which all men are bad and all women are good. Other women, including Medea's substitute daughters, Agameda and Glauke, do not share Medea's victim-only status in that they contribute in their own ways to Medea's mistreatment. For example, Agameda articulates how she uses whatever limited powers of persuasion she can to attach herself to powerful men. As she states, the world of Corinth is one in which "Jede Frau nutzt die Gaben, die sie hat, um einen Mann an sich zu fesseln. Turin hat mir den Weg ins Königshaus geöffnet, Presbon zeigt mir den Weg, mich an Medea zu rächen" (Wolf, *Medea. Stimmen* 85) ["every women uses whatever gifts she has to bind a man to herself. Turon has opened for me the way into the royal household, Presbon is showing me the way to avenge myself on Medea"] (Wolf, *Medea*, trans. Cullen 66). To be successful, Agameda needs to connect herself to men. The implication of Agameda's self-reflection here is that it is in part because Medea is unwilling to play this game that she so easily becomes a scapegoat. As Agameda articulates, it is Medea's lack of ruthlessness that puts her in a victimized position: "Medea in ihrer Verblendung setzt ja auf die Stärken der Menschen, ich setze auf ihre Schwächen" (Wolf, *Medea. Stimmen* 79) ["Medea in her blindness puts her faith in people's strengths, I put mine in their weaknesses"] (Wolf, *Medea*, trans. Cullen 61). Surprisingly, in light of the plethora of feminist discourses celebrating solidarity between women, Medea gains nothing by trying to play to people's strengths or by trying to lift them up alongside herself. Wolf's Medea does not recognize, as Agameda and Irigaray do, that between two women there always seems to be one who gains life, power, and/or autonomy at the expense of the other. That being said, as the example of intersectional feminist movements (such as the Black German movements I discussed alongside Haas's Medea story) prove, feminist emancipation does not have to be the zero-sum gain that Wolf's Medea encounters here. In *Medea. Stimmen*, solidarity between women is an unrealized goal. It should not be necessary for women to become enemies in the process of fighting for social justice, but this is all too often the result when women, specifically white women, try to establish activist communities.

Medea's victimization is furthered not only by the men and women around her, but also by her own acceptance of her status as a victim. Lü goes so far as to argue that "ihr Märtyrertum so unmöglich erscheint wie der Kindermord bei Euripides und Seneca" [her martyrdom appears just as impossible as the child-murder in Euripides and Seneca] (*Medea* 244). As the anger of the mob grows, Medea's resistance to it diminishes. She accepts too easily that there is nothing she can do to quiet the mass of people gathering against her. Medea understands and matter-of-factly states what is happening saying, "Die Menge suchte nach Opfern, um ihren Rachedurst zu stillen" (Wolf, *Medea. Stimmen* 189) ["the crowd began searching for victims to slake their thirst for revenge"] (Wolf, *Medea*, trans. Cullen 155). She also feels that her imprisonment is inevitable remarking, "So hat es kommen müssen" (Wolf, *Medea. Stimmen* 179) ["it had to happen like this"] (Wolf, *Medea*, trans. Cullen 147), and argues that she no longer has any control over the direction of her life lamenting, "alles lief nach einen Plan ab, auf den ich keinen Einfluß mehr hatte" (Wolf, *Medea. Stimmen* 196). ["everything was proceeding according to a plan over which I no longer had any influence"] (Wolf, *Medea*, trans. Cullen 161). These are not the statements of an autonomous subject setting herself up in resistance to the mob or of a woman who is prepared to fight for justice. Wolf's Medea calmly accepts a violent and flagrantly unfair justice system with hardly any defiance. She complies with her own role as victim to a degree that strikes me as at odds with Wolf's efforts to present her to readers as a more realistic Medea-figure.

It is only after her children are killed that Medea finally begins to regret this generally calm acceptance of her fate. At the very end of the text, Medea finally tries to do something in her own defense by making a feeble attempt to curse the people of Corinth. Medea rails against those who have ruined her life and killed her children, but unfortunately Wolf has already stripped her Medea of the magical powers that would make this threat an effective form of revenge. In other versions of the Medea story, this curse would indeed be sinister and worth taking seriously. However, Wolf's Medea can only play at cursing the Corinthians. The impotence of Wolf's Medea is most striking in this final moment, which ends in despair rather than in triumph. Instead of heading off to the court of Aegeus on a chariot pulled by dragons, Wolf's Medea has nowhere to go as she cries: "Wohin mit mir. Ist eine Welt zu denken, eine Zeit, in die ich passen würde. Niemand da, den ich fragen könnte. Das ist die Antwort" (Wolf, *Medea. Stimmen* 224) ["where can I go. Is it possible to imagine a world. A time, where I would have a place. There's no one I could ask. That's the answer"] (Wolf, *Medea*, trans. Cullen 186). Wolf's Medea is a complete and total victim, out of time and place, who faces oppression at the hands of women, men, and ultimately herself.

Dagmar Nick's Medea and Immortality

Medea's fatalistic reflections evolve into meditations on her legacy in Nick's continuation of the story of an innocent Medea. I have spent the majority of this chapter analyzing the significance of the ways in which Wolf's Medea departs from the typical Medea canon. I now want to return to Dagmar Nick's novella. Stephan insists that because of the author's own disinterested attitude toward feminism, Nick should not be included in the category of feminist Medea stories. Stephan argues that Nick's text represents a "dezidierte Abgrenzung vom feministischen Diskurs der damaligen Zeit" [decided separation from feminist discourse of its time] (163). I disagree and will make an argument for the contrary here. The strongest evidence in favor of reading Wolf and Nick's Medeas together lies in the shared victimization and hopelessness of their Medea figures. Nick's Medea shares the fatalism that plays a central role in the undoing of Wolf's Medea. For example, Nick's Medea articulates her belief that "So oder so, die Zeiten würden sich ändern, sagen sie dann—vermutlich ohne zu wissen, was sie da sagen. Ich glaube nicht, daß die Zeiten sich ändern können. Auch die Menschen nicht" [One way or another, the times will change, they say, presumably without realizing what they are saying. I do not think that the times are capable of changing. Neither are people] (33). Both Wolf and Nick's Medeas consider themselves victims of fate, paralyzed and made forever infamous by malicious lies. Change is impossible and Medea is locked forever into a single path of continuous mythologized victimhood.

While Wolf's Medea ends with nowhere to go, Nick's Medea, whose story we enter after the murder of the children and Medea's banishment from Corinth, has a clear destination. Even if she is not exactly sure how to get there, Nick's Medea knows that she must travel to the home of Chiron, the centaur famous for training heroes, including Jason. The primary focus of Nick's Medea story is the question of legacy and infamy. As Medea herself succinctly puts it: "Eine Frage habe ich: nach dem Sinn der Unsterblichkeit" [I have one question: about the meaning of immortality] (33). During her travels, Medea encounters two famously immortal (or eventually not so immortal) beings, the titan Prometheus and Chiron himself. Prometheus endures eternal suffering as a punishment for giving human beings fire. Chiron notably relinquishes his immortality or is forced to relinquish it, when he is pricked/shot by one of Hercules's arrows dipped in hydra venom. Although he is known as a great healer, Chiron ironically cannot heal himself from this injury and eventually dies, after which he is honored by being placed in the sky as a constellation. By drawing these other mythological figures into the Medea story, Nick conceives of the process of mythmaking itself as a kind of immortality. Putting Nick's Medea story into context with Wolf's helps to explain why the question of immortality might be one of central importance to the Medea story in general. While Medea will not become a constellation in the sky, she achieves her own kind of (after)life through the stories told about her. Medea becomes immortal through the process of mythologization and both Nick and Wolf's texts can be subsequently read as a reckoning with the dangers that often arise from repeated acts of storytelling. How can we avoid mythologizing the subjectivity of those already in power and provide space for people who have been historically disenfranchised to have their say?

Stories are what make Medea infamous and immortal. They are ultimately what she has to overcome if she will ever be able to achieve redemption. When we first encounter Nick's Medea, she is traveling to find Chiron because she hopes that it will give her some direction after the horrible events that befell her in Corinth. She describes all that has happened recounting:

> Ich habe den Namen Chiron nicht mehr gehört, seit mich Iason verließ, seit man die Kinder mir nahm und sie steinigte, bis sie starben, seit man die Stadttore hinter mir zuwarf und Geschichten erfand. Aber Geschichten hat man in diesen Gegenden immer erfunden. (Nick 10)
>
> [I no longer heard the name Chiron, since Jason abandoned me, since they took my children from me and stoned them until they died, since they closed the doors of the city on me and invented stories. But, in this area stories have always been invented.]

Writing after Nick, Wolf's text fills in the gaps of the stories invented by the Corinthians. The emphasis Nick's Medea places on storytelling also blends well with Wolf's emphasis on her own storytelling practice. However, Nick also complicates this picture by reiterating the invented nature of stories. Even the stories Wolf tries to pass off as "authentic," are always fictional, and as such, have the potential to victimize the innocent.

Nick's Medea directly expresses her distrust of stories and is determined to believe only what she sees with her own eyes. As in Wolf's novel, sight is easier to achieve than speech. When she hears centaurs in the woods, Medea hides in order to witness their behavior for herself thinking:

> Wenn es stimmt, daß sie Frauen reißen, wie Löwen das Wild—ich will es erfahren. Ich glaube nicht an Geschichten. Man hat zu viele Geschichten erzählt. Am Ende halten die Leute alles für wahr. Auch daß Medea ihre Kinder eigenhändig erwürgt hat. Ich! Eine kolchische Mutter! (Nick 39-40)
>
> [If it is true that they seize women, like lions take game,—I want to experience it. I don't believe in stories. Too many stories have been told. In the end people take everything for truth. Even that Medea strangled her kids with one hand. Me! A Colchian mother!]

Because of the lies that ruined her own reputation, Medea is not inclined to believe the stories that she has heard about the centaurs. She has experienced firsthand just how wrong and damaging fictional accounts can be. Interestingly, she blames not just the storytellers for this misinformation, but also the people who believe such stories. Whether trusting or gullible, Medea connects her suffering to the will of an audience to believe what they are told, lacking the inquisitiveness to seek out a more complete truth. Medea also attributes the impossibility of the accusations against her to her role as a "Colchian mother." While there certainly is evidence that mothers disapprove of the violence that takes place in their communities, time and time again in the works of both Wolf and Nick, these women prove powerless to stop it. The invocation of motherhood here by Nick's Medea proves hollow when combined with Wolf's interrogation of failed motherhood in *Medea. Stimmen*.

When she finally arrives at her destination, Nick's Medea tries desperately to help Chiron heal his wound, but like many ineffectual Medeas (and mothers) before her, she fails miserably and is left with only "die Traurigkeit seiner Augen [und] meine Nutzlosigkeit" [the sadness in his eyes [and] my uselessness] (62). Nevertheless, Medea is determined to carry on. Her life continues, for better or for worse, despite all that has already happened to her: "Ich weiß, daß ich fortgehen soll. In eine andere Landschaft. Zu anderen Menschen. Ich habe noch eine Weile zu leben" [I know that I should go away. To another landscape. To other people. I still have awhile to live] (65). Just like Wolf's Medea, Nick's Medea is not sure where she should go, only that she cannot stay where she currently is. There may be slightly more hope in Nick's invocation of other lands and peoples. However, the future is still not a bright one for the maligned Medea. Barbara Feichtinger characterizes the message of Nick's Medea story when she writes, "Die Menschheit könne dem Untergang entgehen, wenn sie ihrem prometheischen Unsterblichkeitswahn entsage—und Chiron wie Medea in ihren positiven Kräften, ihrem eigentlichen Sein, wiederentdecke" [Humanity could escape downfall, if they renounce their Promethean delusion of immortality and discover again Chiron and Medea in their positive powers, their actual being] (213–214). While this may be inspirational for the reader, encouraging them to live in the moment does little to help Medea escape the burden of her infamy. Medea still has quite a while to live, especially through the multitude of stories that will be told about her. The question then becomes, is there ever a way out for Medea? Is it ever possible for her to escape this dismal fate? What are the stakes of a feminist project that tries to redeem her through storytelling (the process through which she was initially vilified) and what does success in such a project mean in terms of broader feminist political goals?

Authorial Agency

For both Wolf and Nick channeling voices from the past is a powerful rhetorical strategy that lends subjective authenticity to their characterizations of Medea. With this context in mind, I want to return to authorial (or in Spivak's terms intellectual) voices. If, as Butler writes, "narrative capacity constitutes a precondition for giving an account of oneself and assuming responsibility for one's actions," then it would seem that Wolf is trying to fictively give her characters a similar power of self-expression (*Giving an Account* 12). However, these are literary characters and not real people. Therefore, there is always an author behind these voices. *Medea. Stimmen* draws attention to this fact when each monologue is introduced by an epigraph from a variety of literary and intellectual sources. Ranging from Plato to the feminist philosopher Adriana Cavarero, these epigraphs represent another understudied set of voices, intermingled with the voices of Wolf's characters. Our reading of each monologue is guided from the start by the words of other writers; the epigraphs keeping the importance of authorship always in the forefront of readers' minds. For example, we are set up to understand Jason as power-hungry when his first monologue begins with the following comment from Plato: "Mighty is the longing of man to be remembered and to make himself an immortal name forever" (Wolf, *Medea*, trans. Cullen 27). The words of this outside source deliberately undermine Jason's intentions before he even begins to speak. In other words, as much as the prologue claims that this story is about channeling the voices of these characters, Wolf subtly relies on authors, all of whom would qualify as Western intellectuals under Spivak's definition, to dictate our interpretation of this text.

By framing her text as a recovery of truth, Wolf relies on the same universalizing principles against which she also attempts to argue. Spivak warns us about the danger of simply reestablishing the same allegorical quality of the myth through its rewriting when she describes "the unrecognized contradiction within a position that valorizes the concrete experience of the oppressed, while being so uncritical about the historical role of the intellectual" (275). In other words, while taking on the role of the intellectual author and recovering this voice for Medea, Wolf fails to completely examine her own voice and positionality. In *Medea. Stimmen*, Wolf does not merely attempt to present the culmination of a network of Medea stories in order to create a Medea for the present. Her efforts are not to synthesize, but rather to expunge the Medea stories of the past in order to create space for her more *accurate* representation of Medea. In addition to the sorrow that she feels for her children, at the end of Wolf's text, Medea is primarily concerned about the way her story will be told to future generations. She knowingly describes the smear-campaign that will ensue against her saying, "Sie sorgen dafür, daß auch die Späteren mich Kindsmörderin nennen sollen" (Wolf, *Medea. Stimmen* 224) ["they're at pains to assure that even posterity will call me a child-murderess"] (Wolf, *Medea*, trans. Cullen 186). While Wolf does try to speak from an historically excluded perspective, a perspective that she sees herself as sharing with Medea, Wolf fails to account for the way that intersectional constructions of race and of gender also play a role in how voices are either uplifted or silenced.

Channeling Sigmund Freud's work on sexual perversions, Spivak constructs a sentence to illustrate the foundation of "imperialist subject-production" writing: "White men are saving brown women from brown men" (296). Such a subject-generating sentence of Wolf's Medea story might be: East German intellectual author saving classical literary figure from male scapegoating. While this is a stance that seeks justice for the marginalized, it is also uncritically self-indulgent in ways that are similar to the gestures that Spivak critiques in Western intellectual culture. *Medea. Stimmen* co-opts the idea of the heterogeneous marginalized subject and problematically argues that it applies just as much to white Eastern GDR subjects, as it does to the people defined by Spivak as subaltern. While there are certainly similarities between the marginalization of these groups, conflating them without reflecting on their significant differences does not align with the goals of intersectional feminism. While Spivak, as an intellectual embedded in the Western university system, recognizes and acknowledges the limitations of her own critical project, Wolf attempts far less self-reflection. As Weber argues, "Wolf sets up identifications with the victims of anti-Semitism, racism and imperialism, resulting in equivalencies of victimhood that obscure the workings of whiteness" (165). Instead of the more appropriate sympathy, Wolf tries to generate empathy through which white, settler-colonial readers can incorrectly feel that they fully understand Medea's experiences as a victim of colonization and racialized violence.

Instead of allowing Medea's revenge to serve as a dramatic sign of the desperation she feels and the oppression she faces, Wolf transcribes this same desperation onto the act of storytelling itself, placing herself as author, rather than Medea, in the position of the one who performs a dramatic action, while trying to escape cycles of slander. Koskinas makes a feminist argument when he describes the Medea story's penchant for confronting and breaking cultural taboos. Koskinas maintains that

> "Medeas Rache [that is, the killing of her children] ist ihr einziger Ausweg, ihre einzige Möglichkeit, aus dem Kreislauf der zerstörenden Geschichte, aus der patriarchalischen Welt auszutreten und die für sie zugedachte soziale Rolle (dienende Mutter und Ehefrau) zu verweigern" [Medea's revenge is her only way out, her only opportunity to get out of the cycle of this destructive story, to step outside of the patriarchal world and to reject the social role (of subservient mother and wife) for which she was intended] (95).

Wolf sees a decidedly different kind of feminist potential in the Medea story. If Medea, the child-murderess, is an invention of powerful men and an elaborate cover-up used to mask the violence necessary to maintain patriarchal power, then the way to fight back is no longer through murder, but through storytelling. Just like murdering the children in other Medea stories, the act of storytelling is an act of resistance against a long history of insurmountable obstacles. As Wolf describes in the prologue, "das Eingeständnis unserer Not, damit müßten wir anfangen" (Wolf, *Medea. Stimmen* 9) ["confessing our need—we should begin with that"] (Wolf, *Medea*, trans. Cullen 1). The need that Wolf describes is a need to connect with the past, to (re)connect with a Medea who emerges out from the depths of centuries of misunderstanding to speak to us today. The act of writing this book becomes a substitute for the murder of the children in that it serves as a last-ditch effort to break out of the established patterns of power that characterize the Medea myth and our understanding of the gendered nature of who is given permission to tell stories or to serve as a creator of knowledge.

On a more personal level, this also maps onto Wolf's efforts to defend herself as a GDR writer. The confidence, self-assurance, and even at times defiance, of Wolf's narrator in the prologue contrasts with her aesthetics of subjective authenticity in which narrators "constantly question their own assumptions whilst trying to reconcile conflicts between their individual experience and the world around them" (Summers 233). The reader is asked to question their assumptions, but Wolf puts herself, as author, in the position of the omniscient heroine, who is finally going to rescue Medea. Wolf's narrator describes how we as readers will somehow be able to reach across time and warn Medea about the way in which she has been and will be misunderstood: "wir müssen sie warnen. Unsere Verkennung bildet ein geschlossenes System, nichts kann sie widerlegen" (Wolf, *Medea. Stimmen* 10) ["we must warn her. Nothing can refute our misjudgment; it forms a closed system"] (Wolf, *Medea*, trans. Cullen 1–2). Although we might try to let her know about what is to come, false judgments still keep Medea entrapped. Despite her efforts to escape it, Euripides's work still haunts Wolf's Medea story, much like the bones of Iphinoe haunt Corinthian society. Although her efforts are valiant, just like Medea, Wolf finds herself fighting an uphill battle against epistemic storytelling traditions that seek to exclude her. To have her say, Wolf must take on some of the qualities of the hegemonic and authoritarian subject critiqued by both Spivak and Irigaray. Spivak wants to believe that there is some hope in her own work as a "female intellectual" when she concludes her essay insisting that "the female [marginalized] intellectual as intellectual has a circumscribed task which she must not disown with a flourish" (308). Wolf understands and takes seriously her responsibility to represent (*darstellen*) her communities as a female writer and as a GDR writer. But, just because an author is a member of a group that has been marginalized, she is not guaranteed to avoid reifying the same methods of knowledge-production, or in Wolf's case storytelling, that intentionally exclude her.

In Wolf's version of the Medea story, there is, despite the plurality of voices invoked by her title, minimal room for multiple individuals to share the spotlight and to wield power together. In order for Wolf as the author to emerge as a feminist heroine, Medea's agency has to be reduced and her status as a victim emphasized. For Wolf to truly redeem her, Medea has to be a perfect victim, oppressed on all sides and by people of all genders. This gesture was potentially hopeful and empowering for twentieth-century feminist scholars and writers who were seeking to rewrite literary and political history and to recover the stories of the women who helped to shape European and American culture and literature. In addition, it is seemingly empowering for Wolf herself, who certainly felt trapped by the negative narratives that were being told about her after Reunification. That being said, it is important to acknowledge what Bridge calls "a strange reluctance on Wolf's part, both within the novel and in her comments about it, to admit that what she is constructing is a fiction" (36). By shying away from, while simultaneously reinforcing, her role as author, Wolf recreates imperialist approaches to narrative that we, as scholars at least, should try our best to avoid naturalizing. By positing a *real* Medea, Wolf upholds the problematic notion that "it is possible to scrape away the layers of interpretation this work has deposited, in order to retrieve a version of events which antecedes the distortions of myth" (Bridge 37).

Reading Irigaray and Spivak alongside of Wolf and Nick helps us understand why *Medea. Stimmen* ultimately does not provide a lot of hope for women, especially women who are not authors. Both Irigaray and Spivak are justifiable skeptical about any potential for a female or subaltern speaking subject. The multiple voices channeled by Wolf's text start to generate a polyvocal, non-essentialist, more inclusive feminist politics, but they end up running into the limitations of the cultural context in which they find themselves. In *Medea. Stimmen* the author ultimately wields complete power over the victimized, narrated object of the story, thereby ironically realigning Wolf's project with the oppressive model of mythmaking that she initially seeks to subvert. By trying so hard to set Medea free, Wolf encounters constraints due to the hierarchy automatically set up between the actively writing author and the objectified fictional character. While this is true of any work of fiction, these problems are highly gendered in Wolf, Nick, and Irigaray. They highlight the precarious position of mothers within a society that simultaneously needs them to reproduce, but which also does not want to see too much power escape into the hands of women. Wolf and Nick want to believe that we can overcome these oppressive conditions by writing ourselves out of them. While I respect such optimism, unfortunately the act of writing finds Wolf and Nick right back where they started, replicating the very power structures they seek to circumvent. The gendered problems of voice, agency, and subjectivity that perturb Wolf, Nick, Spivak, and Irigaray are not solved simply by making Medea less murderous.

CHAPTER 3

Performance and Gender Performativity in Dea Loher's *Manhattan Medea*

ἀλλ᾽ ἐσμὲν οἷόν ἐσμεν, οὐκ ἐρῶ κακόν, γυναῖκες

—Euripides 364

[Well, we women are, I will not say bad creatures, but we are what we are.]

—Euripides 365

In this line, Euripides's Medea articulates a very closed view of what it means to be a woman. Women are what they are, and there is nothing that they or anyone else can do to change it. However, within the context of the play it is clear that Medea does not really believe in any intractable qualities of womanhood. She expresses this idea within a series of lies, which she uses to trick Jason into believing that she is no longer angry about his betrayal. Domnica Radulescu sums this situation up nicely when she argues that Medea "embraces the concept of a 'female nature' in an ironic way, in the sense that she lucidly uses its stereotypes in conjunction with those of the 'male nature,' as a way of accomplishing her revenge and punishing those who have caused her misery" (89). Medea uses the possibility that the category of woman might be fixed and stable to lull Jason into a false sense of security. Medea acts the role of a passive, forgiving, and stereotypically deferential woman in order to prepare the way for its contrast, her violent revenge. In doing so, Medea draws attention to the potential disconnect between what one does or says and who one is, forcing readers and viewers to confront the socially constructed nature of identity categories. Even in Euripides, the figure of Medea contributes to debates about the fixity of gendered roles and models identity as performative.

Although my focus up to this point has been on novels, in this chapter I will return to Euripides's original medium, namely the theater. Dea Loher's play, *Manhattan Medea*, was written for the *Steirischer Herbst* avant-garde art festival in Graz, Austria, where it premiered under the direction of Ernst Binder in October 1999. The drama consists of ten scenes written in a combination of free verse and of prose, thereby drawing attention to the script of the play as a text in and of itself. Subsequently, *Manhattan Medea* has been translated and performed in numerous countries in Europe and in North America.[1] However, for the purposes of my analysis, I will focus on this play as a text, examining only the published written script. This is intentional because my argument centers around the fact that Loher's script does unique feminist work, regardless of how the play may or may not be staged. Many of the novels I examine in this book include theatrical elements and so by reading Loher's play in much the same way, as a dramatic text, rather than a theatrical event, I analyze this play in a comparable manner to those novels.

Loher is a feminist and a Marxist known for her politically engaged and often controversial plays. In her work, she takes up a variety of complex themes and causes including child abuse, sexual violence, unemployment, and poverty. Loher demonstrates her interest in left-wing politics by using her adaptation of *Medea* to critique capitalist exploitation. All the other Medea texts I have examined thus far are set in Ancient Greece. Loher, however, transplants her Medea story into a highly fictionalized version of New York City in the 1990s. The United States becomes a metaphor for the capitalist West, while Medea and Jason represent the East. Loher depicts them as Eastern European immigrants fleeing the Yugoslav Wars, thereby historicizing the violence of this story within a wartime context. Significantly, Jason and Medea are also presumed to have the same racial and ethnic background, thereby negating one of the major differences between them that is featured in numerous other Medea stories. Although the time and place are drastically altered from the classical Medea story,

1 There have been notable productions in places such as Germany (Stuttgart 2013), France (Paris 2009 and Marseille 2012), Greece (Athens 2013), and Canada (Quebec 2011), indicating a transatlantic and perhaps, slightly Francophone, interest in this material.

the plot remains largely unchanged from Euripides's text. Medea is still betrayed by Jason and banished. She still kills her child and Jason's new wife.

Although the play's action follows this familiar trajectory, Loher's cast of secondary characters is unrecognizable from any previous version of the Medea story. Keeping with Loher's tendency to critique capitalist systems of exploitation, King Creon takes the form of the Sweatshop Boss, a wealthy businessman who has married off all of his daughters except one. This eclectic group of added characters also includes the artist and doorman, Velazquez (a reference to the Baroque portrait artist Diego Velázquez [1599–1660], whose work was famously copied and adapted by such artists as Pablo Picasso [1881–1973] and Salvador Dali [1904–1989]), and Deaf Daisy, a deaf transvestite who, like Medea, struggles to overcome a violent history. In a nod to postmodern critiques of stable meaning-making through language, both of these significant character additions represent the blurring of binaries: Velazquez, a binary between original and copy in art, and Daisy, a binary between male and female. By putting these binaries and others, such as the binary between East and West, under scrutiny, Loher advocates for a model of storytelling that is not based on a hierarchy of speaking subject and silent object. Instead, through the interaction of these characters, she generates collaborative models for performance, political action, and representation.

Unlike the victimized herbal healer we encounter in adaptations of *Medea* by Christa Wolf and Dagmar Nick, Loher's Medea truly lives up to the title of this book and acts the part of a murderous mother. Medea murders her son on stage (a rare stage direction, despite Medea's typically violent behavior) and engages in acts of self-harm in order to publically display her grief and guilt. Loher's Medea refuses to become invisible or unheard, acting out her emotions with her body. Instead of taking away Medea's capacity to perpetrate violence and replacing it with victimhood, Loher's Medea displays her violence on a grand scale, emphasizing the performative aspects of this aggression. Loher pushes her Medea to the extreme, interrogating the implications of a world in which Euripides's Medea might actually be telling the truth. Women are unquestionably what they are, or at least what their societies have made them. However, in Loher's play what women are proves to be more complex than it initially seems. Loher uses her self-reflexive and exaggeratedly performative Medea to suggest that even though we might appear to be stuck with one version of a narrative, it could have been otherwise. The past is linked to the future through our interactions with others in the present. Even if we cannot fully escape them, myth and narrative are mutable if we engage in a process of collective agency and collaborative storytelling.

Medea and Performance

Although I will not be analyzing actual performances of *Manhattan Medea*, the concept of performance is central to my reading of this play as a text. In my analysis, I use the term "performance" and the related adjective "performative" in two ways: first as a communicative practice (as in performative language) and second, as a process of identity formation through repeated actions (as in gender performativity). The audiences both internal and external to the play are important for Loher because these spectators ultimately help to shape the story that is told to them. In other words, not only is Loher's work itself a play, presumably performed for an audience, but it is also a series of performances by the characters for and with each other. Erika Fischer-Lichte defines performance as an "autopoietic feedback loop," meaning that a performance is co-created by all of its participants, whether "performer" or "spectator" (3). This understanding of performance is self-reflexively depicted in *Manhattan Medea* through the carefully crafted interactions between pairs of characters.

Over the course of the play, Velazquez, Jason, and Daisy each serve as an audience for Medea's calculated (and often violent) performances. By looking closely at how Medea's performances change depending on her audience, the stakes of Loher's political and literary project come into focus. Because performance is a shared experience, it is difficult to think of the performer as a completely independent subject acting in a way that asserts only their individual agency. As Fischer-Lichte articulates, performance "opens up the possibility for them [the performer] to experience themselves as subjects able to co-determine the actions and behavior of others and, at the same time, whose actions and behavior are determined by others" (4). The only way that Medea can truly assert herself is through collaborative performance. She must recognize that her voice is not entirely her own and embrace her audiences as collaborators. Medea's performances internal to Loher's play are a self-reflexive investigation of the nature of performance itself and they help us to see how even the identity categories that we think are the most fixed are actually co-created with the people around us.

This understanding of performance connects to two of Judith Butler's most cited and noteworthy contributions to the field of feminist theory, namely gender performativity and compulsory heterosexuality. In the preface to *Gender Trouble* (1990) Butler asks, "Does being female constitute a 'natural fact' or a cultural performance, or is its 'naturalness' constituted through discursively constrained performative acts that produce the body through and within the categories of sex?" (viii). Nine years after the publication of Butler's book, Loher considers a similar question in her reworking of the Medea material, albeit her line of questioning is less broad. Loher asks: Does being Medea, does being an Othered, child-murdering mother constitute an inescapable and "natural fact," or is being Medea rather a cultural performance that can be manipulated by performers and audiences to serve their own political ends? Loher's work forces her readers to confront the question of what it actually means to play a role or to establish an identity in the first place, to fit oneself into a category through performative acts. Where Butler's work thinks about the construction of the category of woman, Loher invites us to think more specifically about different female character *types* and to consider how one performs as a wife, as a mother, and most uniquely, how one performs as a specific literary, mythological, or dramatic character.

When considering how we account for ourselves and our identities in the world, Butler returns to her notion of performativity, writing that "an account of oneself is always given to another, whether conjured or existing, and this other establishes the scene of address as a more primary ethical relation than a reflexive effort to give an account of oneself" (*Giving an Account* 21). By making Medea perform not just for, but with other characters, Loher highlights the ethical relations involved in performance. Medea's efforts to understand who she is are necessarily collaborative and in her performances she finds both antagonists and allies. By structuring interpersonal relationships in this way, Loher highlights the constructed nature, not just of gendered identities or of political actors, but of mythological figures as well. It might seem obvious that fictional characters are performative and constructed, but I argue that Loher's play unpacks this constructedness in ways that expand on Butler's work and more fully reveal the feminist political stakes of understanding gender as performative.

By exposing the literary world of myth and the process of mythmaking to the same scrutiny and contingency that Butler's theoretical work gives to gender, Loher further exposes the way that gendered roles in literature, and in life, become limiting for women and genderqueer people. At the same time, Loher contends that it may be possible through performance to assert a productively queer and collective agency that starts to push beyond these binary categories. Reading Butler and Loher together generates a unique model for feminist performance. Birgit Haas (not to be confused with Ursula) cautions against reading Loher primarily as a feminist author, arguing that it is materialism that ultimately dominates her plays: "Vielmehr vertritt Loher die Position des feministischen Materialismus, d.h. die Performanz von Weiblichkeit ist mehr oder weniger offen an die soziale Situation der Figuren geknüpft" [Loher represents more often the position of feminist materialism. This means that the performance of femininity is more or less openly tied to the social situation of the characters] (B. Haas, *Das Theater* 234). In my reading of *Manhattan Medea*, I make the case that Loher's engagement with gender performativity is equal to if not greater than her critique of materialism and capitalism. Furthermore, I contend that Loher's play insists that readers treat the various identity categories of the characters (gender, nationality, social class, etc.) as inseparably intertwined. Performance is always intersectional, not just in terms of the performers' identities, but also in terms of the spectators'. Loher's deconstruction of performance provides avenues for reconsidering how these identities are negotiated and narrated as well as how the affect-driven relationship between audience and performer applies to Butler's understanding of gender performativity.

Medea and Velazquez

Through the interactions between Medea and the doorman/artist Velazquez, Loher directly confronts what it means for a work of art to be an original versus a copy, thereby interrogating her own process of adapting the Medea material. In addition to engaging in this meta-reflection on the repetition inherent in the process of retelling mythological stories, Loher's decision to take up this line of questioning gives us a model for thinking about how gender performativity plays out in the supposedly timeless landscape of mythology. One of the major concerns that Butler highlights at the beginning of *Gender Trouble* is that, if we argue that gender is culturally constructed, we run the risk of merely replacing a "biology-as-destiny" mentality with a culture-as-destiny understanding of gender (8). Loher pushes this idea of culture-as-destiny to its limits through her Medea character, who over the course of the play rejects and simultaneously embraces the implications of her role and her name.

Before Loher's Medea can even try to establish herself as a subject, she needs to establish the roles that she can and cannot play. As the audience of Medea's first performance, Velazquez helps Medea establish the ground rules for her subsequent interactions with others. Velazquez initially worries that Medea thinks he is a criminal, simply for doing his job. He remarks, "Sie beobachten mich, als ob es ein Verbrechen wäre" [You are watching me as if it were a crime] (Loher 9). Although it is Velazquez who first describes feeling on display, it is Medea who ultimately tries to play a part in this opening scene. Instead of immediately revealing her identity to him, Medea presents herself as a petty criminal (not unlike the one Velazquez projects onto Medea's observation of him) calling herself, "eine Diebin, Dealerin. Vielleicht nur Hure, harmlos" [a thief, a dealer. Perhaps only a whore, harmless] (9). Medea wants information about Jason and his new fiancé, the Sweatshop Boss's daughter Claire, but fears that if she reveals her true identity the doorman will resist telling her the truth. Unfortunately, her efforts to perform believably as a *normal* figure from within this inter-city milieu is too much of a stretch to be believable. Velazquez initially thinks that not only is she not who she says she is, but also that she is not quite human when he exclaims "Als ich die Augen aufschlug in der Morgendämmerung, glaubte ich an ein Phantom" [When I opened my eyes at dawn, I believed in a phantom] (9). In trying to be anyone else but herself, Medea barely appears real. The play veers into the melodramatic in this moment in which the attempt to name leads to, as Peter Brooks would have it, "irresolvable conflict and contradiction" (100). The being that stands before the doorman in this first scene consistently evades categorization.

Although it subverts all attempts to label her, Medea's initial performance with the doorman lacks conviction and, therefore, never ends up being particularly persuasive. She is not good at pretending to be normal and Velazquez confirms her difference by never seeing her as she deceptively tries to represent herself. As Medea continues to resist giving her name, Velazquez mistakes Medea again, this time for a journalist. He assumes that Medea is interested in uncovering some tabloid-ready information about the Sweatshop Boss and his family. However, Medea's imitation of a journalist is short-lived because she does not know information that any interested journalist would already have. After Medea expresses a lack of knowledge about the weddings of the Sweatshop Boss's other daughters, Velazquez comments, "Hören Sie Ma'm, Sie sind gar nicht von der Presse, wie—sonst wüßten Sie doch Bescheid" [Listen Ma'am, you are definitely not from the press, like—otherwise you would already know] (Loher 12). Medea cannot blend in with the other New Yorkers and she is finally forced to admit: "Ich bin nicht von hier" [I am not from here] (12). The fact that her lack of celebrity knowledge marks her as an outsider within this community stands in contrast to other Medea adaptations in which Medea's knowledge of magic is part of what sets her apart. In this more contemporary setting, the problem is not that Medea knows too much, but rather that she knows too little about the people who are valued in this particular society.

At the end of this first scene, Medea gives up her failed attempt to perform the general role of the every-woman. However, she has learned from this encounter and will persist in her efforts to mold performative language and narration to her will and desires. In her efforts to merely be anybody other than herself (a thief, a dealer, a whore, a journalist), she cannot succeed in coming across as authentic. The character that she tries to play here is difficult to perform because that character has no backstory. She cannot connect to others through her performance if her character has no depth. It is impossible for Medea to convincingly play the role of merely anyone who is not Medea because that role is defined by lack. Medea might be able to confuse Velazquez for a little while, but ultimately, as the literary scholar Sebastian Wogenstein argues, even mastery of the language of the everyday person is not enough for Medea to achieve a "dauerhaften Aufenthalt in ihrer physisch wirklichen Welt" [lasting stay in her physically real world] (303). As it turns out, perhaps Velasquez was correct to believe in phantoms. At one point he asks to touch Medea and she answers him "Kommen Sie nicht näher.—Wir sind uns nicht vertraut.—Und ich bin keine, die man sich erwählt, zu seiner Anvertrauten, schnell" [Don't come any closer.—We are not intimately acquainted.—And I am not a person, who one quickly elects to be their confidant] (Loher 9). In her interaction with Velazquez, Medea is untouchable in both the physical and the emotional sense. The barriers that she puts up keep her from successfully communicating and collaborating with Velazquez.

In order to move forward, Medea must embrace her own Medea-ness, her own destiny as a perpetrator of violence and of revenge. In an act whose drama is heightened by the fact that she has withheld the information up to this point, Medea eventually reveals herself as Medea to the doorman. After Velazquez expresses that he sympathizes with the mother of Jason's child, Medea finally asks him to fetch her husband saying:

> Sagen Sie ihm—
>
> Sagen Sie Jason—
>
> Ich bin hier.
>
> Seine Frau ist hier. (Loher 16)
>
> [Tell him—
>
> Tell Jason—
>
> I am here.
>
> His wife is here.]

Although she reveals her true identity, Medea still does not refer to herself by name. When she tells Velazquez who she is, it is in terms of her position as Jason's wife. Medea still tries to be absolutely anyone other than Medea. She attempts to establish herself as a presence in the play without having to attach herself to the implications that come from being Medea, from being set on a course toward revenge, destruction, and violence. Nevertheless, this course is ultimately unavoidable and since she cannot overcome it, she quickly learns to embrace it. As the scholar Stephanie Catani argues, "Sie versucht nicht, sich vom tradierten Mythos zu emanzipieren, sondern beruft sich konsequent auf diesen. Lohers Medea ist, was Medea immer schon war—und anders kann sie nicht sein" [She does not try to emancipate herself from the myth as it was handed down, instead she consistently relies on it. Loher's Medea is, what Medea always already was—and she cannot be otherwise] (326). Catani's language mirrors that of Euripides's Medea, suggesting that while Medea might not be able to control the fact that she is Medea, she can control the manner in which she acts out this role through language-play and acts of performance. Medea can reconfigure and blur the binaries between performer and audience, subject and object, original and copy.

A closer examination of the character of Velazquez underscores the fact that Medea's first diegetic performance also highlights the repetition inherent in the process of adapting mythological stories. In his art, Velazquez copies the work of the artist Diego Velázquez, not in order to become a new Velázquez, but so that he will become the only Velazquez (Loher 11; Wogenstein 305). His goal, paradoxically, is to create a "Nachahmung, um unnachahmlich zu werden" [an imitation in order to become inimitable] (Wogenstein 306). Instead of trying to copy the emotional intentions of the original artist, Velazquez merely copies the forms that he sees, his own artistic and creative innovation being the act of copying itself. He endeavors to create "eine Kopie, die keine ist" [a copy, which isn't one] (Loher 11). In order to become the artist left standing over the course of history, Velazquez believes it is best not to add any of one's own emotions to one's art. Medea tries to adopt this same blankness in her initial self-presentation for the doorman. However, she cannot achieve Velazquez's artistic ideals. She ultimately has too much of a desire for a deeper, more emotional connection.

Velazquez prefers to let Medea replicate her vengeful path without interference because he cannot stomach the incorporation of emotions into artistic reproduction. At the end of the play, he effectively absolves himself from the guilt of having to watch Medea suffocate her son with a garbage bag saying, "Ich kann keinen Abschied sehen" [I cannot see any farewell] (Loher 60). Yet it is actually his failure to watch over her that gives Medea the opportunity to kill her son in the first place. If Wogenstein is right and Medea's subjectivity is characterized by the combination of her "rationale Willen" [rational will] and her "Affekte und die beschriebenen Zwänge" [affects and the described forces] (302), then Medea's character completely goes against Velazquez's own aesthetics of emotionless copies. Velazquez is the "Meister der Kopie" [master of the copy] (Loher 11), and yet he cannot watch Medea's reproduction, her *Nachahmung* [emulation] of her most noteworthy action as Medea, the killing of her child. Velazquez's copies of shapes and of colors may stand the test of time, but when we copy stories and create mythologies such emotional distance is impossible to achieve. Velazquez's final action in the play is giving Medea his copy of the Diego Velázquez painting *The Infant Philipp Prosper* (1659). When he gives Medea the painting, he resists any emotional reaction that she might give in response, saying that the painting "soll kein Trost sein" [should be no comfort] and that Medea should not even thank him for the gift (60). The painting should only serve as a reminder that in his capacity as a doorman, he will be responsible for the safety of Medea's child. No emotion necessary; as he says from the start, he is just doing his job. However, by leaving the son with his mother, Velasquez fails at even this professional task. The stage directions make it clear that Velazquez vacates the scene before Medea takes up the same garbage bag that was used as a wrapping for the painting and suffocates her child to death. Velazquez facilitates, but does not participate in the murder of the child. The act of copying (as represented by Velazquez) creates the means for, but is not a co-creator of Medea's final performance, which is actually a performance with and for Deaf Daisy (as I will explain in detail later).

Scholars such as Catani and Wogenstein have drawn particular attention to the way that Velazquez's copy of *The Infant Philipp Prosper* (1659) transforms into one of Picasso's mid-twentieth-century recreations of another famous Diego Velázquez work, *Las Meniñas* (The Ladies-in-Waiting) (1656), within the fire that consumes the home of the Sweatshop Boss at the end of the play. This layering of copies on copies adds to our understanding of Loher's interrogation of the process of mythmaking itself. Wogenstein argues that the fire symbolizes an authentic representation in the sense that the physical changes caused by fire are undeniable and cannot be faked: "Das, was verbrennt, verwandelt sich im Verbrennen, wird zerstört und *spielt* nicht bloß sein Verbrennen" [that which burns, changes itself by burning, becomes destroyed and does not merely *play* its burning] (Wogenstein 311; emphasis in original). There is an authenticity in this alteration because the changed object bears little to no resemblance to the original. The painting that disappears into the fire looks nothing like the painting that emerges out of it. Furthermore, Picasso's cubist rendition of this work looks very little like Velázquez's baroque original. As Birgit Haas articulates, the point here is that, "Aus einem Abbild kann in der Nachdichtung nicht nur stilistisch, sondern auch inhaltlich etwas völlig Neues hervorgehen" [Something completely new can emerge through the process of adaptation out of a copy, not only stylistically, but also in terms of content] (*Das Theater* 259–260). Contrary to Velasquez's understanding, the best copy or adaptation may be one that changes the original entirely and develops something completely new.

This understanding of adaptation more closely reflects what Loher sets out to do in her own retelling of the Medea story. By copying *Medea* and having Medea copy previous versions of herself, albeit in an entirely new setting, Loher generates her own distinctive work of art. Both of the paintings in the play are copies, just copies of different sorts. Velazquez's copy of the Velázquez painting duplicates the shapes and colors on the canvas as closely as possible. Picasso's copy of another Velázquez painting is a reinterpretation of older material that is personalized to Picasso's unique artistic style and historical context. What emerges then from the fire of authenticity is not the work that most closely resembles the original visually, but the work that has taken the original as a starting point and imbued it with the artist's own emotions and artistic vision. In her process of self-reflection on the art of copying and adapting older works of art, Loher argues that the most authentic copies are surprisingly those which stray the most from the original, the copies that most reflect the time and individual style of the copier. Loher's Medea models for readers that not only is the most successful copy a subjective one, but it is also a collectively subjective one, which combines the affects and interests of a variety of individuals.

Medea and Jason

Jason is the character with whom Medea shares the most history and so her performances with him are more communicative and effective than those with Velazquez. Together Jason and Medea have been through a number of traumatic experiences. Both Medea and Jason are immigrants and therefore outsiders in the United States. In other versions of the Medea story, we have seen the problematic ways in which Medea has been Othered, racialized, and dehumanized, even by authors supposedly sympathetic to her plight. Therefore, it is significant that in Loher's play, Jason is allied with Medea through this shared outsider status. Jason cannot use Medea's difference to dismiss any claims that she has on his attention, affection, and respect. Instead of being placed solely on her shoulders, Medea shares the burden of ostracism, oppression, and sacrifice with Jason. Their bond is forged by the struggles required to build a new life for themselves in a new country. Despite Jason's efforts to deny this connection, Medea insists that because of their history, their destinies are irrevocably linked.

For Jason, rejecting his past literally means rejecting the maternal body when he helps to drown his own mother in an effort to escape the violence of war. According to Butler, in addition to being constructed through performance, subjectivity is also generated through exclusion and rejection. As we saw in Luce Irigaray's work in the previous chapter, psychoanalysis describes the rejection of the maternal body as a part of the process for establishing subjectivity. As Butler explicates for us, other feminist psychoanalytic scholars such as Julia Kristeva build on a foundation established by Jacques Lacan, in which language itself represents a rejection of the maternal body because "language, in turn, structures the world by suppressing multiple meanings (which always recall the libidinal multiplicity which characterized the primary relation to the maternal body) and instating univocal and discrete meanings in their place" (Butler, *Gender* 79). Multiplicity links back to the maternal, while clear expression from one voice or a singular subjective position invokes the paternal. Therefore, Jason's desire to forget the past by ridding himself of his mother and Medea's insistence on remembering it connects to contemporaneous feminist understandings of the relationship between motherhood and subjectivity within an androcentric system.

In one of Loher's most striking alterations to the Euripides plot, Medea insistently reminds Jason that he drowned his own mother in order to save himself. In a performance of his own that directly parallels Medea's killing of her son, Jason recounts the tragic events of the past, describing his mother's death as a sacrifice that she, herself, desired for the sake of her son. In his story, mother and son are running away from soldiers and a home that lies in ruins when they encounter a river that Jason, who has been carrying his mother up to this point, cannot cross with her on his shoulders. He relates her subsequent death with a strange combination of morbid detail and tenderness saying:

> [Ich] nehme ihren Kopf in beide Hände sacht wie sie
> es mit mir getan als Kind und
> küsse ihre Augen und
> halte den Kopf fest unter Wasser. (Loher 21)

> [[I] take her head in both hands gently as she
> did with me as a child and
> kiss her eyes and
> hold her head firmly under the water.]

It is challenging to imagine the effort and the force required to hold someone underwater as their body instinctually fights for its own life as occurring with the delicate tenderness Jason uses to describe it here. He retells this story in this way to assuage his own sense of guilt for his past actions. In her reading of another Loher play, the controversial *Unschuld* (Innocence) (2003), Katrin Sieg argues that "guilt saps characters' life energy, shrinks their libido, turns love to hate and violence, and elicits rituals of remorse and atonement that are as extravagant as they are futile" (124). In *Manhattan Medea* many of these same markers of guilt are at work (except for perhaps the shrunken libido, since Jason appears to have no trouble wooing Claire). Nevertheless, having Medea as his audience complicates Jason's elaborate efforts to atone for his past through performative storytelling. Medea knows the truth about their violent histories and thus serves as a contrarian, but not entirely unsympathetic audience for Jason.

The juxtaposition of Jason killing his mother and Medea killing her son draws further attention to the idea that any effort to establish independent subjectivity means that the mother must be metaphorically, if not literally, cast off. The initial implication being that we must act as Jason does, or the mother will destroy us, as Medea does. While seemingly necessary, at least symbolically, the act of casting the mother aside is also difficult to live with. At the conclusion of his story, Jason describes how after killing his mother,

> da
>
> gab es niemand mehr
>
> der mir näher war als ich mir selbst
>
> und keinen der mir fremder war als ich mir selbst (Loher 22)

> [there
>
> was no longer anyone
>
> who was closer to me than myself
>
> and no-one more foreign to me than I to myself]

Jason's expression of both closeness and distance from himself upon killing his mother serves as a parallel to what Medea feels after performing the reverse action and killing her own son. After suffocating her son Medea declares, "Von jetzt an / werde ich / eine lebend[e] Tote sein" [from now on / I will / be the living dead] (Loher 61). Just as Jason experiences the feeling of being inbetween two extremes after killing his mother, Medea also exists in a nebulous space in-between life and death after killing her son. In both of these deaths what should be the intimate love between mother and child breaks down into extreme violence, and both Jason and Medea experience the discomfort of guilt over their past actions. However, because Medea is a feminist killjoy, as defined by Sara Ahmed, who "poses a problem because she keeps exposing a problem" (*Living a Feminist Life* 99), Medea is willing to live with the discomfort that Jason wants to ignore. The difference between Medea and Jason is that Medea owns her guilt, whereas Jason tries to mask his.

Medea's ability to confront her guilt even extends beyond deeds for which she is directly involved. Although Medea and Jason had not even met when Jason's mother drowns, as an early co-creator of Jason's performance of this story, Medea comes to feel as though she participated in it. Medea describes herself as initially drawn to Jason because of his "schönen Mund, / mit dem du gut reden konntest" [pretty mouth / with which you were able speak well] (Loher 22). She is so captivated by his rhetoric as he relates the story of his mother's death that "es war als ob ich mitgeholfen hätte, / sie zu ertränken" [it was as if I had helped / to drown her] (22). Jason's persuasive tongue is an example of the manipulative power of performative speech for a willing audience. Although Medea remembers her empathy, these feelings ultimately stay in the past, locked away in Medea and Jason's war-torn homeland. Their relationship changes when Medea is no longer willing to serve as a collaborative audience for his guilt-assuaging performances. Medea eventually comes to understand the death of Jason's mother as an example of a woman (not dissimilar to Claire), who is problematically willing to sacrifice everything for Jason. He does not want true companionship or collaboration, but rather women who "sich selbstlos opfern wollte[n]" [want to sacrifice themselves selflessly] for him (23).

Family dynamics in *Manhattan Medea* are heavily influenced by gender roles, particularly through the contrast between Medea and Jason's new bride, Claire. Jason is quick to set up a stark and gendered contrast between the two women in his life. Medea believes so deeply in her bond with Jason that she does not initially understand that Jason has betrayed and abandoned her. At first, she thinks that Jason has concocted a plan to swindle the Sweatshop Boss out of money and asks him when they will run away together, calling his engagement "ein guter Fang" [a good catch] (17). Medea's description of Claire as a valuable possession to be exploited is shared by Claire's father, the Sweatshop Boss. As he crudely puts it, "Meine Tochter ist eine Geldheirat, und jeder Schwanz in der Stadt ist scharf auf sie" [my daughter is a money match and every dick in the city lusts after her] (47). Claire never gets to speak for herself in the context of the play, thereby establishing her as a feminine object for the projections of the other (primarily male) characters. Claire's femininity and sexual desirability prevent her from serving as a co-creator of any performances within the play.

As many Jasons before him, Loher's Jason is attracted to women who show him absolute devotion. Jason describes the bond that he has with Claire saying dramatically, "Sie vertraut mir jetzt schon. Nicht einmal drei Wochen—/ und sie würde sich ein Brandmal geben lassen mit meinem Namen" [she trusts me already now. It is not even three weeks—/ and she would let herself get branded with my name] (17). If what Jason says is true, which is impossible to judge since we never hear from Claire herself, this level of unquestioned devotion and trust is deeply problematic from a feminist perspective. If this is what Jason desires from a partner, Medea might count herself lucky to be free from such a self-effacing relationship. The only other perspective we get on Claire comes from Velazquez who insists: "Die hat was im Kopf. Ist nicht eine von diesen abgefuckten Park Avenue chicks, wenn Sie wissen, was ich meine. Die ist am Julliard, studiert Violine. Und—eine echte Schönheit noch dazu" [She is quite smart. Is not one of these fucked up Park Avenue chicks, if you know what I mean. She is at Julliard, studying violin. And—in addition a real beauty] (13). One wonders what this accomplished young woman sees in the manipulative Jason! What is clear is that when Medea insists on being treated as an equal and is no longer willing to sacrifice everything for Jason, she fails to exhibit the refinement and feminine appeal that both Jason and Velasquez use to characterize Claire. Medea's androgyny, or improper femininity, makes her the opposite of Claire, but she is also not entirely unappealing. Jason, in a statement of unmitigated ego, concludes his comparison of the women by lamenting that "wenn ich leben könnte mit zwei Frauen, wäre ich glücklich" [if I could live with two women, I would be happy] (29).

Jason's desire to have everything for himself, no matter the inconvenience or even the violence that it does to others, is something that Medea latches onto and exaggerates through performative acts of self-harm.

While Jason's performance in front of Medea is directed at assuaging his own guilt, Medea recreates the pain of her past indiscretions in front of Jason by attacking her own body. After Jason claims to love Claire, Medea pulls out the knife that was used to kill her brother, an act of violence jointly committed by Medea and Jason during a competition over limited food during their voyage to America. Medea proceeds to cut her own palm and both of her cheeks with the knife. Jason recognizes that this performance is intended for him when he inquires, "Was willst du mir beweisen" [What do you want to prove to me?] (33). At first Medea avoids his query, directing his attention to the way the knife is permanently marking her face. After cutting her first cheek she sarcastically appeals to Jason's appreciation of her appearance asking, "Ist es dir egal geworden, / wie ich aussehe" [Have you become indifferent / to how I look?] (33). After proceeding to cut her other cheek, Medea also goes for a jealous response remarking, "Dir ist es egal geworden, / wer mich ansieht" [You don't care / who looks at me] (34). Medea tries to seduce while in the process of cutting up the very means through which that seduction might be successful. She uses her physical beauty to gain an upper hand, while at the same time acting to destroy that beauty, marking her own body with the signs of the emotional pain that Jason has caused her.

Jason and Medea's shared guilt for the death of Medea's brother also confuses the boundary between victims and perpetrators of violence. Christine Künzel argues that the violence in Loher's plays is a violence that comes "von innen [...] wie ein Trieb" [from inside, like a drive] (360). However, even Künzel herself points out that this would imply a naturalization or a biological determinism of violence when in fact, in *Manhattan Medea* at least, we are presented with quite the opposite (363). Violence is what is used to mark the unnatural and unacceptable nature of the perpetrator's past actions and, in the case of Jason, the current denial of responsibility. Through the shock value of her performed violence, Medea draws attention to her status as a victim, as someone who suffers because of Jason's betrayal. Within a legal justice system that requires evidence, that requires signs of harm done; Medea takes it upon herself to mark her physical body in ways that reflect her emotional pain. A similar moment of lashing out physically in order to represent inner pain occurs in Hans Henny Jahnn's *Medea*, when Medea plucks out the eyes of the messenger who comes to tell her of Jason's engagement. "Von meinem Zorn verstehst Du nichts. Von meinem Leid verstehst Du nichts. Von Deinem Untergang verstehst Du nichts. Ich aber sehe, sehe, sehe" [Of my anger you understand nothing. Of my suffering you understand nothing. Of your demise you understand nothing. But I see, see, see] (28), proclaims Jahnn's Medea. The dark humor in Medea's insistence on her own metaphorical vision just as she has removed the messenger's own means of sight is similar to Medea's efforts to get Jason to come back to her and to admit their shared guilt by cutting open her face. By perpetrating these acts of self-harm, Medea makes herself visible as a victim. Similarly to Wolf's depiction of Medea, Loher's Medea ascribes to the logic that sympathy is derived from victimhood, even if that victimhood is self-imposed. However, unlike Wolf's Medea, when Loher's Medea acts as a victim, it is not a passive victimhood, but more like Jahnn's Medea in its extreme aggression.

Although Jason does not abandon his marriage plans, Medea's bloody performance does allow her to communicate more openly with him. By cutting herself up in front of him, Loher's Medea channels Butler's contention that:

> Indeed, if, in the name of ethics, we (violently) require that another do a certain violence to herself, and do it in front of us by offering a narrative account or issuing a confession, then, conversely, if we permit, sustain, and accommodate the interruption, a certain practice of nonviolence may follow. (Butler, *Giving an Account* 64)

Medea literalizes Butler's metaphor by manifesting the violence of her past on her body, thereby forcing Jason to account for it. By confronting this traumatic past, Medea hopes that they might both be able to overcome it and live in peaceful unity. Even though she is ultimately wrong about any potential for peace, Medea's efforts represent an attempt to engage in collaborative performance with Jason. Fischer-Lichte argues that performance is an "interplay between intention and emergence, planning and contingency" (9). Medea certainly encounters both when she cuts open her body for dramatic and communicative effect. In order to perform together, Medea and Jason must relinquish some control to each other. When Jason fails to respond to her dramatics in the way that she would like, Medea returns to his initial question about the audience of her performance and answers it. The knife, she tells him, binds the two of them together:

> Das verbindet.
> Diese Nacht.
> Und alle die Nächte danach,
> in denen wir in dieser Schuld lagen,
> die wir teilen.
> Für immer (Loher 34)
>
> [That unites.
> This night.
> And all the nights thereafter,
> in which we lay in this guilt,
> that we share.
> for always]

The use of the German word "teilen" here is particularly interesting because it can mean both separation or division, as well as sharing, the primary meaning invoked by this passage. Shared guilt is ultimately what divides Medea from Jason. The soon-to-be scars on Medea's face, as well as the knife itself, serve as reminders of the violence in which both Medea and Jason have already been complicit in order to secure their future in the United States. Medea argues through her performance that these bonds of mutual violence and of mutual guilt are inescapable, just as the scars that will form over the places she has cut herself may fade over time, but will never completely vanish from the canvas of her skin. Medea has taken her interaction with Velazquez seriously and created a copy of past violence that simultaneously is not one. As Medea demonstrates, the past is never gone, but will perform itself over and over again, casting a shadow over the present that one can either reject or embrace.

Medea and Jason represent two different kinds of storytellers: those who use stories as a way to alter the past, thereby absolving themselves for their actions like Jason, and those who use stories to bring the pain of the past back into the present like Medea. Fischer-Lichte articulates how time is related to performance writing that "performative processes are realized in the present by referencing the past and bringing forth the future" (7). Medea proves to be the one who understands this relationship between time and performance because by bringing her past into the present, she finds some degree of success in her future. By working with and not against the dictates of her past, Medea establishes herself as an artist, as a masterful creator of performances. If Velazquez is the master of copies, Medea is the master of remembrances, a different, but potentially more progressive and productive type of copying. As Antje Roeben writes, "die Figur Medea lebt in und durch ihre Erinnerung" [the figure of Medea lives in and through her memory] (94). Medea insists that the violence of the past cannot be whitewashed by pretty words retold until one is convinced that they are true. Instead, it must be brought into the present and truly accounted for in all of its violence. While there are certainly many limitations to German *Erinnerungskultur*,[2] including the continued erasure of Germany's colonial past (as we saw in Ursula Haas's *Freispruch für Medea*), Loher's Medea represents the best of such impulses because she recognizes that the memory of violence is brutal and uncomfortable. Through the interactions between Medea and Jason, Loher argues that instead of trying to erase a violent past through storytelling, one must deal with it together, in the present,

2 This term, literally meaning "memory culture," is most frequently used to describe Germany's cultural engagement with the Nazi past and the Holocaust. In recent years the successes and failures of these efforts to confront a violent past and present have been used (sometimes problematically and sometimes more productively) as examples for how the United States might deal more effectively and deeply with its own history of slavery and structural racism. See for example Yuliya Komska's nuanced take in *The Washington Post* "What to Do With Confederate Monuments: Seven Lessons from Germany" (2017); and Susan Neiman's overly optimistic book *Learning from the Germans: Race and the Memory of Evil* (2019).

and without shying away from difficult conversations. The problem that remains to be addressed is whether or not such performative remembrance must always come at the expense of the bodies of women onto which past violence is, in the case of Loher's Medea, literally inscribed.

Medea and Deaf Daisy

After forcing Jason to acknowledge the shared bond of guilt that inextricably links them together, Medea turns to a third and final audience for her most violent performance yet. In collaboration with Deaf Daisy, Medea's revenge finally plays itself out on stage. Because of Daisy's deep connection to performativity and to grief, they[3] are Medea's most collaborative and influential audience. Deaf Daisy is the most unique character in any of the Medea stories I have discussed thus far and to understand their relationship with Medea, we need to closely examine their identity as both a transvestite and a person with a disability.

In her conversation with Jason, Medea fails to live up to the standards of femininity as represented by Claire. Medea's non-normative gender identity is only accentuated by her collaboration with the transvestite Deaf Daisy. Although Daisy's status as a transvestite never becomes a focal point within the dialogue of the play, the stage directions clearly describe them as such. The choice of this word "transvestite" (rather than transgender or transsexual), classifies Daisy as similar to a drag queen, presumably dressing their assigned male body in feminine-coded clothing. In other words, Daisy does not appear to experience gender dysphoria, at least not directly,

3 I will use the gender-neutral pronouns they/them when referring to Deaf Daisy to mark their multi-faceted gender identity. Pronouns are never used to refer to this character in the play itself. At one point, they are gendered female through the use of the article "die" (Loher 43), but they are also represented in the character list by the masculine form of "ein tauber Transvestit" (8). Since the writing of this play in 1999, the use of gender-neutral forms in the German language has become more common, but this character predates the increased visibility of such activism.

but rather takes pleasure in adorning their body as they see fit depending on the context. In *Bodies That Matter*, Butler cautions her readers not to understand drag as exemplary of gender performativity, but rather as just one instance of it (175). Nevertheless, drag has an important role to play in Butler's analysis. She writes that drag makes visible to us a kind of "heterosexual melancholy" (*Bodies* 180), in which the straight subject mourns the loss of the same sex person that he/she never loved by becoming that man/woman. Butler tells us that

> what drag exposes, however, is the "normal" constitution of gender presentation in which the gender performed is in many ways constituted by a set of disavowed attachments or identifications that constitute a different domain of the "unperformable" (*Bodies* 180).

Essentially, Butler argues that gender performativity does not mean that there is a pre-existing subject on top of which gender is assembled, like putting on a mask or an outfit, but rather that it is the performance of gender itself that creates a subject. The art of drag celebrates the idea that there is nothing inherent or natural about gender or heterosexuality. However, drag also highlights the fact that gender performativity stems from the melancholic. It is because of existing social or cultural prohibitions on certain activities, such as having a romantic partner of the same gender as oneself, that these acts and/or the rejection of them become integrated into our own gender performance and are thereby constitutive of our own subjectivity. Although we learn nothing about their sexuality, Daisy's status as a transvestite makes them a clear ally of Medea, who, as we saw through her interactions with Jason, also mourns significant losses, which eventually manifest themselves through corporeal performance.

In a nod to their identity as a transvestite, Daisy uses clothing to communicate. For example, they remark on the class dynamics of the city, saying to Medea: "Sie haben hier nicht zufällig interessante Kleidung herumliegen sehen, Hüte Schuhe Taschen. Man sollte meinen, die Leute in dieser Straße wären großzügig, wenn schon nicht verschwenderisch, im Wegwerfen ihrer Garderobe" [You see here, not by chance, interesting clothing lying around, hats, shoes, bags. One should think, the people in these streets would be generous, if not also wasteful in the discarding of their wardrobe] (Loher

42). Daisy uses the indifference of the wealthy people who throw away their clothing to better position themself to take advantage of what others overlook. Clothing is so essential to Daisy's understanding of identity that they also describe their parents' clothing as substitutes for the people themselves:

> Mein Vater war eine rostbraune taillierte Jacke mit Samtkragen, unecht, und einem Manschettenknopf am linken Ärmel seines Hemdes. Meine Mutter hauptsächlich ein mauvefarben geblümter Winkelrock mit Totenköpfen am Saum. (Loher 42)

> [My father was an auburn fitted jacket with a velvet collar, artificial, and a cufflink on the left sleeve of his shirt. My mother essentially a mauve, floral chevron skirt with skulls on the hem.]

By describing their parents through clothing, Daisy highlights their mom and dad's efforts to elevate their social rank through aesthetics, for example, the artificial velvet of the father's jacket. Daisy also highlights their parents' inner turmoil, as in the combination of floral and skulls in their mother's attire or their father's single cufflink. Daisy uses these clothes to protectively distance themself from their father's violence. When Medea asks how they became deaf, Daisy grimly responds that "Die Jacke schoß dem Winkelrock das Gehirn aus der Fassung" [The jacket shot the chevron skirt's brain from its casing] (Loher 43). By reducing their parents to clothing, Daisy can dissociate somewhat from the brutal murder of their mother by their father. When Daisy offers up this story to Medea, it becomes clear that their deafness is a psychosomatic reaction to the trauma of bearing witness to this domestic violence. It is in this moment of horrific murder, as pieces of their mother end up in their hair, that Daisy experiences their "Hörstürz" [acute hearing loss] (43). Daisy has been traumatized and, therefore, needs to remove their parents' bodies, reducing them to clothing in order to be able to tell this story. Butler rightfully argues against the notion that the clothes make the woman (Butler, *Gender* 140–141), but it cannot be denied that clothing often plays an important role in establishing Medea's identity as an outsider. In Ursula Haas's novel, for example, Medea and her family make a point of dressing like Greeks when Jason arrives (Haas 56), and in Franz Grillparzer's Medea play, the titular character eventually tears off her Greek clothing to go back to her native style of dress (Act 2). When they use clothing as a coping mechanism, Daisy highlights how gender performativity connects identity to melancholy and trauma.

This is not to say that Medea and Daisy get along right away just because they share a history rife with violence and grief. Because Daisy is a deaf person, they force Medea to respond differently to them, initially upsetting and destabilizing Medea's usual mode of interacting with others. Daisy forces Medea to engage in acts of deconstruction on a number of levels. Daisy's presence reminds not just Medea, but also the readers of the play as well, that the choices available to a given person may look different depending on that individual's class status or their ability to engage with a world that only accounts for certain types of bodies. When they first meet, Daisy has to remind Medea several times to face them when she is speaking, so that Daisy can read Medea's lips: "Sprechen Sie klarer, ich lese von den Lippen" [Speak more clearly, I am reading from lips] and later "Wenden Sie mir Ihre Lippen zu" [Turn your lips toward me] (Loher 41). This insistence on accommodations upsets Medea and she initially resists changing her behavior, only giving in when it becomes clear that Daisy can get her what she wants. These tense initial interactions between Daisy and Medea are an example of what in disability studies is called the social model of disability. Daisy struggles to interact because Medea does not face them when she talks. Medea eventually accommodates this request, but only because it is also in her best interest, because she needs something from Daisy. Medea's initial refusal to face Daisy when speaking is what causes Daisy to experience disability, not the fact that they cannot hear. When Medea chooses to engage with Daisy on Daisy's terms, the two have no trouble interacting. The problem is not Daisy's body, but Medea's initial refusal to make the space conducive to communication.

I want to pause over Loher's depiction of Daisy as a person with a disability and connect it to their experiences of grief and loss in a world that is not built for them. Through the character of Daisy, Loher uniquely introduces a figure into the Medea story who is even more of an outsider than Medea herself. Daisy is quick to pick up on Medea's sorrow in being denied husband, child, and brother because they themselves have experienced a great deal of loss. As they describe the trauma through which they lost their hearing, Daisy tells Medea that "das erste Lied, das ich lesen lernte, heißt 'Accidents will happen.' Daran halte ich mich" [the first song, that I learned to read is called "Accidents will happen." I adhere to this] (Loher 43). As Christina Crosby[4] writes of her own paraplegic body, for Daisy, "the affective pain of grief remains stubbornly beyond address" (623). As illustrated by their psychosomatic symptoms, Daisy cannot really contend with the loss for which they grieve, whether truly by accident or passed off as accident. In this way, they resemble Jason, except for the fact that their expression of grief is not purely self-interested. Crosby places her grief in a multiplicity of locations writing that "my grief is written on/in/above/below/beside/throughout my body" (626). Feminist scholar Eve Kosofsky Sedgwick argues that the space "beside" can be read as a queer resistance of dualism because it "permits a spacious agnosticism about several of the linear logics that enforce dualistic thinking: [...] cause versus effect, subject versus object" (8). Loher and Crosby apply this queer spatial understanding to grief by placing grief in a multiplicity of positions with relation to the bodies of people who have disabilities. Deaf Daisy (and for that matter Crosby), as a person who is both queer and disabled, reminds us that pain, loss, and grief are not experienced within fixed spaces or on a straightforward timeline.[5] Again borrowing from Crosby, Daisy demonstrates that "mourning is not an ideally progressive affect, oriented toward a vanishing point on the shared horizon of a united social field. We are not all headed in the same direction, on the same clock" (627). Daisy, as Medea's most influential audience member, provides a clear counterbalance to Medea's seemingly fateful trajectory toward violence and murder. If Medea is encumbered

4 I met Christina Crosby when she presented an early version of this work at the Feminist Theory Workshop at Duke University in 2017. She was one of the kindest, most generous scholars I have ever met, and I was very sad to hear of her passing in January 2021.

5 The combination of queer studies and disability studies is again fruitful in that both have notions of alternative time structures. I am thinking here especially of Jack Halberstam's understanding of queer temporalities and subsequently, Robert McRuer's notion of crip time. These efforts to rethink temporality also resonate with Loher's anti-capitalist goals. In this vein, I would be remiss if I did not also highlight the work of Kathi Weeks and Maggie Rosenau. I am particularly indebted to the latter for first introducing me to the idea of crip time.

with the baggage of literary history, Deaf Daisy reminds us through their disability and mourning that history and grief do not move in a straight line. Unlike Jason, who only wants to go forward, Medea and Daisy are implicated in cycles of loss that highlight the intersecting perspectives and histories that come together in their co-constitutive identities.

Deaf Daisy and Medea are further united through a common enemy, the Sweatshop Boss. In addition to Daisy's gender performance and psychosomatic deafness, their conflict with capitalism and its representative, the Sweatshop Boss, proves to be a relevant force in their alliance with Medea. Loher is well known as a playwright who is sympathetic to the ideologies of Marxism, and so it is no surprise that she highlights differences in wealth and in social class through the juxtaposition of two characters with disabilities. In the character list and stage directions the Sweatshop Boss is described as someone who uses a wheelchair and in his conversation with Medea, he reveals that he grew up poor and that an accident with an iron beam eventually forced the amputation of his legs (Loher 50). However, in a gesture that again underscores the social model of disability, his wealth and social status shield him from many potential negative consequences of these amputations. He can surround himself with provisions that smooth his way through the world, a luxury not shared by either Medea or Daisy. As he himself describes, "meine Beine haben sich in Geld verwandelt" [my legs turned themselves into money] (49). Although this exchange of legs for money might seem like a poor deal, the Sweatshop Boss appears satisfied with the trade.

With a Peruvian mother and a Russian father, the Sweatshop Boss's rise to prominence is an embodiment of the American Dream, a capitalist fantasy that proves unattainable for figures such as Daisy and Medea, whose differences, especially gender identity, preclude them from attaining the same upward mobility through financial success. It is this inequity that ultimately leads Daisy to take pleasure in watching violence play out against the power structures represented by the Sweatshop Boss. As Daisy struggles to cope with the violence committed against their mother, they encourage similar levels of violence from others, in this case, Medea. Medea and Daisy bond over an ability to manipulate bodies, both their own bodies and the bodies of others. When describing the corporeal punishment awaiting those who attempt to steal from the Sweatshop Boss, Daisy scoffs at the possibility of having their ears cut off remarking, "Nicht, daß es mir auf die Ohren ankäme" [Not that I depend on my ears] (45). In a moment that harkens back to Medea's mutilation of her own face, Daisy too expresses a willingness for their body to be marked by violence in the service of their vengeful political goals.

When Medea engages in a truly collaborative performance with Daisy, *Manhattan Medea* uncovers a new feminist potential for the Medea story based on a process of performative storytelling. Butler asks us to "consider gender, for instance, as *a corporeal style,* an 'act,' as it were, which is both intentional and performative, where '*performative*' suggests a dramatic and contingent construction of meaning" (*Gender* 139; emphasis in original). Similarly, Loher invites us to think about literary roles and our own acts of retelling certain stories as contingent. The culturally constructed nature of mythological stories is supposed to be obscured because their repetition naturalizes them. Relatedly, the constructed nature of the genders we perform is often normalized and naturalized away. It is then a kind of deconstructionist violence to reveal this underlying constructedness. This is precisely the project that Loher's self-reflexive Medea undertakes. As Butler reminds us, what we might like to consider "normal" or "timeless" is, in fact, little more than a "*stylized repetition of acts*" (Butler, *Gender* 140; emphasis in original) and "a norm that can never be fully internalized" (Butler, *Gender* 141). Whenever Medea acts out her violent revenge on stage, she repeats and reinforces the fact that these actions constitute the character of Medea. Loher's Medea may not be able to escape the implications of her role, but she is, through her interactions with Deaf Daisy, able to establish a collective agency that puts pressure on understandings of subjectivity which necessitate that complete control be placed in the body of a single subject. In her work on trans art Eva Hayward writes that

> to some degree, being trapped in a body is an existential crisis for all of us, trans or not. This is not another mind/body split; rather, our bodies are not endlessly available to intentionality. Bodies exceed intention, even as our intentions are always predicated on embodiment. (Hayward 273)

By having Medea interact with a character who is a transvestite with a disability, Loher highlights this understanding of how bodies can work both for and against our intentions. Just as in performance, living in a body itself is a process of co-creation in which our individual desires and goals cannot always be met. Loher's Medea learns to appreciate this and to use it to her advantage through her interactions with Deaf Daisy.

By the end of the play, Deaf Daisy helps Medea to truly become a collaborative performer. Returning again to the importance of clothing, Medea seeks out Daisy in order to ask them to procure a red leather dress that will kill its wearer. As in Euripides's play, Medea intends to kill her rival Claire with this gift. In an exploration of the connection between trans performance and protest, Treva Ellison invokes the ballroom culture of the late twentieth-century United States. Ellison defines "werquing it" on the ballroom floor as "a relational gesture of world-making at the spatial scale of both the body and the community that aligns sender and receiver in a momentary network of fleshly recognition" (1). It is through their negotiations over the dress and over their own bodies that Medea and Daisy become allies. The "dress" that Medea describes is actually more of a skin-tight bodysuit: "Es muß eng sein, eine zweite Haut vom Hals bis zu den Fußknöcheln und den Handgelenken" [it must be tight, a second skin from the neck to the ankles and the wrists] (Loher 44). The kinky fleshiness emphasized by this garment would fit right in on the ballroom runway, in which the creation of new worlds and of communities is channeled through the body and through fashion. When forced into red leather, Claire is pushed out of the role of the naïve classical musician described by Jason, Velasquez, and the Sweatshop Boss. Through the outfit provided by Deaf Daisy and Medea, Claire potentially becomes destructive to herself and to others. The choice of a red leather body suit as a means for taking down Claire, and through her the Sweatshop Boss, is an act of werq in that it disrupts power hierarchies and destabilizes identity categories. By werquing it, Medea and Daisy also invoke a cultural history of appropriating the world-making strategies of Black, trans, and People of Color communities to which Medea, at least ostensibly, does not belong. That being said, Loher's goal is ultimately the performative, collaborative, and vengeful destruction of the many norms that also prove limiting to these historically excluded communities.

When Claire and the Sweatshop Boss's house burns down, it is an indictment of the capitalist system that only comes about through a performative negotiation between Medea and Deaf Daisy. One might think of negotiation as itself a deeply capitalist enterprise, but the negotiations between Medea and Daisy seek to subvert this combative paradigm. Daisy agrees to help Medea, but reminds her that "Das hat seinen Preis" [That has its price] (Loher 45). Medea acknowledges her willingness to pay, but no price is settled until Daisy returns. When they arrive with the dress in a trash bag, Daisy finally reveals what this service will cost saying, "Sagen wir, ich gebe diesen Müllsack für ein Schauspiel. Wird es Komödie, wird es Tragödie, es tut nichts, wenn es nur ein echtes Spiel ist" [Let's say, I give this trash bag for a play. It doesn't matter if it becomes comedy or becomes tragedy, as long as it is a real game/play] (54). As payment for the dress, Medea has to perform for Daisy. She has to act out her role as Medea by taking her violent revenge and she must do so in a way that also incorporates Daisy's desire to see a real (i.e., subjective and collaborative) performance. Far from trying to hide from the implications of her name any longer, Medea now owns her role saying, "Ich werde dir ein Feuerwerk zu sehen geben. Die Unschuld soll brennen" [I will give you a firework to see. Innocence shall burn] (54). Medea is ready to give a repeated performance centuries in the making. Unlike the Sweatshop Boss's negotiations in which he uses his daughter as a commodity, Medea's and Daisy's negotiations are a part of their mutual performance. Medea and Deaf Daisy have established the terms for these acts of revenge and Medea is prepared to follow through, even if it means living up to the name that she initially fought so hard to deny.

Unlike most other versions of the Medea story, it is another character, namely Daisy, who stokes Medea's vengeful fire, instead of trying to calm her down. Rather than presenting Medea as an angry and rash figure, Loher depicts a Medea whose interactions with her audiences internal to the play, both literally and figuratively, give her the tools she needs to carry out her calculated, vengeful acts. Because it is the result of a collaboration, Medea's revenge becomes simultaneously about something specific to her and about something bigger than herself. If she acts both for herself and willingly on behalf of Deaf Daisy, her actions become not just about the anger of one jilted woman, but about the frustration of all people who have been mistreated and overlooked by an unfair system. If Medea cannot fully assert her agency as a single individual, then she will do so as a figure representing a collective group. As the audience of this performance, Daisy goads Medea on. In a moment of doubt, Medea questions whether or not murder is the correct path, wondering, "Sollte ich Mitleid mit der Schönheit haben" [Should I have sympathy with beauty] (55). Meanwhile though, Daisy revels in the total destruction that is to come saying, "Ein Feuerwerk—das die Engel dieser Stadt zu Asche macht, die längst ihre Seelen verloren haben. Ihre blassen Gesichter werden rot, brennen, und wehen, grauer Staub, ins Nichts" [a firework—which turns the angels of this city to ashes, those who long ago lost their souls. Their pale faces becoming red, burning and sore, gray dust, into nothing] (55). This is Deaf Daisy's revenge just as much as it is Medea's.

Daisy's social isolation (because they are a transvestite, deaf, and impoverished) renders them even more eager than Medea for the downfall of the Sweatshop Boss and his family. In this performance, the internal audience has just as much influence as the performer herself in terms of initiating these violent acts of revenge. The stage directions further highlight Daisy's role as observer when they describe how Daisy "zieht sich in eine Ecke zurück und wartet, beobachtend" [withdraws into a corner and waits, observing] (54). Marcela Požárek argues that in *Manhattan Medea*, "das Verhältnis zwischen Sichtbarkeit und Erkenntnisgewinn ist dabei zentral" [the relationship between visibility and gaining knowledge is central] (114). Although Požárek makes this statement about Medea and Velazquez, it is even more true of Medea and Deaf Daisy in that Daisy's role as an observer co-creates Medea's own identity. By playing her role properly, Medea generates something approaching justice for Deaf Daisy, even though this revenge does nothing to help either of them truly escape the difficult conditions in which they find themselves.

Medea, Revenge, and the Reader

Deaf Daisy is such an effective audience for Medea because they prompt her to engage with her own internal conflicts and multiplicities. One question that circulates around Medea's murderous acts in this and other Medea stories is: Against whom does Medea actually exact her revenge? While it seems clear that Jason is a target, cases can be made for Medea's ire toward Creon, Creon's daughter, Medea's children, and most strikingly Medea herself, who feels guilt for leaving her homeland and for her brother's murder. Loher's play expresses this ambiguity within the structure of one of Medea's final monologues. After Medea makes the decision to go through with her revenge, Medea's relationship to language undergoes a temporary, but significant change. After the stage directions describe Deaf Daisy assuming their observatory position, Medea delivers a long speech before her final confrontation with Jason. Her monologue begins in free verse as she directly addresses her child, who has yet to appear in the script, saying, "Manchmal glaube ich / die Augen meines Bruders zu sehen / in den deinen" [Sometimes I think / I see my brother's eyes / in yours] (Loher 56). After invoking the connection between child and brother, her speech shifts into prose as she describes the events of their ocean voyage to the United States. As the monologue goes on and Medea describes the hunger that leads her and Jason to decide to kill Medea's brother, the punctuation of the text falls away leaving behind a block of unorganized words.

Medea proceeds to have a language breakdown as she retells the story of her brother's death. Her sentences run together making it difficult to determine where one thought ends and another begins:

> ...Sie ißt für zwei Mein Bruder Feines Paar Das sagt ihr jetzt Jason Nicht dein Geschäft Mein Bruder Wir sind zu dritt auf dieses Schiff gegangen Wir werden dieses Schiff verlassen zu dritt Ich sage Schwein Mein Bruder Wir haben nicht das Geld für vier Ich Ich habe es Mein Bruder Das reicht nicht für ein viertes... (Loher 57)
>
> [...She eats for two My brother Fine pair That you say now Jason Not your business My brother We are three of us went onto this ship We will leave this ship as three

> I say pig My brother We don't have the money for four I I have it My brother It is not enough for a fourth…]

Unlike Jason, who alters the story of his mother's death in a way that makes it more comfortable to tell and absolves him of his guilt, there is nothing soothing about Medea's narration of her brother's murder, especially when a reader sees it presented on the page as a text that increasingly loses its organizing structure. Medea uses this act of storytelling as an opportunity to engage deeply with the trauma of her past (and present), rather than trying to suppress it. Furthermore, the form of her reflections passes some of that discomfort onto the readers of this play who must figure out for themselves how to engage with this confusingly unpunctuated section of text.

Because Medea's words resist organizing themselves into punctuated sentences, this format highlights the role that the reader (or the actor performing this role) already plays in terms of generating a subjective meaning from any passage. The transition from free verse, to prose, to unpunctuated prose draws attention to the process of interpreting texts more broadly. In this way, Medea, the character, also performatively collaborates with the reader external to the play. We create meaning with her. For instance, in selecting quotations to pull from this passage in order to talk about Loher's technique here, I made somewhat arbitrary and subjective decisions about where thoughts begin and end. In this speech, Loher's Medea re-invokes the problem of the copy and the original, identified first through the character of Velazquez. If there is no decipherable original, then every performance or reading of this speech is a copy that also is not one. We are allowed some degree of creativity within the confines of a system of grammar that still plays an ordering function. There is no singular voice, but a variety of voices that can be drawn from Medea's speech.

In addition, the structure of this monologue invokes the theater itself as it also takes on the qualities of someone reading the script of a play out loud. The interjection of character names into the sentences gives the impression that this monologue could actually be a very literal reading of dialogue. For example, the lines "Jason Sie ißt für zwei Mein Bruder Feines Paar Das sagt ihr jetzt Jason Nicht dein Geschäft Mein Bruder Wir sind zu dritt auf dieses Schiff gegangen" [Jason She eats for two My brother Fine pair That you say now Jason Not your business My brother We are three of us went onto this ship] (Loher 57) might be punctuated as follows:

> Jason: Sie ißt für zwei.
>
> Mein Bruder: Feines Paar. Das sagt ihr jetzt.
>
> Jason: Nicht dein Geschäft.
>
> Mein Bruder: Wir sind zu dritt auf dieses Schiff gegangen. (Loher 57; punctuation mine)
>
> [Jason: She eats for two
>
> My brother: Fine pair. So you say now.
>
> Jason: None of your business.
>
> My brother: We three of us went onto this ship.][6]

This punctuation turns Medea's monologue into a dialogue between her brother and Jason, which Medea mechanically reads out, as if directly from a script. By invoking the theater here, Loher reminds us that it is impossible for Medea to tell an independent story or to generate a non-collaborative subjectivity. The theater is a means of expression, but it is one in which performance creates multiple voices that are always intruding into any individual's effort to speak. This is not to say that all such intrusions are negative. Loher draws out both the violence and the politically productive nature of these intrusions by highlighting them in her anti-capitalist adaptation of the Medea story. Since our voices can never be completely tethered to our individual bodies, we must work together through performance to build more collaborative identities and future solidarities.

When she finally suffocates her son, the tone of Medea's speech continues in this style of uncertain address to multi-layered internal and external audiences. While Velazquez refuses to be Medea's audience, Daisy

6 When restructured and ordered in this way, I also feel compelled to make minor alterations to my original more literal translation. This further highlights the dynamic I describe in which the reader imposes their own order on the text depending on context.

continues to observe carefully as Medea proceeds to kill her son. Again, Medea establishes a dual diegetic audience for this, her final performance saying:

> Mein Bruder. Du hattest recht.
> Es reicht nicht für vier.
> Es reicht nicht einmal für drei.
> Ich gebe dich zurück.
> Und dann wird Frieden sein.
> Und ich werde endlich
> allein sein mit mir.
> Nur für mich.
> Für mich.
> Für mich. (Loher 61)
>
> [My brother. You were right.
> There is not enough for four.
> There is not even enough for three.
> I give you back.
> And then there will be peace.
> And I will finally
> be alone with myself.
> Only for me.
> For me
> For me.]

Medea delivers this speech to her brother, but what starts out as an act of deference to him, quickly turns into an affirmation of herself. In a stark contrast to the Medea at the beginning of the play who introduces herself as anybody but Medea, this Medea ultimately takes ownership of her own actions, articulating that they are done for her. She kills her son and she does so for herself, or at least, so she claims. Medea's claim to autonomy here is undermined when one remembers that this action is also a performance for Daisy as direct payment for the dress that kills Claire. However, Medea's articulation of her own subjectivity here still represents an important, albeit limited, moment of self-recognition. Her final words before she actually suffocates her son are "Ich liebe dich" [I love you] (Loher 61). Here again, Loher's Medea uses her voice to connect with others, but she does so through an ambiguous statement in which it is unclear whether she is expressing her love for her brother, her love for Jason, her love for her son, or even her love for herself. She recognizes that even in performing this act of violence "for herself," there are other presences and audiences who will always have some influence over her performance. This realization is powerful because it ultimately allows Medea to move forward. Instead of becoming stuck in the misremembrance of the past, as Jason seems to be, Medea maintains an awareness of the influence of the past on her present and future. After she kills her son, she is both dead, in that a part of herself dies along with her child, and yet alive in that she will now finally move (in Crosby and Sedgwick's terms) on, in, and beside her grief. Obviously this act is most harmful to the child, who will never have a future, but Medea's actions are also another act of self-harm. Like Daisy, Medea demonstrates that true self-reflection requires productive discomfort and that grief is not a straight line, but rather a cyclical process.

The reader is ultimately asked to consider the violence that we have potentially perpetrated against Medea and, by extension, other immigrant women like her, through the process of mythmaking and storytelling. In dramas about the story of Medea, it is very rare for Medea to kill her son(s) on stage. More often than not, this act of violence happens off-stage with Medea reappearing afterward, bloody weapon in hand, to tell the audience about her feelings now that the deed is done. Loher's play is one of the few exceptions to this in that the stage directions specifically call for Medea to suffocate her son while still in view of Daisy. However, Ahmed cautions us against too readily condemning Loher's positioning of Medea as a figure who uses aggression to draw attention to structural violence when she writes that "part of the work of the killjoy is to keep pointing out violence. In making these points, killjoys are treated as people who originate violence" ("Affinity of Hammers" 228). If one takes a step back to examine the origins of Medea's violence, as Loher does, one sees that it begins with the violence of the Yugoslav Wars, during which both she and Jason were displaced. For Medea, Jason is a harbinger of war as she describes saying, "Du warst der erste, der erste von vielen, / die in unser Dorf geflohen kamen vor dem Krieg, / bevor der Krieg zu uns kam" [you were the first, the first of many / who came fleeing into our village before the war / before the war came to us] (Loher 19). Violence is not something that Loher's Medea instantiates herself, but is instead something that her world, including Jason, brings down upon her. Loher employs Medea's dramatic and murderous actions to draw attention to the violent world to which we all contribute.

Medea's fight throughout Loher's play is primarily one for identity and for visibility. She wants to be seen and she engages her full body in that effort. To reduce her to only one gruesome act, however violent and reprehensible, fails to account for the whole story, or the whole person that is the figure of Medea so richly crafted here. Loher invites her readers to consider the performative nature of Medea's role and to consider how Medea becomes exactly what we have made her through repeated storytelling, a murderous mother. Ahmed writes that "violence is so often reproduced by not being understood as violence" ("Affinity of Hammers" 225). Loher's Medea forces us to recognize that she also experiences violence through the act of committing the filicide that leads her to be recognizable as Medea. Confronting the process of mythmaking in this way attacks the reader's assumptions about what mythology means. Medea as killjoy asks us to question if myth cannot be a kind of hidden violence, not understood as such because, like Jason, it repeatedly distracts and shocks us with the horrors of what people are capable of when pushed to their limits or when they are not socially visible as human beings.

At the very end of the play, Medea's violence is overshadowed when Daisy breaks free from her role as audience member and becomes the focal point. It is the dress that Daisy provided that sets fire to the house of the Sweatshop Boss, burning Velazquez's copied painting into yet another copy. The stage directions deliberately connect this moment to Daisy's perspective by emphasizing that the burning of the house should be primarily seen and not heard: "In der Tür des Hauses erscheint eine Fackel, menschengroß, lodernd. Man hört sonst kein Geräusch. Keinen Schrei. Nur Stille" [In the door of the house, there appears a torch, human-sized, blazing. One hears otherwise no sound. No scream. Only stillness] (Loher 61). Loher describes visual, rather than auditory signs of Claire's demise and of the burning of the Sweatshop Boss's house. The relatively aggressive depiction of filicide and this quieter depiction of the murder of Claire stands in sharp contrast to Euripides's version of the play in which the death of the children is described in far less detail than the death of Creusa, which a messenger relates over 94 graphic lines. When Claire fades soundlessly away into a fire, it is quite different from the Euripides's graphic description of Creusa and how "from the top of her head blood dripped, mingled with fire, and her flesh dropped from her bones like resin from a pine torch, torn from the unseen jaws of the poison" (Euripides 391). In Euripides, the death of Creusa is linguistically performed for Medea and she takes great pleasure in hearing this story of her rival's extreme suffering. In Loher's play, Medea performs Claire's death for Daisy and it therefore remains seen and not heard. Once again, the intended audience plays a crucial role in how a performance takes shape.

Daisy is the one ultimately tasked with interpreting Medea's final performance. As the house burns to the ground, Daisy sings a Macedonian folk song about taking revenge on one's former lover after having been jilted. As they sing, it is unclear whether or not they sing for themself or for Medea. As we have seen, it is most likely a mixture of both. What is clear is that the prophecy of the song, that betrayal will end in flames, just like the prophecy inherent in the name Medea, that she will kill her children, comes to fruition at the end of this play. Even (or perhaps especially) in performance, every character in Loher's play is exactly who he/she/they seem(s) to be: Medea is Medea, Jason is Jason, the Sweatshop Boss is an exploitative capitalist, and Velazquez is the artist imitator. Daisy, the deaf transvestite, is ultimately the paradigmatic performer who ties them all together and destructively cleanses the scene with fire at the end. Daisy is the one who best understands how performance works, and so they are given the last word. As the figure furthest on the margins of this society,

Daisy is best equipped for this task; for as Ahmed writes: "we learn about worlds when they do not accommodate us. Not being accommodated can be pedagogy" ("Affinity of Hammers" 221). In this final scene, Daisy instructs us based on her hard-earned knowledge. Collaborative performance is about disarming your oppressor; it is about creating a spectacle that generates loss and destruction. In this final moment, Deaf Daisy brings the anti-capitalist undertones of the play out into the open singing, "Was du besitzt, mein Herz, will ich in Flammen sehen" [What you own, my heart, I want to see in flames] (Loher 62). Revenge is about collaborating with others to destroy the possessions, both physical and mental, of the people who have wronged you, even if those things, as in the case of Medea, are also near and dear to your own heart. It is only this kind of sacrifice, the sacrifice of being willing to destroy it all, the sacrifice of being willing to destroy a piece of oneself, which truly achieves vengeance.

Conclusion

This is not to say that Loher's play explicitly endorses revenge as a political strategy. After all, Medea and Deaf Daisy are actually worse off by the end of the play than they were at the beginning, both potentially facing criminal charges for their deeds. When describing another of Loher's plays, *Adam Geist* (1998), Künzel writes that "der Protagonist scheint hier eher Objekt der Handlung als selbst Handelnder zu sein" [the protagonist seems here more as an object of the plot rather than himself an actor] (364). At first, Loher presents Medea as a similar victim of fate. It appears that because she is called Medea, her destiny is already mapped out for her and there is little that she can do to control it.

However, when one looks closely at the way that Loher's Medea tailors her performance of this role to each of her diegetic audiences, it becomes clear that there is more going on than the simple creation of a character who becomes the object of a plot that literary history has created for her. Because of Medea's performances, Velazquez sympathizes with Medea's plight and brings Jason down to talk to her; Jason relives the night that he killed his mother and has second thoughts about marrying Claire, and Deaf Daisy witnesses the anti-capitalist revenge that they so desire. Through performance, Medea negotiates her way into a story that, on a certain level, tries to exclude her. Despite the fact that she is still the titular character, all of the figures in *Manhattan Medea* have individual goals and desires, which initially have nothing to do with Medea. By the end of the play, she has taken on a central role in all of their lives. Jason tries to start a new story by marrying Claire, but he cannot do this because Medea intercedes. The Sweatshop Boss has a narrative in his mind about the marriage of his final daughter and Medea is not included in that script until she forces her way in. Medea interferes with these and other narratives, mixing in her own perspective with theirs through the use of violent and dramatic performances.

Medea's aestheticized violence, especially in collaboration with Deaf Daisy, gives her the power of narration, the power to collaboratively dictate whose stories matter and who has a voice. When Butler connects performativity and subjectivity, arguing that there are no subjects which are not already gendered and which do not already have to repeat that gendered performance in order to remain subjects, she reminds us that subjectivity relies on ever-changing culturally constructed notions of what it means to be a specific kind of human being (*Bodies* 177). Similarly, in *Manhattan Medea*, Loher shows us that there is no mythology, no literary history, without the repetition of certain roles and characters. Yet, these characters too must be seen as adaptable to different audiences and to different times and places. Just as there is no standard gender, there is no essential literary role. There are only performances, which are simultaneously geared toward and influenced by the audiences to whom they are directed. Fischer-Lichte articulates how performance forces us to engage with the world differently, writing that "performance in this respect marks the limits of the Enlightenment by undermining the Enlightenment's reliance on binary oppositions to describe the world and its belief in the total controllability of natural and cultural processes" (10). Performance cannot be created in isolation and one person cannot dictate or predict the full extent of its outcomes. With *Manhattan Medea*, Loher has indeed created a feminist Medea who is prepared for the twenty-first century, a Medea who is forced to recognize and to come to terms with the fact that her subjective voice will always represent a collaboration with both her past and her various present audiences. Even if we are what we are, that being is actually a process of becoming, one that only happens in community with the people around us.

CHAPTER 4

A Forcible Return to the Womb: Elfriede Jelinek's Melodramatic Medea

Melodrama traditionally traces its roots to the eighteenth-century French stage. The word itself, with the combination of the Greek roots μέλος (*mélos*) and δράμα (*drama*), suggests a juxtaposition of tune/tone and dramatic theater.[1] The music (literally and figuratively) of intense emotional expression distinguishes the melodramatic mode from other storytelling forms. In her first lines in Euripides's play Medea sings of her suffering: "Oh, what a wretch am I, how miserable in my sorrows!" (Euripides 293). From the start, Medea engages in two foundational melodramatic gestures: the expression of emotional pain and singing. It should then be no surprise that one of the most popular works of early German *Melodram* was Friedrich Wilhelm Gotter's *Medea* (1775). The scholar Yixu Lü convincingly argues that in Gotter's theatrical work the titular character's internal conflict becomes its central, melodramatic focus ("Transformations" 152). Medea's internal struggle as she decides whether to kill her children transforms Gotter's play into a melodrama of maternal sacrifice and the rejection thereof.

Gotter's *Medea* proves that from some of its earliest manifestations in the German-speaking context, melodrama and Medea were well suited to one another. Lü elaborates on the melodramatic engagement with exaggerated emotional states in Gotter writing that "Gotters Leistung besteht vielmehr darin, in seinen Quellen bereits offenbare oder latente Gefühle ins Extrem zu führen, so daß das Irrationale zum durchgängigen Modus

1 Please note that I published an earlier and shortened version of this chapter as an article titled, "A Forcible Return to the Womb: Elfriede Jelinek's *Lust* and the Melodramatic Mode," *The German Quarterly*, vol. 91, no. 2, 2018, pp. 108–122. doi: 10.1111/gequ.12062.

seiner Exposition wird" [Gotters achievement, in fact, is to take emotions already obvious and latent in his sources, and lead them to the extreme so that the irrational becomes a universal mode of his exposition] (*Medea* 51). Medea is a woman so severely oppressed and with options so limited that she considers, and ultimately performs, unthinkable and deplorable deeds. As we have seen in other adaptations (including Dea Loher's play from the previous chapter) these deeds are often traumatic for Medea as well as for the people she aims to hurt. Melodramatic Medeas invite us to experience the conflict of a woman divided against herself.

In 1989, over 200 years after Gotter's *Medea* hit the stage, the Austrian author Elfriede Jelinek appeared on the cover of the feminist magazine *Emma*, shortly after the publication of her controversial novel *Lust*. In the cover story, *Emma* founder and editor Alice Schwarzer tries to soften Jelinek's tough, dominatrix image. Schwarzer strategically begins the interview with a question about Jelinek's makeup and returns several times to the topic of Jelinek's supposedly feminine clothing and personality. Although Jelinek performs the need to apologize for any transgression of gendered boundaries in her life and her work, she also playfully resists Schwarzer's efforts to domesticate her by insisting on her identity as both a delicate woman and a masculine writer. She teases Schwarzer, saying:

> Ja, aber Alice, ich *bin* sehr weiblich. Leider. Wenn ich eine Domina wäre, da könnte ich noch abräumen, dann hätte ich ja mit Männern überhaupt keine Schwierigkeiten. Aber dann hätte ich auch nicht schreiben müssen. (Jelinek, qtd. in Schwarzer 51)
>
> [Yes, but Alice, I *am* very feminine. Unfortunately. If I were a dominatrix, I could sweep up the profits; I wouldn't have any difficulties with men at all. But then I would also not have to write.]

Jelinek goes on to affirm *Lust* as a literary achievement, applauding herself for her expert combination of content and of form: "*Lust* ist das, was ich ästhetisch immer erreichen wollte beim Schreiben. Diese Art von Komprimiertheit und Ineinanderfallen von Sprache und Inhalt habe ich eigentlich immer angestrebt" [*Lust* is what I always wanted to achieve aesthetically in my writing. I have always aspired to have this level of compactness and collaboration between language and content] (51). In her self-presentation, Jelinek refuses to conform to any prescribed notions of male or of female, or any traditional (i.e., masculine) understanding of what it means to be an author. Even though (or perhaps because) Schwarzer tries so hard to soften her image and make her more palatable to a mainstream audience, Jelinek defies her by coming across as witty and deliberately provocative. *Emma* readers confront a Jelinek who, like the character of Medea, is defined by multiple, seemingly contradictory layers.

Jelinek's resistance to picking a side in her gender-bending self-stylization in the interview with Schwarzer is also reminiscent of Jonathan Goldberg's contention that the mode of melodrama resists (neo)liberalism by creating space to move "beyond minority, separatist identity" (16). By exploding our understanding of Medea as a murderous mother, *Lust*, like Loher's *Manhattan Medea*, puts pressure on the notion that identity is ever a singular thing. Unlike the other texts I have examined thus far, *Lust* is not explicitly a Medea story. It does not take place in Corinth or Colchis and it does not contain any recognizable figures from Euripides's play. However, it does contain brutal familial betrayal that culminates in a mother killing her child. Published after Ursula Haas and Dagmar Nick's Medea stories, but before Christa Wolf's and Loher's, Jelinek's *Lust* falls chronologically right in the middle of the works I examine in this book. This temporal centrality and more abstract connection to the Medea material makes *Lust* an ideal work for summing up my interrogation of the ways in which Medea stories and feminist political aims collide in the late twentieth century.

Jelinek's story explodes the boundaries of mythological adaptation, taking the themes of the Medea story and applying them to a drastically different context, thereby revealing new stakes for both mythological stories and her contemporary feminist political landscape. One of the few other scholars to write about *Lust* and myth, Daniel James Bowles, draws on the work of Roland Barthes to describe how Jelinek both breaks down and builds up semantic and social systems. Bowles argues that through word play "*Lust* both defuses and disassembles constitutive myths—such as sports, music, and capitalism—while constructing others—like the frigidity of women and their lack of agency" (121). Although I do not directly engage with Bowles's semantic understanding of myth in my reading of *Lust*, I agree that on the levels of both story and language, Jelinek's text generates almost as much as it destroys. *Lust* is a further example of the Medea material's refusal to be contained by a single context, frame, or genre. Although Jelinek's novel has primarily been discussed on the basis of its successes and failures as a work of (anti)pornography, I contend that the melodramatic move away from stable binaries of difference and toward heightened emotional states is where Jelinek's true feminist innovation lies. In *Lust*, Jelinek both repeats and engages critically with the tropes of pornography and of melodrama, highlighting the oppression of women inherent in these literary modes, and thereby altering her readers' experiences of them. Reading this novel as a melodrama and as a Medea story, while never providing us with direct solutions to the problems it exposes, deepens our understanding of the ways in which women are abused not only by men, but also by literary discourses and modes. By forcing readers to grapple with unsolvable, inescapable violence, Jelinek's reworking of the core plot of Euripides's *Medea* makes us aware of our problematic genre-based expectations and how they contribute to cycles of gendered aggression. In *Lust*, Jelinek uses melodramatic depictions of violence to generate moments of productive discomfort, moments which force her readers to reflect on their inability to think outside of hegemonic genre and gender categories.

Lust tells the story of Gerti, a housewife in rural Austria who is sexually abused and exploited by her husband Hermann and by a law student named Michael. To cope with her situation she gets drunk, stumbling around her snowy, mountainous factory town. When she eventually tries to run away to Michael, he refuses to take her in and watches as her husband rapes and recaptures her.[2] At the end of the novel, Gerti kills her young son, placing his body in a river and thereby symbolically reabsorbing him into her womb. In response to Hermann and Michael's betrayal, Gerti becomes a murderous mother, a Medea figure, compelled by domestic

2 I use the term "rape" to highlight my reading of these scenes as acts of penetration to which Gerti does not explicitly consent. This is an interpretation based on my understanding of the power structures and interpersonal dynamics in Jelinek's text. The use of this term does not adhere to contemporaneous legal definitions of rape. In Austria, spousal rape was not explicitly outlawed until 1989, the same year that *Lust* was published. The Federal Republic of Germany did not officially outlaw spousal rape until 1997.

abuse to commit unthinkable acts of violence. In addition to the theme of filicide, *Lust* depicts sexual violence within several different familial and extra-familial power dynamics, combining two literary modes often thought to be incompatible—pornography and melodrama. Instead of focusing on the relationship between Gerti and the adult men in her life (as the majority of scholarship on this text does) and identifying *Lust* only as a work of anti-pornography, I argue that Jelinek's aggressive approach to the conventions of both pornographic and melodramatic narrative compels her readers to recognize the political potential of self-analysis. In *Lust*, Jelinek uses the Medea plot to engage with contemporaneous feminist politics surrounding pornography and sexuality, while also experimenting with narrative practices that engage a multiplicity of perspectives and encourage self-reflection.

Pornography

The artistic modes of pornography and melodrama are difficult to define because they appear in a variety of styles and of media. When considering how these modes interact in *Lust*, Linda Williams's contention that pornography is sadistic and melodrama is masochistic is a useful starting place ("Film Bodies" 7). While these designations often overlap, Williams's distinction highlights the importance of perspective and of identification within these narrative modes. In both melodrama and pornography, according to Williams, someone takes pleasure in the presence of suffering and exploitation—the question is simply who is enjoying it and why.[3]

3 I want to note that Williams (and most of the other scholars I cite in this chapter) makes this point primarily about hard-core heterosexual pornography. This makes sense because this is the kind of pornography also referenced by Jelinek in the novel. Obviously, pornography as a mode has taken on many unique forms and expanded as a category (especially with the growth of the internet) in ways for which Jelinek's text (published in 1989) cannot possibly account. In my analysis here, I hope not to place a wholesale value judgment on all pornography, but rather to demonstrate

In the pornographic scenario invoked here, the person perpetrating the abuse—and even more importantly, the person watching the abuse being perpetrated—is the one who achieves pleasure. Therefore, it makes sense that Silvia Henke describes pornography as deeply rooted in the visual, as a mode dominated by "optische Überzeichnungen, das Phantasma totaler Sichtbarkeit […] und eine fast ausschließlich männliche Blickrichtung" [excessive optics, the phantasm of total visibility […] and an almost exclusively masculine line of sight] (252). The clearest representation of this dynamic in *Lust* occurs when Michael refuses to let Gerti into his cabin, watching from the window and masturbating as her husband rapes her. Michael's presence as a voyeur makes this the most salient example of pornography in the novel. All of the figures required for this brand of hard-core heterosexual pornography are present: There are two "performers," Hermann and Gerti, and a viewer, Michael, who derives sadistic pleasure from the act of viewing. According to Nancy Bauer, "the world as pornography depicts it as a utopia […] in which to use another person solely as a means to satisfy one's own desire is the ultimate way to respect that person's humanity" (4). In other words, "the porn world encourages us to treat ourselves and others as pure means" to an end (Bauer 5). This is exactly what Michael does when he refuses to help Gerti and instead takes advantage of the situation to satisfy his own sexual desire. As the narrator describes it, "Michael späht aus dem Fenster und strengt sich an, erneut zu wachsen, um aus sich das Beste, das meiste zu machen" (Jelinek 248) ["Michael peers out of the window and makes an effort to grow once again in order to make the most and best of himself"] (Jelinek, trans. Hulse 201).[4] Michael's selfishness is a perfect example of the behavior that is normalized and seen as laudable within the pornographic landscape, misogynistic behavior that alarmed many late twentieth-century feminists.

Exploitative behavior based on gender difference is also central to many depictions of Jason within the Medea story. In fact, Jason's heroics are largely

how Jelinek's novel engages with contemporaneous anti-pornography discourses and the so-called sex wars within twentieth-century feminist movements.

4 Please note that all translations of *Lust* are taken from Michael Hulse's translation from 1992. All other translations in this chapter are my own.

based on his abilities as an imperialist exploiter, especially of women. It is sometimes overlooked, as adaptations tend to focus on Medea's violence, but Jason is by no means a peaceful man. He is a conqueror. As we saw in Ursula Haas's *Freispruch für Medea*, for instance, Jason's heroic deeds almost always come with Medea's help and he is quick to use her devotion for personal gain. Inge Stephan reminds us that the history of Jason and his search for the Golden Fleece has become deeply connected to colonial and sexual violence (79). This is not to say that absolutely all pornography is sexual violence, but rather that pornography and sexual violence are deeply intertwined in Jelinek's novel, just like sex and violence are linked in the Medea story. Stephan cites Christoph Hein's *Das goldene Vlies* (The Golden Fleece) (2005) as an example of how in the story of Jason and the Argonauts: "das erotische Begehren führt zu sexueller Gewalt, die in der Suche nach Gold mühsam kompensiert wird" [erotic desire leads to sexual violence, which is painful compensation in the search for gold] (Stephan 79). The Fleece itself is symbolically a "Goldschatz, Eroberungskarte, magisches Potenz—und Verjüngungsmittel, reales Objekt, bloßer Vorwand im Herrschaftskampf der Männer oder Symbol menschlicher Hybris" [golden treasure, ticket to conquest, magical virility – and means of regaining youth, real object, mere pretense in the fight among men for domination or a symbol of masculine hubris] (Stephan 84). In other words, in the Medea material we encounter numerous examples of men exploiting women in order to achieve their desires, whether physical, sexual, financial, or emotional. In more traditional Medea stories, these desires intersect in the symbol of the Golden Fleece. In *Lust*, these desires intersect through the pornographic relationships between the adult characters.

The (second wave) feminist concern that heterosexual sex itself might be inherently objectifying is certainly at the heart of Jelinek's novel, in which we are provided with no examples of sexual behavior that is not brutal, violent, and abusive. Through her male characters, Jelinek engages the history of Jason as the quintessential masculine exploiter and directly engages with contemporaneous debates surrounding the politics of pornography. What is less clear is the side of these debates that Jelinek ultimately champions. With *Lust*, Jelinek jumped into both sides of the so-called sex wars within feminist movements of the 1970s and 1980s. A year before the novel came out, she published an excerpt of it in Claudia Gehrke's pro-pornography collection *Frauen und Pornographie* (Women and Pornography) (1988). That same year, Jelinek also participated in *Emma* magazine's anti-pornography PorNo campaign. However, to understand the nuances of Jelinek's engagement with pornography, it is crucial to consider if and how the book enables readers to take sadistic (and in Williams's terms, at least, pornographic) pleasure in the act of reading. In other words, are we as readers positioned as Jason (the exploiter) or Medea (the exploited, turned potential exploiter)?

Successful pornography assumes that we can see clearly, and that is exactly what *Lust* so often denies its readers. The first half of *Lust* consists primarily of sexually explicit scenes in which Gerti is repeatedly raped by her husband. Her body is constantly penetrated and torn apart as she is forced to comply with a variety of increasingly degrading and humiliating commands. There is little indication that Gerti takes any pleasure in this treatment and her self-destructive actions suggest quite the opposite. Each description of sexual violence bleeds into the next, denying the reader the ability to process any one of these encounters as a unique or meaningful experience. Particularly at the beginning of the text, the episodes in which Hermann abuses Gerti blend into an endless stream of penetration, biting, thrusting, and tearing. It is this overload of sexually explicit content that actively prevents readers from becoming aroused—ironically, overexposure resists an optimal pornographic point of view. Unlike Michael, readers of the novel are unable to adopt a voyeuristic perspective because they are too busy sorting through the confusion generated by the lack of coherent scenes or images within the text.

Hard-core pornography frequently presents viewers with an objectified victim of exploitation. In order for the sadistic style of the type of pornography being critiqued here to be effective, that victim needs to suffer. In *Lust*, Gerti takes on this role, becoming a de-individualized stand-in for all women who experience (sexual) violence. As her husband abuses her, Gerti often goes numb, seemingly acquiescing to the abuse, rather than protesting against it. The narrator accentuates Gerti's objectification in the following scene:

> Neben der Frau fallen Kleidungshaufen zusammen wie tote Tiere. Der Mann, immer noch im Mantel, steht mit seinem starken Glied zwischen den Falten seiner Kleidung,

> als fiele Licht auf einen Stein. Strumpfhose und Unterhose bilden einen feuchten Ring um die Hausschuhe der Frau, aus denen sie steigt. Das Glück scheint die Frau schlaff zu machen, sie kann es nicht fassen. (Jelinek 17)
>
> [Beside the woman, clothing falls in a heap, like dead animals. The Man, still in his coat, is standing with his member standing firm amidst the folds of his clothing. Like light falling on a stone. The tights and panties make a moist ring around the woman's slippers as she steps out of them. Happiness seems to be making the woman go slack. She can't grasp it.] (Jelinek, trans. Hulse 16)

As she is raped, everything about Gerti goes limp, starting with her clothing as it is removed. Gerti is no more alive than her stockings. The narrator subtly suggests that this experience is actually not sexually pleasurable for Gerti through the ironic use of the term "Glück" [happiness or, I think more apt here, luck] in combination with the adjective "schlaff" [flaccid/limp]. It is her husband's pleasure, his "Glück," that necessitates her going "schlaff." In this heteronormative world, there is not enough room for two active participants in this sexual encounter. These language choices indicate that, in this scene at least, we are in an androcentric, pornographic space in which all positive sexual response is thought to mirror the male erection. Instead of becoming erect (as her husband presumably does), Gerti lies limp throughout the event. At the end of this passage, readers enter briefly into Gerti's thoughts. However, even this narratorial access to Gerti's mind does not generate any profound or emotional reflection. "Sie kann es nicht fassen"—she cannot grasp it; she cannot take the action necessary to process what is happening to her. In this moment, Gerti is completely passive, an object. Like Wolf and Nick's Medeas she is the epitome of victimhood. The primary access we have to Gerti is the knowledge of what is happening to her body. Even when the narrator enters her mind, Gerti's deepest thoughts and feelings are obscured, placing her in the position of a universalized victim of violent abuse, a passive woman indistinguishable from so many others.

One might argue that this explicit content, however overwhelming, still provides some space for the reader to take pleasure in watching Gerti's suffering. However, *Lust* takes further steps to deny its readers the comfortable viewing position and sadistic voyeurism required for pornographic arousal. In one of the most brutal scenes in *Lust*, Michael and his friends assault Gerti. In the description of this gang rape, the narration vacillates between third and first person, constantly changing the perspective through which these events are focalized, and thereby preventing the reader from attaining any attachment to the characters beyond their roles as symbols within a vicious power dynamic. At first, readers confront detached third-person narration ("Die Buben halten ihr die lebendigen Hände oben unter dem Kopf zusammen"(Jelinek 196) ["The lads hold her living hands together above her head"] (Jelinek, trans. Hulse 160), only to be suddenly jerked into the first person-plural perspective, which implicates the readers in the rape as well: "Na, gehen wir nicht so weit, da wir, selber Knechte, mit Gewalt das unsere nehmen von der Gerti" (Jelinek 198) ["Well now, let's not go so far, slaves ourselves, as forcefully to take what is ours from Gerti"] (Jelinek, trans. Hulse 161). Readers are thus forced to confront their previous roles as sadistic voyeurs when they are unexpectedly removed from a position of comfortable distance and thrust into the roles of violent perpetrators. Not only does the narration fluctuate between these two voices, but various acts of narratorial reflection also interject into the scene. "Das tut doch weh, denkt keiner daran?" (Jelinek 197) ["That hurts, doesn't that occur to anyone?"] (Jelinek, trans. Hulse 161), the narrator inquires at one point, adding later, "Na also, warum treten sie dann nicht zurück [...]?" (Jelinek 198) ["So why not get out of the way [...]?"] (Jelinek, trans. Hulse 162). Jelinek's narrator even gives the impression that these violent actions are inevitable by describing how "es ist unglaublich, was man mit den dehnbaren Schamlippen alles anfangen kann, um sie, als wär's ihr Schicksal, in der Form zu verzerren" (Jelinek 197). ["It's unbelievable how you can stretch and flex the labia to change their shape, as if that were what fate intended for them"] (Jelinek, trans. Hulse 161). In this quotation Gerti is reduced to her anatomy. This objectification normalizes the acts of violence committed against her to the point of making them awe inspiring, at least from the narrator's perspective. Nothing can be done because it is the fate of the labia to be brutalized in this manner. All readers of this scene are challenged by narrative voices who refuse to explicitly side with any of the characters, be they assault victims or perpetrators. This narrative situation is uncomfortable for readers who are likely more familiar with being guided toward sympathetic attachment to one character or another.

Since readers feel lost and confused, rather than titillated and aroused, Jelinek disrupts the fulfillment-driven voyeurism of pornography, despite her novel's graphic sexual content.

As with Jason and the Golden Fleece, economic concerns also play a role in Gerti's pornographic and melodramatic relationships with adult men. For the abuse of her body by her husband, Gerti receives a capitalist prize in the form of financial security and a closet full of clothes. For the abuse of her body by Michael, Gerti receives a melodramatic prize, the impression of being in love. In other words, instead of a commodified (read pornographic) prize, Gerti receives an emotional (read melodramatic) prize through the abuse she endures at the hands of Michael. Even though Michael is no less violent than Hermann, for example, the narrator describes how he "zerrt die Frau an den Haaren herüber, bis sie wie ein Vogerl darüber flattert" (Jelinek 120) ["hauls the woman round by the hair till she's flapping above him like a great bird"] (Jelinek, trans. Hulse 100), Gerti has a very different emotional response to his aggression. With Hermann, she remains dead inside only to later relish all of the skirts she can now buy. Contrastingly, after an encounter with Michael, Gerti "spricht von ihren Gefühlen" (Jelinek 120) ["speaks of her feelings"] (Jelinek, trans. Hulse 100) and displays affection when she "bedeckt Michael mit flaumigen flauschigen Küssen" (Jelinek 124) ["covers Michael with soft and downy kisses"] (Jelinek, trans. Hulse 102). Inexplicably, what she gets from Michael is, at least initially, a feeling of being loved. This feeling completes her emotionally in the same way that Hermann supports her financially and draws on a melodramatic understanding of the relationship between suffering and love.

Often cited as a response to Georges Bataille's *Historie de l'oeil* (*Story of the Eye*) (1928), *Lust* draws on and challenges established pornographic literary traditions. My argument, however, is that these anti-pornographic gestures ultimately move Jelinek's text firmly in the direction of melodrama. Scholars including Henke, Brenda Bethman, Ulrich Struve, and Chieh Chien claim that Jelinek's primary goal in *Lust* is to critique the genre of pornography through exaggeration. I argue that this emphasis on excess actually places Jelinek's novel more accurately in the realm of melodrama. Jelinek's innovation lies in the way she melodramatically pushes the claims of pornography to their extremes, thereby drawing her reader's attention to how these conventions encourage women to accept their own suffering. *Lust* has also been compared to the pornographic work of the Marquis de Sade because of its detailed description of a plethora of sexual acts, without any real interest in the characters or the complex emotions and motivations that underlie them. Annette Doll argues that in both de Sade and Jelinek we see "Welten ohne Subjekte" [worlds without subjects], an accusation that, if true, would insist that Jelinek's characters are more like representative types, stand-ins for all people of their nationality, gender, and/or class (176).[5] Peter Brooks connects such de-individualizing gestures to melodrama when he writes that as a literary mode melodrama seeks "to make the world we inhabit one charged with meaning, one in which interpersonal relations are not merely contacts of the flesh, but encounters that must be carefully nurtured, judged, handled as if they mattered" (22). Characters, such as the limp Gerti as she is raped, are not unique individuals, but rather representatives of larger groups. This is a hallmark of both melodramatic and pornographic excess in which the individual's dynamic inner life takes a back seat to elaborate corporeal expressions of emotion. Although Jelinek occasionally breaks down this de-individualization by giving her readers fading glimpses of the unique psychic life within her characters, her exaggeration of the pornographic erasure of the individual is a large part of what makes this novel so melodramatic.

5 Doll goes on to say that in Jelinek's novels the characters are often so flat that even "Mann und Frau sind bei Jelinek austauschbar" [man and woman are interchangeable in Jelinek] (168). While I recognize that both men and women perpetrate acts of violence in *Lust*, I do not agree that the identity category of gender does not matter in this novel. Gerti's position in the inherently gendered role of "mother," for instance, makes her gender and her relationship to her reproductive body crucially important.

Melodrama

Anna Seghers sets her short story about Jason, "Das Argonautenschiff" (The Ship of the Argonauts) (1948), after Medea's revenge and departure from Corinth. Seghers depicts a defeated hero, a wearied Jason still clinging to the Golden Fleece and without a functioning ship, unable to travel or to move forward. As Stephan writes, Seghers foregrounds "ambivalente Bilder eines männlichen Heldentums" [ambivalent images of masculine heroism] (123). In one scene, Jason encounters a wife whose husband beats her. Trying to play the hero, Jason asks her to run away with him and the woman responds by laughing at him:

> Die Frau lachte auf, wenn auch freudlos. Ihr Lachen machte sie aber jung und freudeversprechend. Sie antwortete: "so etwas denkt man vielleicht einmal, aber man tut es nicht. Ich sage dir doch, Ich bleibe des Kindes wegen." (Seghers 255)
>
> [The woman burst out laughing, albeit joylessly. Her laughter made her young and promising of joy. She answered "one sometimes thinks about something like this, but doesn't do it. I say to you, I stay because of the child."]

Medea is usually the one who endures the brutal betrayal of a husband for whom she has sacrificed everything. Seghers universalizes this same dilemma by placing it into the mouth of another woman, one who strongly resembles Gerti in her approach to her own suffering. While a woman suffering at the hands of a man can be a pornographic gesture, a mother suffering for her child is a quintessentially melodramatic one.[6] Just like the joyless laughter of the abused woman in Seghers's story, ambivalence surrounds the figure of the suffering mother. While we are sad to see her suffer, we also feel that such sorrow is part of her maternal responsibility,

6 The most prominent example of this being the 1937 film *Stella Dallas*, written by Harry Wagstaff Gribble, Sarah Y. Mason, Victor Heerman, and Joe Bigelow, directed by King Vidor (Los Angeles: United Artists), and based on the 1923 novel of the same name by Olive Higgins Prouty, from which Linda Williams draws much of her astute work on melodrama in film.

a responsibility that Medea eventually denies when she kills her children. Stephan writes of Medea that

> Leidenschaft und Intellektualität, Gewalt und Verbrechen auf der einen, Demütigung und Verrat, Opferung und Vernichtung auf der anderen Seite bilden ein explosives Gemisch, das den Medea-Mythos bis heute zu einer ambivalenten Erbschaft macht. (Stephan 2)
>
> [passion and intellect, violence and crime on the one side, humiliation and betrayal, victimhood and destruction on the other side, create an explosive combination that makes the Medea mythology, even today, an ambivalent inheritance.]

This ambivalent feminine inheritance of both victimhood and violence is one of the themes that also drives Jelinek's novel. In her book on real murderous women (whom she labels "Medea's daughters") Jennifer Jones argues that women who kill "are women who did not put others first, whether husbands, parents, or children. They violated the primal patriarchal condition of femininity itself: self-sacrifice" (100). This is an accusation that often applies to Medea and most certainly applies to Gerti. When readers truly consider Gerti's relationship to her child alongside her relationship to her husband, the melodramatic nature of Jelinek's Medea story becomes clear.

The denial of satisfaction and the emphasis on desperate longing that we see in *Lust* are not characteristics of pornography, but rather of melodrama. In melodrama, it is the victim's pleasurable suffering that takes center stage, depriving us of the release we come to expect at the conclusion of a pornographic scene. The importance of thwarted desire as a foundational aspect of melodrama functions as a counter to the pornographic experience of exploiting others for self-fulfillment. Melodrama can thus be seen as the "feminine" side of pornography. It is pornography from the perspective of the person being exploited, the person whose wants and needs are denied. Heike Bartel writes that the characters in Franz Grillparzer's *Medea* are caught in a cycle of "destructive self-denial and aggressive self-assertion" ("Dressing" 173). Similar contradictory qualities are shared by the characters in *Lust* and reflect the melodramatic nature of both stories. Although Jelinek is quick to criticize the melodramatic portrayal of women as happy victims, she also uses the tools of melodrama to uncover the political potential of emotion-driven self-reflection. In other words, Jelinek exposes the benefits of being forced to see oneself in a different light.

In his book *Melodrama: An Aesthetics of Impossibility* (2016), Goldberg argues for an understanding of melodrama that is also decidedly queer. Instead of providing us with moral clarity, Goldberg argues that melodrama rejects singularity in terms of both media and identity. The "re-mediated, mixed-media" of melodrama allows us to move past such simple and straightforward identity categories (Goldberg xi, 16). Similar to the character of Deaf Daisy in Loher's play, melodrama asks us to experience something that defies easy binary categorization as real or imaginary, personal or impersonal. Melodrama is politically intriguing because of its adaptability and its insistence that nothing and no one is ever just one thing. Jelinek uses shifting narrative voices and the surprise murder at the end of her novel to destabilize her readers and their understanding of the power dynamics of narration. Not only does Gerti perform an act of melodramatic violence when she kills her son, but Jelinek also perpetrates an act of melodramatic violence against her own readers when she makes them culpable in the novel's acts of sexual violence.

Melodrama has traditionally been defined as a counter to realism, with "realism signifying rationality, order, pragmatism, and clear-headedness, while melodrama stands for feeling, excess, sentimentality, and grandiose gestures" (Kelleter and Mayer 10). For this reason, the melodramatic mode has, until recently, been unnecessarily denigrated as a *feminine* or *popular* genre, not worthy of serious critical attention. One of the fields that has been instrumental in changing such perceptions is feminist film theory. Scholars such as Williams, Christine Gledhill, and Monique Rooney argue that melodrama is actually modernity's "dominant aesthetic form" (Rooney 3) and that instead of a "conservative genre that tends to reinforce the status quo," melodrama is an adaptable mode characterized by "disruptive elements of unpredictability and uncertainty" (Rooney 2). Melodrama's tendency to engage directly with negative emotions such as discomfort, anger, and shame, becomes politically productive when such emotions reveal injustices that cannot be overcome within the current social system and power structure. This characterization of melodrama resonates deeply with the discomfort and ambiguity represented by all of the Medea stories discussed in this book. As Goldberg puts it, melodrama is "an aesthetics of impossibility" that shows us "the productive possibilities in the impossible situation that remains impossible" (79, 29). Medea's acts of violence cannot be undone and she usually fails to improve her lot through her revenge. Although melodrama may not always be a strong catalyst for revolutionary social change, it forces us to reckon with our own limits, inviting us to dream, to wish, to struggle, and to imagine different possibilities for ourselves. This, in and of itself, is a valuable lesson for social justice movements, especially ones seeking to alter policy and public opinion, such as the German New Women's Movement.

Melodramatic tropes pervade the initial characterizations of the figures in *Lust*. Using his exclusive and total possession of her body to protect himself from HIV/AIDS, Gerti's husband, Hermann, violently assaults her and, in exchange, takes care of her financially: "Dem Mann genügt eine allein nicht, doch die drohende Krankheit hemmt ihn [...] Er versucht das Beste: zu leben und geliebt zu werden" (Jelinek 14) ["one woman isn't enough for the Man. But the threat of disease restrains him. [...] He tries to make the best of it: to live and be loved"] (Jelinek, trans. Hulse 13). Despite his displays of aggression and masculine dominance, Hermann is just as emotionally needy and uncertain as any female character. To cope with the terms of this exploitative bond, Gerti gets drunk and stumbles through a dismal alpine landscape, acts of self-harm similar to those practiced by Euripides's Medea who initially "lies fasting, giving her body up to pain" after Jason betrays her (Euripides 287). These conditions invoke a well-known trope of domestic melodrama, the unhappy housewife. Gerti is trapped in a loveless marriage and is driven to drink in a desperate attempt to escape her condition.

This setup also connects Gerti to characterizations of the domestic strife between Medea and Jason. Just like Hermann, Jason often suffers an identity crisis and lashes out because of Medea's role as a source of his protection. In Euripides, Jason desperately tries to tip the scales in his favor, arguing that bringing Medea with him into Greek civilization is a far greater gift than any service she performed for him: "So far as you *did* help me, you did well. But in return for saving me you got more than you gave" (Euripides 331; emphasis in original), he argues. In Grillparzer's version of the story, Jason's insecurity goes a step further when he laments to Kreon: "Ich bin nur Jasons Schatten, nicht er selbst" [I am only Jason's shadow, not him, himself] (Act 3). The primary difference in *Lust* is that, instead of Medea being the one to lash out with physical violence, in the end *both* Gerti and Hermann become more violent as a result of their toxic relationship with each other. Rooney argues that melodrama involves "perpetuating a restless, endlessly dissatisfied way of being" (3). This striving dissatisfaction is an unsympathetic, but melodramatic quality, that we often see in both the relationship between Jason and Medea as well as in the relationship between Hermann and Gerti.

An engagement with melodrama is also pervasive in Jelinek's language. One of Jelinek's most characteristic literary moves is her word play and excessive expansion of common metaphors and symbols. She simultaneously reinforces, manipulates, and undermines her readers' expectations and knowledge of the symbolic connotations of various words and idioms. To use a straightforward example from *Lust*, when talking about genitalia, Jelinek sometimes uses the rather conventional and recognizable pornographic language of "Glied" (27) ["cock"] (Jelinek, trans. Hulse 23) or "Schwanz" (20) [dick][7] and "Muschi" (145) ["pussy"] (Jelinek, trans. Hulse 119). However, Jelinek also gets rather creative and excessively metaphorical at times, also speaking about the "spuckender Spender" (32) ["spitting dispenser"] (Jelinek, trans. Hulse 28) and the "elektr. Leitung" (26) ["electricity main"] (Jelinek, trans. Hulse 23)] or the "Büchse" (114) ["socket"] (Jelinek, trans. Hulse 95), and the "saugfähiges Tuch" (46) ["absorbent cloth"] (Jelinek, trans. Hulse 40), just to name a few examples. Bowles contends that this "linguistic playfulness [serves] as a counterbalance to the violent hierarchies of the plot" (127). I argue that Jelinek's word play is equally aggressive in that Jelinek simultaneously builds up a pornographic vocabulary with which her reader is likely familiar and also pushes them outside of their comfort zone, forcing them to accommodate a wide variety of euphemistic genital vocabulary that establishes connections between

7 Hulse translates this passage in such a way that the word "penis" does not appear, so this is my own translation.

sexual hierarchies and everyday objects. With these metaphors and euphemisms, Jelinek both naturalizes and challenges existing pornographic vocabulary. Furthermore, this process of engaging critically with pornographic language is reminiscent of Brooks's contention that melodrama, through its excesses, generates a feeling that "the represented world won't bear the weight of the significances placed on it" (11). The saturation of the sexualized linguistic world that Jelinek creates, in which every truck or rag also represents the brutality of sexual violence, is then both pornographic and melodramatic in its pervasive over-signification.

Although much of the response to *Lust* focuses on the abusive relationships between Gerti and adult men, her most exaggerated and over-signified relationship is actually her relationship with her son. The very presence of the son works to disrupt the pornographic story world. He represents a resistance to the telos of pornography—namely, the climax—because the child signifies a potential future beyond that event, something that comes after the sexual climax. Although the son is easy to miss until his death in the final five pages of the book, his importance in Gerti's life is established in one of the novel's first scenes, a scene that is rich with emotional weight and symbolism. Walking through the snow, mother and son discover the carcass of a dead bird. The child's desire to engage in athletics and snowball fights rather than walk calmly by his mother's side is described as a parallel to the "natürliches Schauspiel" (Jelinek 8) ["natural business"] (Jelinek, trans. Hulse 8) of the half-eaten bird, with its blood strewn all over the ground. The narrator casts a dark shadow over the boy's seemingly innocent childhood games, equating them with the instinctual and sensational violence of this representation of the animal world. We are in the realm of melodramatic over-signification from the very beginning of this novel, and more specifically, from our entry into the relationship between Gerti and her son. Through her depiction of aggression and of abuse, Jelinek draws her readers' attention to the systemic violence inherent in interpersonal relationships. This link between larger structural concerns and familial bonds relates directly to melodrama's insistence that interactions be loaded with an excess of larger interpretive meaning. Gerti's final act of filicide, though overdetermined when one rereads this first scene, still shocks readers. Through the tense and heavily symbolic relationship between mother and son, Jelinek upholds the melodramatic convention of pushing everything to its limits, thereby highlighting the impossibility of moving any further.

Although Medea's sons do not appear as speaking characters in Euripides, Jelinek draws on a long German-language tradition of highlighting the fraught relationship between Medea and her son(s). For example, Grillparzer links Medea's emotional transformation and desire for revenge to her abandonment by her own children. Kreon gives the children a choice, to either go back with their mother or to stay with his daughter Kreusa. In a seeming condemnation of Medea's status as an unwanted foreigner, the children themselves select the latter option. Medea takes this rejection extremely personally calling one of them "Undankbarer! Ebenbild des Vaters!" [Ungrateful (one)! Spitting Image of the father!] (Grillparzer, Act 3). This specific critique of the sons as a reproduction of the father is crucially important for understanding Gerti in Jelinek's novel as she struggles to reconcile her husband's behavior with the potential future behavior of her son, who resembles both of his parents in uncomfortable ways.

The son is the most mysterious figure in *Lust* in that Jelinek provides her readers the least access to his interior life and motivations. Significantly, he is the only major character for whom no name is provided, the most direct sign of a figure that has been de-individualized or reduced to a type.[8] In many ways it is true that the son becomes whoever Hermann or Gerti want him to be, displaying very little personality of his own, apart from their projections onto him. In addition to the many instances in which the son is represented as a future Hermann, a capitalist exploiter and an abuser of women, in select moments he is also like his mother, that is, feminized and passive. When he sleeps, the child briefly escapes the violence between his parents and the example that this behavior is destined to set for him. In one such instance the narrator asks:

8 It is a hallmark of Jelinek's work to delay naming her characters and to describe them first according to their roles as wives, husbands, mothers, workers, etc. This is one more reason that critics of her work tend to see her characters as types. However, when she does eventually give them names, it is often as if Jelinek is baiting her readers, demonstrating how easy it is to forget people's individuality in our efforts to place them into normalized identity categories.

> Wer in diesem Land ist ein Kind und hat einen Raum, wo es sich ausgeht, daß der Körper hineinpaßt? Wer kann Bärlis und Sportbilder dabei anschauen und die Popstars? Dieses Kind ist aus dem Anlaß des Sexgebrülls seiner Eltern an einen ruhigen Ort hingelegt. (Jelinek 126)
>
> [Where is the child in this country who has a room his body will fit into? And where he can look at teddy bears and pictures of sport and pop stars? Because of the sexual ruckus of his parents, this boy has been transferred to a quiet spot.] (Jelinek, trans. Hulse 105)

Even as the child is always already enmeshed in the cycles of violence and oppression inflicted by his father on his mother, he takes refuge from this violence in the comforts of his own room and amid his personal possessions. Nonetheless, it is unclear how much these possessions serve to construct an individualized identity for him, or how much they actually serve to differentiate him from other children, thereby making this scene an odd mix of individuality and typification. The son is old enough to have individual possessions and tastes, but the reader is not provided much information about the specifics of these items or of his opinions. At best, we can say that he seems to have an interest in sports and that he is something of a bully with regard to the other children. The narrator combines these two qualities to remark that "das Kind fährt gut Schi, die Dorfkinder vergehen wie Gras darunter" (Jelinek 10) ["the child is a good skier, the village children are like grass beneath him"] (Jelinek, trans. Hulse 9–10). Beyond that, very little can be conjectured about the son as an individual. This mirrors the way in which his mother comes to consider him only in terms of the man he will become, not in terms of his own unique personality.

Even the psychoanalytically symbolic act of breastfeeding is demystified in Jelinek's account of this maternal relationship: "Fast würde der Mutter die müde, die Muttermilch aus den Brüsten stürzen vor Schreck, daß dieses Kind keine unsterbl. Seele zu haben scheint, denn es macht seine Mutter nicht selig" (157). ["It's enough to make Mother's breasts squirt milk: the boy just doesn't seem to possess an immortal soul. At least, he gives his mother no joy"] (Jelinek, trans. Hulse 129). This quotation begs for a psychoanalytic reading following in the footsteps of Jacques Lacan and Luce Irigaray. In this relationship between mother and child, it is as if the pre-Oedipal unity of the two through the act of breastfeeding is impossible because of some specific deficiency on the part of the child. Symbolically, even at this early stage, the son is already a potential violent abuser of Gerti just like his father. When she (prematurely) characterizes him as a type, Gerti negates any pre-existing spiritual bond between mother and child. Gerti wants to experience a deeply resonant mother-son connection, but this is impossible because, according to the narrator, there is something off about her son's soul, which prevents him from being a blessing to her by association.

Gerti cannot see her son as a blessing, only as a burden, as something for which she must care. For example, the narrator describes the attention and the detail with which Gerti prepares her son's food saying, "Die Mutter hat einen ganzen Teil des Vormittags Karotten fein durch ein Sieb gedrückt, damit sie den Augen des Kindes nützen. Das Essen fürs Kind macht sie selbst" (Jelinek 60) ["For much of the morning, Mother had been straining carrots through a sieve, for the boy's eyes. She cooked the lad's food herself"] (Jelinek, trans. Hulse 51). Gerti puts a lot of labor into nourishing her son, despite their lack of a spirito-physical bond through breastfeeding. Gerti's son is in the precarious position of being both a vulnerable child and a future violent male abuser. It is this tension and ambiguity that causes Gerti to fixate so much of her emotional energy on him and ultimately, I argue, one explanation for why she finally murders him.

Through this combination of pornographic and melodramatic plotlines, Gerti becomes a perpetrator of the same kind of objectification through which she herself is victimized. She is unable to see her son as anything other than a potential substitution for Hermann, leading her to commit the brutal act of filicide. Throughout the novel, the narrator describes Gerti as deeply concerned about the effect of her husband's abuse on her son. After a scene in which the son walks in on his mother being raped, the narrator indicates to the reader that even amid her own suffering, Gerti thinks only of him:

> Sie strampelt mit den Beinen und hält die Augen ins Ungewisse ihres Kindes gerichtet, was wird wohl aus ihm werden? Ein junger Adler, der an einem Kleinwagon nagt? Mit Schnabelhieben in die Brust eines Menschen hackt? Der beim Slalom, der hinterm Haus, zum Spaß und damit die Menschen sich an Umwege gewöhnen, gesteckt ist,

sich besiegen lassen kann? Alles, was dieses Kind und dieser Mann sich wünschen, ist auf seine Weise gefährlich. (Jelinek 54)

[She thrashes her legs, her eyes fixed on the uncertainty that is her child: whatever will become of him? An eaglet gnawing at a sportscar? Beak hacking into the flesh of a human breast? Will he accept defeat in the slalom, which is staked out behind the house and is meant for fun and to accustom humankind to detours? Everything this Man and his manchild wish for is dangerous in one way or another.] (Jelinek, trans. Hulse 46)

The narration shifts into *erlebte Rede* [free indirect speech] as Gerti expresses the potential for her son to become like his father, a bird of prey, out for blood. She distracts herself from her current circumstances by imagining her son's future, only to discover that this line of thought leads her right back to her current position, as a woman victimized by violent sexual abuse at the hands of a more powerful man. She concludes that the desire for domination in all men, whether adult or child, is dangerous in its own way. More than any physical or emotional distress directly caused by her husband's behavior, it is the perpetuation of this abuse in future generations that truly frightens her.

Gerti refuses to accept the fact that this cycle of male violence will continue uninterrupted. Reflections similar to the one above appear throughout the text, for instance when Gerti/the narrator thinks, "wie wird dieses Kind erst aufgeigen, wenn es, nach Papas Vorbild im Reisespaß, ein Mann und Vater geworden ist!" (Jelinek 38) ["how much better will he perform on his fiddle when one day, like his daddy, he's learnt to work the fiddles of manhood and fatherhood and perform the parts!"] (Jelinek, trans. Hulse 33), or when she refers to him as her "Schicksalssohn" (Jelinek 176) ["fateful son"] (Jelinek, trans. Hulse 144). These reflections are reminiscent of Grillparzer's Medea, who says of Jason: "Die Kinder liebt er, sieht er doch sein Ich, / Seinen Abgott, sein eigenes Selbst / Zurückspiegelt in ihren Zügen" [He loves the children, sees his self in them / His idol, his own self / Mirrored back in their traits] (Act 4). Although similar in the sense that both women are concerned about the male characters projecting their own identities onto their children, Jelinek's text is distinct in that she centers this concern around the son, rather than its more accurate source, the father. In Jelinek, this projection of the traits of the father onto the son comes from the mother. While Grillparzer understands this conflation of father and son as a flaw of Jason's, Jelinek's text is harder to pin down. Gerti sees her son, at least partially, as responsible for the cycle of masculine domination in which she is trapped. Gerti's experience of motherhood activates what little emotional life the narrator grants her. However, in her efforts to be a good mother, she ends up treating her son like a de-individualized type. Gerti can only see him as either an extension of her victimized self or as a representative of his abusive father, the naturalized perpetrator of masculine violence.

Who is "We"?

The pronoun "we" ideally generates a sense of solidarity. However, Jelinek's *Lust* destabilizes the identity of "we." Jelinek uses multiple narrative voices to directly attack potential connections between characters or between readers and the text, thereby mirroring Medea's frequent struggles to form feminist coalitions (one major exception being Loher's Medea as explicated in the previous chapter). Jason and Medea's relationship almost always comes down to picking sides, to a choice between saving their marriage or their children. In Seneca's "Medea," Jason defends his actions toward Medea saying that his sons would surely die if he does not seek out the security that comes from marrying Creusa. Ultimately, he claims that "the sons won out over the father. Indeed, I think even she, fierce-hearted though she is and unyielding, would place her sons' interest before her marriage" (Seneca 355). Jason argues that the social conditions of his environment force him into a choice between wife and children, one that if the roles were reversed, Medea would make in favor of the children, just as he does. As we saw in Wolf's *Medea. Stimmen*, Medea fails to form connections and establish solidarity with others because the power structure in Corinth pits people against one another. Medea's failed coalition building is narrativized through Jelinek's insistence that the solidarities we think we establish through the use of the pronoun "we" are not nearly as stable as we might believe them to be. Medea, like a reader of Jelinek's novel, is forced to contend with the fact that a failure to establish solidarity with others makes it difficult to secure one's bodily integrity and often leads to slanderous narrative attacks.

In addition to Jelinek's thematic citation of melodramatic tropes, her language itself takes on melodramatic characteristics, generating impossible narrative situations for the reader to attempt to untangle. Stephan writes that "Jelinek's Prosastück ist kein psychlogischer Roman, sondern ein Text, in dem die Vorstellung des autonomen Subjektes in Anschluss an Diskurse der Postmoderne verabschiedet wird" [Jelinek's work of prose is not a psychological novel, but a text in which the conception of the autonomous subject is dismissed in alignment with discourses of Postmodernity] (181). Instead of gaining access to the interiority of these characters, readers of *Lust* confront complicated narrative perspectives that question binaries and the process of meaning-making itself. Jelinek's characters are not the only ones responsible for the violence perpetrated by and against Gerti; Jelinek also implicates the readers of her text in this violence through the use of shifting narrative referents. By challenging her readers to work hard to keep track of their constantly changing position in relation to the narrated events, Jelinek entangles readers not only in the violent actions of the plot, but also within a phallocentric violence attached to language itself. Jelinek's "we" has different referents throughout the novel, sometimes indicating a group of men (as in the gang-rape scene discussed at the beginning of this chapter), sometimes the townswomen, and sometimes an even more abstract and nebulous collective. Just as scenes of sexual violence often confusingly blend into one another, the narrative voices in *Lust* overlap and combine in complicated ways that destabilize the reader.

Scenes of sexual violence in *Lust* often begin in a traditional third-person narrative style. In one such scene, the narrator describes how "der Vater hat einen Haufen Sperma abgeladen, die Frau soll alles ordentlich wegputzen. Was sie nicht aufleckt, muß sie aufwischen gehn" (Jelinek 40) [Father has shot a wad of sperm and now it's up to his wife to clean it up properly. What she doesn't lick up she'll have to wipe up] (Jelinek, trans. Hulse 35). Although the content is explicit, the narrative voice that introduces this scene is unremarkable. As the scene goes on, the narrative voice switches from third person to first person rather abruptly:

> Übrigens, wenn sie schon die Beine aufgeklappt hat, kann sie sich gleich über ihn stellen und ihm in den Mund pissen. Was, sie kann nicht? Stoßen wir ihr das Knie nach oben und treffen klatschend (Applaus, Applaus!) ihre weichen Futlappen, die sich gleich leise schmatzend öffnen werden, und wir Männer müssen sofort mit dem Maßkrug auf den Tisch hauen. Wenn sie dann noch nicht seichen kann, zerren wir ihr ganzes weibl. Geschlecht an den Schamhaaren nach unten, bis sie in den Kniegelenken einknickt und, aufs äußerste gespreizt, auf den Brustkorb des Herrn Direktor hinuntersinkt. (Jelinek 41)
>
> [Oh and while she's at it with her legs apart like that she can stand over him and piss in his mouth. What, she can't? Let's see. Up with her knee. There we are (applause, applause!)—the tender lips of her cunt, we'll part them with a soft smacking sound and we men'll be banging our tankards down on the table with a thump. If she still can't pee we'll drag her privates down by the short and curlies till she bends the knee and splays across the Herr Director's chest.] (Jelinek, trans. Hulse 35–36)

There is a lot to unpack stylistically in this dense passage. It begins, as is typical, in the third person. The reader is informed about Gerti's actions and engages with them from a comfortable position as an external observer. Hints of access to Gerti's interiority slowly become perceptible through the use of the modal verb "kann" [can], which the narrator employs to draw attention to the limits of Gerti's perceived capabilities, both physical and emotional. This transitions to a moment of narratorial commentary, in which the narrator asks, "Was, sie kann nicht?" [What, she can't?]. The reader's experience as observer is suddenly interrupted by the interjection of a question, marking a further shift, this time to something Dorrit Cohn calls "psycho-narration," a space where the narrator makes direct comments about the consciousness of a character, often revealing something that the character is not able to vocalize (46). With this question, the narrator casts doubt on Gerti's ability to perform the actions required of her by her husband, further reinforcing the brutality of the moment. Before the reader has time to adjust to these shifts, the narrative perspective changes again, to the first-person plural. All of a sudden, we (the readers) are involved in the violence, dragging Gerti down and banging our beer steins on the table. We (men) even get a little extra-diegetic celebration of our brutality as cries for applause appear, applause from an audience whose location and identity remains ambiguous. Finally, it is important to note that although this "we" is separate from both Gerti and Hermann, it ultimately sides with Hermann. The "we" works for him, forcing Gerti's body on top of Hermann in a violent manner. Not only that, but the rather clinical abbreviation of *weibliches* [feminine] in the German version of this passage further reinforces the notion that the actions of this "we" are a kind of labor, a service performed by "us" for Hermann. It is as if this text were a workplace report, rather than a work of fiction.

In just this one passage, we see examples of the plethora of stylistic choices with which any reader of *Lust* must contend. The effect of these shifting narrative voices only becomes more destabilizing when, pulling back and looking at the text as a whole, it becomes clear that the "we" in *Lust* refers not only to this group of men, but also to several other groups of people at different moments throughout the novel. Each time the narrator talks about "we," the reader must figure out who is included in that "we." In a move that calls into question any stable gender identity for the narrator as well as the reader, the "we" in this text also references groups of women—either all women generally or, more specifically, the townswomen. Furthermore, this change of referents often takes place within a single scene. For example, when Michael and his friends assault Gerti, the narrator starts by employing a masculine "we" to refer to the men perpetrating the violence. Eventually though, the narrative shifts, and the "we" begins to refer to all women:

> Wir Frauen müssen uns halt selber besser einrichten und dann der fernhin hallenden Stille aus ihren leblosen Gerten, meine Herren, lauschen, die noch unter der milden Spannung des Garantiescheins beben, da ihre Frist nicht ablaufe. An uns denken die Männer zuletzt! Fremd ist Michael eingezogen, fremd zieht er ihn wieder heraus. (Jelinek 203)
>
> [We women have to fix ourselves as best we're able, and then hark to the distance, echoing silence from your lifeless gadgets, oh gentlemen, still trembling slightly at the thought that the guarantee might have expired. Of us the men think last of all! A stranger Michael came, a stranger he must away, and so must his thing.] (Jelinek, trans. Hulse 165)

If readers thought themselves secure in their knowledge of a presumed male narrator speaking to a presumed male reader, this quotation turns those assumptions on their head. The narrator, who in this moment self-identifies as a woman, argues that women need to position themselves better in regard to men. These men, now the opposing force to the "we," never really think about the women with whom they interact. As much as Gerti claims to love him, Michael both enters and leaves his encounters with her as a stranger. Jelinek's narrator implies that this experience is the norm for interactions between women and men. Because the readers of *Lust* struggle to position themselves vis-a-vis the "we" invoked by the narrator, they are unable to achieve the perspective required to become comfortable voyeurs and are thus unable to derive (pornographic) pleasure from the reading experience. When "we" becomes a perpetrator of violence, readers are also denied the melodramatic and masochistic pleasure of identifying with and relating to the depicted suffering. Both of these positions are ultimately shut down by Jelinek's narrative techniques, generating a refusal of satisfaction that underscores this text's dedication to broader melodramatic principles. By forcing her readers into the uncomfortable positions of both the unfeeling perpetrators of sexual violence *and* the passive victims of abuse, by whipping them around between pornographic and melodramatic narrative perspectives, Jelinek critiques the oppression of women inherent in both storytelling modes.

Filicide

This brings us to the most significant, and yet under analyzed, event in *Lust*, the murder of Gerti and Hermann's son. Jelinek could have ended her novel with Michael's betrayal and Hermann's recapture of Gerti, effectively demonstrating the inescapability of the cycles of gendered power and violence dramatized in her novel. That being said, *Lust*'s final scene, a depiction of filicide, represents the culmination of the tension between the passive, pornographic Gerti, who goes numb as her husband rapes her, and the emotionally active, melodramatic Gerti, who desperately seeks out Michael, no matter the cost or the humiliation. Jelinek presents readers with a Medea-like provocation, namely a re-figuration of motherly affection. As Stephan writes of Medea "dieser Mythos der

Mutterliebe macht eine Figur wie Medea bis heute zur Provokation" [this myth of motherly love makes a figure like Medea a provocation through the present] (180). Just as in many versions of the Medea story, by killing her son, Gerti is not able to achieve full liberation from her circumstances. She only temporarily delays an inevitable repetition of violence and betrayal. Both Gerti and Medea are unable to find resolution to their suffering, and even potentially make their situations worse through their acts of violence.

There is a temptation among scholars to read both the Medea story and Gerti's act of filicide as tales of emancipation. For example, Bowles argues that in *Lust* "the final infanticide amounts to just as liberating a deed of identity formation as it is a horrifying perpetuation of the patriarchal violence perpetrated against Gerti" (135). With such emancipatory readings in mind, it is imperative to consider from what exactly Gerti and Medea might attempt to seek liberation. Ina Hartwig calls Gerti's act of filicide a "konsequente Liquidation des Biologischen" [forceful liquidation of the Biological] (83). I, however, read the murder of the son not as an end of biological reproduction (there is no indication that Gerti is incapable of becoming pregnant again), but rather as a destruction of the reader's expectations of genre-based repetition. Corporeal reproduction is still possible. What Jelinek actually pushes back against is the reproduction inherent in the process of mythological storytelling.

What Medea and Gerti gain through their acts of filicide is a renewed, and perhaps more realistic, sense of self. Connecting Gerti to Medea, however, demonstrates that such self-knowledge does not necessarily translate into liberation, as Bowles suggests above. Grillparzer's Medea woefully remarks, "Nicht traur' ich, daß die Kinder nicht mehr sind / Ich traure, daß sie (waren) und daß (wir) sind" [I mourn not because the children are no more, I mourn because they were and because we are] (Act 5). The children mirror what Medea has become through her relationship with Jason and so killing them is about killing off the part of herself that was devoted to him. When Gerti kills her son, her story resists both a pornographic ending of climactic pleasure, as well as one of melodramatic martyrdom and endless suffering. In one final act of narrative violence, both of the reader's expected endings are denied them. This act of melodramatic violence is not really an escape from oppression or an assertion of agency, but rather a critique of both of these genre expectations. Jelinek's novel moves beyond neoliberal feminist discussions of individual empowerment, instead shedding light on the structural models within our own narrative modes and genre conventions that undermine female subjectivity. There may be no hope to escape them, but at least we are able to pause for self-reflection and recognize these structures for what they are.

In a metaphorical representation of this process of self-reflection, tension between motion and stillness forms the thematic foundation of the novel's final scene. After entering her son's room late at night, Gerti kisses him before placing a plastic bag over his head to suffocate him. As the boy's life comes to an end, Gerti considers all the activities in which her son will no longer participate. She reflects on how he will no longer be "mobil bei Arbeit, Sport und Spiel" (Jelinek 254) [mobile "at work, rest and play"] (Jelinek, trans. Hulse 206). She notes that she has made him passive, rather than allowing him to grow into a man who would force other women into passivity. Earlier in the text, the narrator describes how "dieses Kind, dem frischen Geschlecht zugehörig, ist von der Mutter aufgezogen worden, und jetzt kann's nicht mehr zum Stillstand gebracht werden, es läuft und läuft!" (Jelinek 218) [this child, a member of the fresh generation, has been brought up by his mother, wound up, and now he can't be stopped, he just keeps going!] (Jelinek, trans. Hulse 177). When she kills him, Gerti is finally able to pause her son, to keep him from running away. By stopping her son (and ending the novel), rather than indulging immediately in the next iteration of the cycle of violent reproduction, Gerti keeps him from becoming the aggressive animal referenced in the opening scene. Just as in the Medea material, filicide brings the continuation of the father's legacy to a halt, at least temporarily. This pause allows us to see the structures that support his power more clearly. Gerti is no longer resigned to being passive, to being a dead bird waiting for her flesh to be torn open, but this does not mean that she is emancipated in the sense that she can fully overcome her objectification and oppression.

Instead of a bird of prey, her dead son becomes a harmless plant in Gerti's arms. Like a fetus, this plant-son needs constant nourishment and attention. As the narrator describes, "Sie trägt den Sohn auf ihren Armen dahin wie einen knospenden Strauch, der einzupflanzen ist" (Jelinek 254) ["She is carrying her son in her arms like a budding cutting that has to be planted"] (Jelinek, trans. Hulse 207). Employing a similar metaphor, Britta Schmierer writes of Hans Henny Jahnn's Medea that "der Kindermord an sich wird von Medea instrumentalisiert, um die Kinder wieder zu den ihrigen zu machen [...] Medea verhindert den endgültigen Reifungsprozess ihrer Söhne, in dem sie beide umbringt" [the filicide in and of itself is instrumentalized by Medea in order to make the children hers again [...] Medea impedes the maturation/ripening of her sons when she kills them both] (149). Now more than ever, Gerti's son is in her care—the maternal bond is impossible to break. Killing the child, a favorite of his father, will certainly not end the sexual abuse that Gerti endures. In the same way, killing her son does not end her responsibilities as a mother. She has made him motionless, but she must continue to care for him. No matter what, Gerti cannot escape the burdens of motherhood. This plant imagery is also reminiscent of Sylvia Plath's final poem, "Edge" (1963), in which she describes Medea's flight away from Corinth:

> Each dead child coiled, a white serpent, [...]
>
> She has folded
>
> Them back into her body as petals
>
> Of a rose [...]. (Plath 272–273)

Plath likens Medea's dead children to plants and to serpents, rose petals that can now re-enter the body of the mother, re-enter the womb. Medea, often associated with magical, life-giving plants, represents both growth and destruction. What she gives, she can also take back into herself. These dead children becoming plants depicts the impossible desire for some mothers to take back as theirs that which their bodies have nourished and given into the world.

In *Lust*, this reabsorption is characterized by icy, liquid metaphors. Jelinek's readers are assured that the child's dead body will be preserved for a long time in the icy river, while "die Mutter lebt" (255) ["the mother is alive"] (Jelinek, trans. Hulse 207). The scene reaches a temporary stasis in which Gerti's role as a mother endures, just as her child's body is preserved by the cold water, the flowing of which simultaneously suggests movement. As she tries to decide whether or not to murder her children, Seneca's Medea experiences a similar moment of frozenness saying, "My heart is struck with horror, my limbs freeze, my breast trembles" (397). In Jelinek's text, Gerti also begins her journey frozen and in pain on her drunken walks. However, by the end, it is the son and not Gerti who is encased in ice. Although she has not managed to change any of the essential conditions of her situation, she has managed to freeze things for a second before she must continue with the exploitative labor that characterizes her life.

It is important to emphasize that this frozen moment is only temporary. Eventually, time and oppression carry on. The narrator argues of women that "sie wissen nicht, wo sie all die Zeit hinter sich verstecken können, damit keiner sie sieht" (Jelinek 255) ["their mistake is not knowing where to hide all the time that lies behind them so that no one sees it"] (Jelinek, trans. Hulse 207). As in Loher's play, the past is presented in this final scene as a force that is impossible for women like Gerti to hide, or to hide from. It will always come out to spoil the perfection of any peaceful moments that women are able to generate for themselves. The narrator metaphorically connects mother and child asking, "Sollen sie sie etwa verschlingen wie die Nabelschnüre ihrer Kinder? Mord und Tod!" (Jelinek 255) ["What are they to do, devour it like the umbilical cords of their children? Hell and damnation!"] (Jelinek, trans. Hulse 207). The mother is bound up in time and in history, just as her child was bound to her in the womb. She cannot escape this bond, just as killing her son does not negate, but rather enhances his connection to her. All that Gerti is able to do is shift her position slightly within already existing binaries between men and women, mothers and children. She cannot remove herself entirely from them. Just as in the community chorus that Hermann directs, in which all of the "schreklich schwachen Stimmen" (Jelinek 9) ["awful feeble voices"] (Jelinek, trans. Hulse 8) of the townspeople fail to harmonize because of Hermann's tyrannical leadership, all hierarchies, whether sexual or not, disrupt the ability of individuals to come together and to form harmonious group identities. Group or familial unity is extremely difficult, if not impossible, to achieve in such a climate of violence, thereby limiting our ability to generate politically effective solidarity. If descriptions of our collective identities are uncritically shaped by the expectations of narrative modes (such as in pornography and melodrama), such modes can never be used as a means of resistance against oppressive social discourses and structures.

As I have shown, the narrative confusion generated by Jelinek's text makes it difficult to establish a comfortable perspective for the reader. This makes it surprising that the scene in which Gerti performs her most unexpected and aggressive act is narrated in an (almost) uninterrupted third-person voice. In fact, the scene of filicide is one of the more poetic in the text, employing both metaphoric language and narrated monologue (*erlebte Rede*).[9] The beginning of the scene in which Gerti suffocates her child is narrated as follows:

> Unbequem liegt das Kind unter dem Auge der Mutter, die an sein Bett tritt und es geraderückt. Welk ist das Kind und dennoch ihre ganze Welt: es schweigt wie diese. Es freut sich gewiß aufs Wachsen, ähnlich dem Glied seines Vaters. Zärtlich küßt die Mutter ihr kleines Boot, das die Welt umschifft. Dann ergreift sie eine Plastiktüte, legt sie dem Kind über den Kopf und hält sie unten ganz fest zu, damit der Atem des Kindes darin in Ruhe zerbrechen kann. (Jelinek 254)
>
> [Comfortless he lies there under the eye of his mother, who comes to his bed and smooths the covers. The boy is flaccid and yet he is her whole world: he is silent, and so is her world. He is no doubt looking forward to growing up, like his father's member. Tenderly Mother kisses her little boat sailing around the world. Then she takes a plastic bag, slips it over the boy's head, and draws it tight at the bottom so that the child's breath will perish in peace.] (Jelinek, trans. Hulse 206)

Jelinek presents this scene in a straightforward manner, from the third person perspective: Gerti goes up to the bed, fixes it, grabs a plastic bag, puts it over the child's head, and holds the bottom tight. However, the narrator also comments on the situation, noting how this weak child has somehow become Gerti's entire world. In addition to the narrator's point of view, we are given limited access to Gerti's perspective. Considering the conflicted

9 Dorrit Cohn draws a distinction between narrated monologue and the German *erlebte Rede*, arguing that narrated monologue specifically refers to the exploration of only one consciousness by the narrator, while *erlebte Rede* can include multiple voices. I am choosing to group them together here because, as I have shown, in *Lust*, the positionality of the narrator is often ambiguous.

relationship that Gerti has had with her son up to this point, the metaphor of the child as a boat, in addition to keeping with the fluid ebbs and flows of this scene, speaks to Gerti's anxiety that her husband's behavior will be continued by her son. Seneca's Medea uses similarly nautical metaphors to describe her internal debate about whether filicide is the correct choice saying, "Conflicting currents whirl me from side to side. Just as, when the whirling winds wage savage warfare, the contending waves drive the seas both ways, and the waters seethe in confusion" (397). Medea and Gerti see no alternative to the son's death because he, too, is controlled by the waves of society's inescapable, gendered power dynamics. This scene is both deeply melodramatic in its description of a mother's tender kiss, as well as violent in the brutal depiction of Gerti suffocating the child. This combination of tenderness and of violence in *Lust* is reminiscent of the drowning of Jason's mother in *Manhattan Medea* and further demonstrates the ability of Jelinek's narration to encompass stark contradictions.

Gerti's act of filicide becomes even more interesting when it transitions into a moment of clear narrated monologue, giving the reader even more direct access to Gerti's consciousness:

> Üppig entfalten sich unter dem Zelt des Sackes, auf dem die Adresse einer Boutique aufgedruckt ist, noch einmal die Lebenskräfte des Kindes, dem vor nicht allzu langer Zeit Wachstum und Sportgeräte versprochen wurden. So geht's, wenn man die Natur durch Geräte zu verbessern wünscht! Aber nein, es will doch nimmer leben. Dann treibt der Sohn hinaus ins offene Wasser, wo er gleich ganz in seinem Element (Mutti!) ist [...]. (Jelinek 254)
>
> [Under the tent of the back, on which is printed the address of a boutique, the boy's life force burgeons richly one more time, this boy to whom not long ago growing up and sports gear were promised. That's how it goes when one tries to improve on Nature with mechanical implements! But no, the child still wants to live. Then the son drifts out into the open waters where he is immediately quite in his element (Mummy!) [...].] (Jelinek, trans. Hulse 206).

The exclamations in this passage draw attention to the odd and difficult relationship between mother and child. As in the previously cited rape scene, which is interrupted by demands for applause, this passage features calls from an unspecified source, once again set off in parentheses. A voice, likely the son himself, but potentially also another narrator, calls out,

"Mutti!" [Mummy!] just as the son is described as returning to his element. In contrast to the commercial objects described here, which imply selfish, capitalist exchanges, in his death the child returns to a watery womb where he is forced into a relationship of mutual dependency. He is again a part of Gerti, the mother. In what Jelinek ironically frames as the ultimate act of mothering, Gerti metaphorically reabsorbs her son back into herself, shielding him from any identity that is not subsumed by his intimate relationship with her. Instead of melodramatically suffering for her son, he and Gerti become one and the same. Gerti remains the passive victim, but in this moment, she also adopts the role of abusive perpetrator. She enacts violence by suffocating her son and taking away his life, yet, like Medea, she does so out of feelings of maternal care, out of a desire to return to a state in which mother and son are inseparably bound together.

When Jelinek reinforces Gerti's motherhood, it stands in contrast with many versions of the Medea story, which suggest that Medea negates her own womanhood through her deeds. In Euripides's play, Jason and Medea blame each other for what has happened shouting: "Children, what an evil mother you got!" and "Children, how you have perished by your father's fault!" (Euripides 407). Each claims that the other is a bad parent. Seneca's Medea takes this a step further, placing even more blame on herself when she declares, "The crime is having Jason as their father, and the worse crime is having Medea as their mother" (397). In Jelinek's novel, Gerti is both a bad and a good parent rolled up into one, as the ultimate expression of motherhood takes on an unexpectedly fatal form. Rather than fighting over who is the bad parent, Jelinek's text seeks to redefine our understanding of motherhood and parenting through a violent return to pregnancy and the womb.

In many versions of the Medea story, Medea's violent actions are read as a way of reclaiming her identity, especially after she has betrayed her family in Colchis and contributed to the death of her brother. While Jelinek's Gerti has no additional family to betray, at least not that we know about, it is important to consider the effects of this violence on Gerti's identity. In Grillparzer's play, Medea transitions from saying: "Ja, wär' ich noch Medea, doch ich bin's nicht mehr!" [Yes, if only I were still Medea, but I am not her anymore!] (Act 4) before she kills her children to reaffirming her identity after deciding to kill them exclaiming, "Medea bin ich wieder, Dank euch Götter!" [I am Medea again, thank you gods!] (Act 4). Does Gerti undergo the same kind of transformation back into a more confident and independent self when she kills her son? Jelinek's answer is decidedly "no." Instead, Gerti actual comes to resemble her husband, whose abuse she is trying to resist. When she murders her son, Gerti proves her similarity to Hermann in that she too turns to pointless violence in a search for momentary stability and order. Hermann abuses Gerti in order to keep his body and his life stable. Gerti, we see, achieves a moment of similar stasis and stability when she kills her son. As Françoise Rétif argues, "Gertis Mord reproduziert das Opfern als Ursprung der Kunst, aber opfert auch dessen Metaphorik" [Gerti's murdering reproduces sacrifice as the origin of art, but it also sacrifices the imagery of this origin] (117–118). Instead of a beautiful work of art generated by sacrifice, readers of *Lust* are left with an ugly imitation of masculine violence.

Gerti's only recourse is to send her son back to nature, to surround him with the foundation of all life: water—both literally (the water of the river) and figuratively (the amniotic fluid of the womb). Stephan describes the final scene of *Lust* as a negation of pregnancy, writing that Gerti suffocates and then lets her son "in einem Bach 'abtreiben'" [be "aborted" in a stream] (180). Instead of bringing a reproductive cycle to an end, I argue that Gerti pauses and then restarts it. Rather than an abortion, which we explicitly encountered alongside other liquid metaphors in Ursula Haas's novel, Jelinek describes Gerti's actions as a return to pregnancy. Gerti cannot change the gendered oppression generated by the traditional nuclear family, so she sends her son back to a state in which he is prevented from maturing within these gendered social roles. The scene of filicide at the end of the novel also aligns with Goldberg's understanding of how melodrama works not to change the world, but to "change our perception and experience of the world" (35). Gerti's world is the same, but the reader's perspective of that world is changed by Gerti's act of melodramatic violence. By combining pornography and melodrama, Jelinek goes even further than Goldberg to uncover the gendered stakes and systems of power that force this shift in perspective. For Jahnn's Medea, as for Gerti, this means regaining the children that she lost to Jason's betrayal when she says, "Mein sind die Kinder jetzt. Der Leib ist meiner, den seine Schönheit hab ich Helios abgetrotzt. Tot ist Jasons Same" [The children are now mine. The body is mine, whose beauty I wrested from Helios. Jason's seed is dead] (52). Both Gerti and Jahnn's Medea see the death of their children as a restoration for themselves and a loss for their husbands. Paradoxically, what she gave life has become hers again through death.

In the final line of *Lust*, the narrator commands us to rest: "Aber nun rastet eine Weile!" (Jelinek 255) ["But now rest a while!"] (Jelinek, trans. Hulse 207). Restful reflection may be exactly what we need, but Jelinek's text has already shown how difficult, if not impossible, such reflection is to achieve. Of Ursula Haas's Medea, Astrid Messerschmidt and Eva Peters write that "Was Medea in der Beziehung zu Jason lernte, ist die Fähigkeit zur (Selbst)-Reflexion" [what Medea learned through her relationship with Jason is the ability for (self)-reflection] (532). In Haas we see this journey toward self-reflection as difficult, but still based on the choices Medea makes. In Jelinek, however, our rest is commanded, further reminding us that there is a nefarious power dynamic at work here. By the end of the novel, the narration has moved away, yet again, from the specifics of Gerti's situation to extrapolate something about the status of women in general. It is not Gerti who is asked to rest at the end, but all of the women implicated by this second-person-plural command. As Stephan writes, "Gertis Tat ist eine Störung, sie verursacht kurzfristig eine Panne im Getriebe der Welt, so dass am Ende alles eine Weile 'rastet'" [Gerti's deed is a disruption. She creates a short-term glitch in the gears of the world, so that at the end everything "rests" for awhile] (181). This small, temporary resistance against the repetition of violent, gendered oppression has been unduly challenging, and so we must rest, rather than pointlessly trying to generate hope in a world in which justice can never fully be served. As Maria Stehle points out in reference to Jelinek's repetition of injurious speech, "the textual mechanism is circular, which means that there is no room for 'change' on the level of the text itself" (233). As in the melodramatic mode, there is no revolution against the patriarchy here, only an assertion of Gerti's ability to perpetrate acts of extreme, and in many ways useless, violence, much like her male counterparts. Gerti participates in the process of objectifying others in the same way that she has been made into a symbol by her husband, and ultimately by Jelinek as well.

After all that the reader has been forced to engage with in this text, the order to rest is an uncomfortable one. Are we really expected to rest after the violent nature of our most intimate relationships has been revealed to us? Are we not supposed to take action to right the suffering so brutally depicted here? This is Jelinek's final provocation to her readers, a provocation that is ultimately a melodramatic one. She shows us our own complicity and then asks us to reflect on it, to come to terms with our own willingness to accept brutality, not only within the literary modes of pornography and melodrama, but within our own lives. We are forced to confront the limits of what we are willing to allow in terms of human suffering and objectification. However, Jelinek ultimately pushes beyond even melodramatic conventions by arguing that our ability to delay this cycle of oppression, even for a moment, proves that our identities are too complex to be accounted for within the conventions of any one set of prescriptive values.

In addition to avoiding putting her readers in a powerful, masculinized, controlling relationship with her text, Jelinek also refuses to place her characters in a position of complete helplessness in which they can only engage in the behaviors stereotypically associated with the gendered roles that they are fated to play. Nevertheless, this is no real escape from these limiting categories, but rather a reflection on and within them. The most fascinating aspect of Jelinek's novel is the way in which she sets us up to think that the world is both exactly the way that we expect it to be and yet, at the same time, not at all what we thought it was. Depictions of melodramatic violence ultimately force their readers to acknowledge these contradictions and establish a more nuanced picture of gender difference and sexual violence. By simultaneously building up and breaking down her readers' assumptions on the levels of plot, character, language, and narration, Jelinek forces her readers to question the degree to which they are also complicit in the gendered violence that infects even our most intimate relationships. Jones writes that "until we honor the rage that is born of oppression, Medea will haunt us and harangue us, and each night the children will die again" (100). In many ways, it is appropriate to say that Jelinek's text is haunted by the Medea story. Rather than directly adapting this mythological material, Jelinek takes the stakes of the Medea myth and considers how they relate to the feminist debates of her time. The children and our innocence will indeed continue to die if we insist on pushing women to the brink through sexual violence and exploitation.

Epilogue

> Γυνὴ γὰρ τἄλλα μὲν φόβου πλέα
>
> κακή τ᾽ ἐς ἀλκὴν καὶ σίδηρον εἰσορᾶν.
>
> ὅταν δ᾽ ἐς εὐνὴν ἠδικημένη κυρῇ,
>
> οὐκ ἔστιν ἄλλη φρὴν μιαιφονωτέρα.

—Euripides 306

> [In all other things a woman is full of fear, incapable of looking on battle or cold steel; but when she is injured in love, no mind is more murderous than hers.]

—Euripides 307

Although Euripides draws on gendered stereotypes in the above explanation of Medea's behavior, Medea's violent actions are, indeed, almost always connected to love—her love of Jason, which leads her to murder her brother and Pelias, her love of her brother, which in part provokes the murder of her own children, etc. In almost all versions of the Medea story, one of the central conflicts is that Medea loves people who do not love her back. When Medea does occasionally find mutual love, it is often with other women or nonbinary people, for example, the various iterations of Medea's nurse/companion and most significantly in this book, Dea Loher's character Deaf Daisy. Friendship is the truest bond in the Medea story because it is always mutual and collaborative. If friendship is a positive example of love, then heterosexual romance is its negative counterpart. Romantic love between men and women always ends in betrayal for Medea because of power imbalances between her partner and herself. Medea forces us to question how we respond when we are brutally rejected, when we give everything and receive only sorrow and even greater loss in return. This is where Medea's role as a murderous mother comes into play. To be murderous is to attempt to escape. To be murderous is to want to sever the ties that bind and to start again. To be a mother is to nurture, to help new things grow. The juxtaposition of these forces is messy, but these contradictions are generative because they reveal the scars and the trauma that unrequited, one-sided love leaves in its wake.

Another miscarriage of justice identified by feminist Medea adaptations relates to the way Medea's story is mythologized. In her poem titled "Brief an Medea" (Letter to Medea) the East German poet Helga M. Novak describes a Medea similar to the one we encounter in Christa Wolf's novel *Medea. Stimmen*. Novak's Medea has been sold out by Euripides and "seitdem jagen sie [Medea] dich durch unsere Literaturen / als Mörderin Furie Ungeheuer" [since then they hunt you [Medea] throughout our literature / as a Murderess, Fury, Monster] (Novak, reproduced in Stephan 10). Lies about Medea have been repeated so many times that they have become normalized. The idea of hunting someone down through literature also strikes me as strangely similar to the project of writing a book about adaptations of a mythological story. In my own hunt, I hope that I have distinguished between Medea the murderess, Medea the fury, and Medea the monster, and also demonstrated how the figure of Medea can both embrace and slip away from such maligned categories, depending on the political goals of her authors. While I have enjoyed this hunt, I trust that it has not ended in unproductive violence, but rather in a more nuanced understanding of the relationship between this figure and a particular moment in feminist theory and history. Part of the appeal of the Medea figure is that one can never really catch her and so, I end this book satisfied to live in the discomfort of Medea's ambiguities. Novak ends her poem by letting Medea know that "die Callas ist tot" [Callas is dead] (Novak, reproduced in Stephan 10). This provocation points to an important aspect of the history of Medea adaptations that I was unable to cover in this book. I have focused my attention on literary Medeas from late twentieth-century Germany, asking what Medeas on the page, or sometimes the stage, show us about contemporaneous feminist theory and politics. This obviously leaves out an extremely important medium in the history of Medea stories, namely film.

By saying that Callas is dead, Novak refers to the soprano Maria Callas, famous for playing Medea in the opera house and in the well-known 1969 film from Italian director Pier Paolo Pasolini. Novak's poem was written in 1977, which is indeed the same year that Callas died. In a gesture not unlike Wolf's in *Medea. Stimmen*, Novak suggests that Callas's portrayal is an injustice to the *real* Medea to which Novak's poem is addressed. Characterized by close-up shots that show off Callas's piercing eyes, Pasolini's film depicts a Medea who becomes herself again through violent revenge. Our first images of the Colchians in Pasolini's film details their participation in an elaborate human sacrifice. As Inge Stephan writes, the world Pasolini creates for his Medea is "irrational, primitiv, barbarisch" [irrational, primitive, barbaric] (213). Medea's bloodlust marks a return to her true nature. However, as Novak's poem suggests, such a depiction of Medea can easily become a dangerous exoticization that, in many ways, strips Medea of her humanity, making her either god or monster. What distinguishes the feminist Medea adaptations I examine in this book from such contemporaneous Medea adaptations by men is that they all ultimately try to make Medea more human, rather than less. For Ursula Haas, Christa Wolf, Dagmar Nick, Dea Loher, and Elfriede Jelinek, Medea is a complex person with all of the contradictions, traumas, and collaborative identities that such humanity entails.

Our understanding of the role that Medea plays in cultural production is certainly incomplete without continued investigation into these Medeas of the screen. In the German-speaking context, I would point to director Branwen Okpako's *Fluch der Medea* (The Curse of Medea) (2014) as just one example of the many unique filmic works that require our detailed attention. Exploring Christa Wolf's legacy as a prominent cultural figure of the GDR, Okpako's film casts Black performers in the roles of Medea and the other female voices from Wolf's novel. Unlike Hans Henny Jahnn's oversimplified and racist characterization of a Black Medea on the German stage, Okpako's casting provides space for deeper reflections on the ways that societies designate insiders and outsiders to power. This self-reflexivity is evident in the many visible microphones and the tightly framed shots of these performers, as well as through the lack of a visual presence of Wolf herself, except through historical footage. Although Okpako's interview with Wolf is central to the structure of the film, Wolf exists primarily as a voice. Contrastingly, the voices of Wolf's novel are brought to life by Black actors, who we view in their capacity as performers, visibly speaking into a camera and a microphone. The lines that Okpako draws between Medea stories and the shattered promise of democratic socialism experienced after German Reunification reveals Medea's ongoing importance as a cultural representation of power and its abuses.

In *Murderous Mothers*, I have demonstrated the great potential and the significant pitfalls involved in using Medea figures as models for feminist politics. Haas's Medea defies gendered expectations by taking charge of her own body and having an abortion. But, as an author, Haas fails to liberate Medea from the colonial history that has become linked to this myth, especially in the German context. The voice of the author is also crucial in the Medea stories of Wolf and Nick as they try, but ultimately fall short of giving Medea a platform to speak for herself. Analyzing voice and voicelessness in this context also invokes discourses of victimization, where people who have historically been erased (women, the subaltern, etc.) struggle to be heard. Loher's Medea fights hard against her victimization. Through her interactions with symbolic characters such as Deaf Daisy, Loher's Medea comes to realize that her only chance for justice comes through collaborative performances. According to Jelinek's Medea-figure Gerti, to be human is to be in pain. The combination of Gerti's violent response to her suffering and Jelinek's use of uncomfortable narrative voices compels readers to reflect on their own complicity in systems of oppression. Feminist Medeas are murderous mothers and murderous mothers teach us that, even in destruction, we are always connected to each other through complex physical, social, political, and historical threads.

As I was completing the writing of this book in the middle of the global COVID-19 pandemic, the Schauspielhaus Zurich live-streamed a production titled *Medea** (2020). Directed by Leonie Böhm, this adaptation of the Medea story inherits the legacy of the Germanophone Medeas discussed in this book. In this two-person show in which Medea narrates her life story to the (often musical) accompaniment of her "best friend" Johannes, the titular character understands herself as someone who must kill her children in order to fulfill her prescribed role. "So steht's geschrieben" [so it is written] she proclaims early on in the play. This Medea understands her predicament as one in which she has sacrificed everything for an undeserving (male) partner: "Alle Wege, die ich ihm eröffnet habe, sind für mich geschlossen" [All the paths that I opened for him are closed to me]. The theme of self-awareness and the character's own meta-reflections on the act of performing as Medea harken back to the works of Jelinek and of Loher. Simultaneously, the articulation of gender difference and its double standards connects to Haas and Wolf's engagements with this myth.

In many of these late twentieth-century Medea stories, bodies seem to matter quite a lot. Bodily fluids, seductive bodies, and injured bodies abound. In Böhm and her team's twenty-first-century representation, Medea's murderous nature is far less about physical death, than it is about a spiritual killing off. Toward the end of the play, Medea cries out "Ich werde jetzt alle meine Illusionen töten" [I will now kill all of my illusions]. In this pandemic-era theatrical work, the children that Medea kills are no longer real in any sense of the word. Instead, Medea's illusions about the world and her blind faith in others are what ends up dead at the end of the play. The Medeas I discuss in this book all struggle within the confines of a corporeal identity politics that positions them as outsiders because of their bodyminds. By removing the weight of the body from the Medea figure, Böhm and her team create a Medea who feels inspired by, but is not destined to relive, her past. This Medea of 2020 is motivated, but not confined, by the body of work that has come before her. My hope is that I have similarly contributed to the rich history of the Medea material and introduced news ways for thinking about her role within the context of late twentieth-century feminist theory and politics.

Bibliography

Primary Literature (and Translations)

Euripides. *Euripides I: Cyclops Alcestis Medea*. Edited and Translated by David Kovacs. Loeb-Harvard UP, 2001.

Grillparzer, Franz. *Medea. 2005. Project Gutenberg*, <www.gutenberg.org/ebooks/7945>.

Haas, Ursula. *Freispruch für Medea*. Limes Verlag, 1987.

Hein, Christoph. *Das goldene Vlies. Erzählung*. Faber & Faber Verlag, 2005.

Jahnn, Hans Henny. *Medea*. Edited by Manfred Weber, Edition Hentrich, 1989.

Jelinek, Elfriede. *Lust*. 1989. 13th ed., Rowohlt, 2012.

____. *Lust*. Translated by Michael Hulse. Serpent's Tail, 1992.

Kolmar, Gertrud. *Die jüdische Mutter*. Wallstein Verlag, 1999.

Loher, Dea. *Manhattan Medea. Blaubart—Hoffnung der Frauen. Zwei Stücke*. Verlag der Autoren, 1999.

"Medea*." By Helena Eckert, Directed by Leonie Böhm, Schauspielhaus Zürich, May 20, 2021, Theatertreffen Festival, Berlin, Germany.

Müller, Heiner. "Despoiled Shore Medeamaterial Landscape with Argonauts." *Hamletmachine and Other Texts for the Stage*. Translated by Carl Weber. Performing Arts Journal Publications, 1984, pp. 123–135.

____. "Verkommenes Ufer Medeamaterial Landschaft mit Argonauten." *Die Stücke 3*. Suhrkamp Verlag, 2002, pp. 71–84.

Nick, Dagmar. *Medea, ein Monolog*. Eremiten-Presse, 1988.

Novak, Helga M. "Brief an Medea." Reproduced in: *Medea: Multimediale Karriere einer mythologischen Figur*. By Inge Stephan. Böhlau Verlag, 2006, p. 10.

Okpako, Branwen, director. *Fluch der Medea*. Branwen Okpako and JPgotMangos, 2014.

Ovid. *Metamorphoses*. Translated by Charles Martin. W. W. Norton, 2004.

Pasolini, Pier Paolo, director. *Medea.* Janus Film und Fernsehen, 1969. *YouTube*, uploaded by Hellenic History Series, 30 December 2020, <https://www.youtube.com/watch?v= t2f9AjQ2ebc>.

Plath, Sylvia. *Collected Poems.* Harper Collins, 1981, <ebooks-ohiolink-edu.libproxy.kenyon.edu/content/d69a16bc-2bdd-40cf-847b-4a5b6d76d474>.

Seghers, Anna."Das Argonautenschiff." *Anna Seghers: Die schönsten Erzählungen*, selected by Christina Salmen. Aufbau Verlag, 2008, pp. 247–266.

Seneca. "Medea." Translated by Jon G. Fitch. Loeb-Harvard UP, 2018, pp. 303–403.

Wolf, Christa. *Medea. A Modern Retelling.* Translated by John Cullen. Doubleday, 1998.

____. *Medea. Stimmen.* 1996; Suhrkamp Verlag, 2008.

Archives

Archiv der deutschen Frauenbewegung, Kassel, Germany.

Frauenforschungs-, -bildungs-und Informationszentrum (FFBIZ), Berlin, Germany.

Secondary Literature

"374 deutsche Frauen halten den § 218 für überholt und erklären öffentlich:,Wir haben gegen ihn verstoßen.'" *Stern*, June 6, 1971.

Ahmed, Sara. "An Affinity of Hammers." *Trap Door: Trans Cultural Production and the Politics of Visibility*, edited by Reina Gossett, Eric A. Stanley, and Johanna Burton, MIT Press, 2017, pp. 221–234.

____. *Living a Feminist Life.* Duke UP, 2017.

Anz, Thomas. "Christa Wolfs Arbeit Am Mythos: Ihr Roman 'Medea' schreibt die Erzählung 'Kassandra' fort." *Süddeutsche Zeitung*, March 3, 1996. Reprinted at: <https://literaturkritik.de/id/16180>.

Arnds, Peter. "Translating a Greek Myth: Christa Wolf's Medea in a Contemporary Context." *Neophilologus*, vol. 85, no. 3, 2001, pp. 415–428. doi: 10.1023/A:1010332619287, May 9, 2015.

Barnett, David. *Brecht in Practice: Theatre, Theory and Performance.* Bloomsbury, 2015.

Bartel, Heike. "Dressing the 'Other,' Dressing the 'Self': Clothing in the Medea Dramas of Euripides and Franz Grillparzer." *Unbinding Medea: Interdisciplinary Approaches to a Classical Myth from Antiquity to the 21st Century*, edited by Heike Bartel and Anne Simon, Modern Humanities Research Association and Manly Publishing, 2010, pp. 161–175.

____. "A Medea Called Wally: Race, Madness and Fashion in Paul Heyse's Novella *Medea*." *German Life and Letters*, vol. 64, no. 1, 2011, pp. 56–70. doi: 10.1111/j.1468-0483.2010.01519.x.

Bartel, Heike, and Anne Simon. "Introduction: Medea, Meetings in Borderland." *Unbinding Medea: Interdisciplinary Approaches to a Classical Myth from Antiquity to the 21st Century*, edited by Heike Bartel and Anne Simon, Modern Humanities Research Association and Manly Publishing, 2010, pp. 1–15.

Bataille, Georges. *Story of the Eye*. Translated by Joachim Neugroschel. City Lights Books, 1987.

Bauer, Nancy. *How to do Things with Pornography*. Harvard UP, 2015.

Beard, Mary. *Women & Power: A Manifesto*. W.W. Norton & Company, 2017.

Beebee, Thomas O. and Beverly M. Weber. "A Literature of Theory: Christa Wolf's Kassandra Lectures as Feminist Anti-Poetics." *The German Quarterly*, vol. 74, no. 3, 2001, pp. 259–279, *JSTOR*, <www.jstor.org/stable/3072786>.

Berlant, Lauren. *The Female Complaint: The Unfinished Business of Sentimentality in American Culture*. Duke UP, 2008. Project MUSE, <muse.jhu.edu/book/69580>.

Bethman, Brenda. *"Obscene Fantasies": Elfriede Jelinek's Generic Perversions*. Peter Lang, 2011.

Bollig, Barbara. "Zwischen den Gezeiten: Griechische Wikinger, teuflische Götter, natürliche Gewalt in Lars von Triers *Medea* (1988)." *Zeitschrift für interkulturelle Germanistik*, vol. 11, no. 2, 2020, pp. 129–145, doi: 10.14361/zig-2015-0103.

Bovenschen, Silvia. *Die imaginierte Weiblichkeit: Exemplarische Untersuchungen zu kulturgeschichtlichen und literarischen Präsentationsformen des Weiblichen*. Suhrkamp Verlag, 1979.

Bowles, Daniel James. "Elfriede Jelinek's Mythic Lust (1989)." *The Ends of Satire: Legacies of Satire in Postwar German Writing*. De Gruyter, 2015, pp. 119–135.

Brauner, Sigrid. *Fearless Wives and Frightened Shrews: The Construction of the Witch in Early Modern Germany*. U of Massachusetts P, 1995.

Bridge, Helen. "Christa Wolf's *Kassandra* and *Medea*: Continuity and Change." *German Life and Letters*, vol. 57, no. 1, 2004, pp. 33–43, doi: 10.1111/j.1468-0483.2004.00268.x.

Brooks, Peter. *The Melodramatic Imagination: Balzac, Henry James, Melodrama, and the Mode of Excess*. Columbia UP, 1985.

Butler, Judith. *Bodies that Matter: On the Discursive Limits of "Sex."* 1993, Routledge, 2011.

____. *Excitable Speech: A Politics of the Performative*. Routledge, 1997.

____. *Gender Trouble: Feminism and the Subversion of Identity*. Routledge, 1990.

____. *Giving an Account of Oneself.* Fordham UP, 2005.

Catani, Stephanie. "Vom Anfang und Ende des Mythos. Medea bei Christa Wolf und Dea Loher." *Monatshefte*, vol. 99, no. 3, 2007, pp. 316–332, doi: 10.1353/mon.2007.0052.

Chien, Chieh. *Gewaltproblematik bei Elfriede Jelinek. Erläutert anhand des Romans "Lust."* Wiku, 2005.

Cixous, Hélène. "The Laugh of the Medusa." Translated by Keith Cohen and Paula Cohen. *Signs*, vol. 1, no. 4, 1976, pp. 875–893, *JSTOR*, <www.jstor.org/stable/3173239>.

Cohn, Dorrit. *Transparent Minds: Narrative Modes for Presenting Consciousness in Fiction*. Princeton UP, 1978.

Crosby, Christina. 2019. "Faithful to the Contemplation of Bones: Disability and Irremediable Grief." *The South Atlantic Quarterly*, vol. 118, no. 3, 2019, pp. 615–641, doi: 10.1215/00382876-7616187.

Daston, Lorraine. "The Morality of Natural Orders: The Power of Medea." *The Tanner Lectures on Human Values at Harvard University*, November 6, 2002, <tannerlectures.utah.edu/_documents/a-to-z/d/daston_2002.pdf>.

Dietrich, Anette. "Konstruktionen weisser weiblicher Körper im Kontext des deutschen Kolonialismus." *Mythen Masken und Subjekte: Kritische Weißseinforschung in Deutschland*, edited by Maureen Maisha Eggers, Grada Kilomba, Peggy Piesche, and Susan Arndt. Unrast, 2017, pp. 363–376.

Doll, Annette. *Mythos, Natur und Geschichte bei Elfriede Jelinek. Eine Untersuchung ihrer literarischen Intentionen*. Verlag für Wissenschaft und Forschung, 1994.

Doyle, Sady. *Dead Blondes and Bad Mothers: Monstrosity, Patriarchy, and the Fear of Female Power*. Melville House, 2019.

Ellis, Alicia E. *Gender and Identity in Franz Grillparzer's Classical Dramas: Figuring the Female*. Lexington Books, 2021.

Ellison, Treva. "The Labor of Werquing It: The Performance and Protest Strategies of Sir Lady Java." *Trap Door. Trans Cultural Production and the Politics of Visibility*, edited by Reina Gossett, Eric A. Stanley, and Johanna Burton, MIT Press, 2017, pp. 1–22.

Feichtinger, Barbara. "Medea—Rehabilitation einer Kindsmörderin? Zur Medea-Rezeption moderner deutschsprachiger Autorinnen." *Grazer Beiträge*, vol. 18, no. 1, 1992, pp. 205–234.

Fischer-Lichte, Erika. "Culture as Performance." *Modern Austrian Literature*, vol. 42, no. 3, 2009, pp. 1–10, *JSTOR*, <www.jstor.org/stable/24649950>.

Florvil, Tiffany N. *Mobilizing Black Germany: Afro-German Women and the Making of a Transnational Movement.* U of Illinois P, 2020.

Freud, Sigmund. *The Question of Lay Analysis: an Introduction to Psychoanalysis* (1926). Translated by Nancy Proctor-Gregg. W. W. Norton, 1950.

Gehrke, Claudia, editor. *Frauen und Pornographie.* Konkursbuch Verlag, 2016.

Gledhill, Christine, and Linda Williams, editors. *Melodrama Unbound: Across History Media and National Cultures.* Columbia UP, 2018.

Goldberg, Jonathan. *Melodrama: An Aesthetics of Impossibility.* Duke UP, 2016.

Haas, Birgit. *Das Theater von Dea Loher: Brecht und (k)ein Ende.* Aisthesis Verlag, 2006.

Haas, Ursula. "Text für Kompositionen," Personal Website, September 2020, <www.poetessa.de/text-fuer-kompositionen.html>.

Hage, Volker. 1996. "Kein Mord, nirgends: Ein Angriff auf die Macht und die Männer: Christa Wolfs Schlüsselroman 'Medea.'" *der Spiegel,* February 26, 1996, pp. 202–206, <www.spiegel.de/kultur/kein-mord-nirgends-a-8c2bcfad-0002-0001-0000-000008889781>.

Halberstam, Judith [Jack]. *In a Queer Time and Place: Transgender Bodies, Subcultural Lives.* NYU Press, 2005.

Hartwig, Ina. "Schwere Arbeit am Moment des Sexus: Über Elfriede Jelineks Lust." *Elfriede Jelinek. Text + Kritik,* Zeitschrift für Literatur, vol. 117, 3rd ed., 2007, pp. 74–84.

Hayward, Eva. "Spiderwomen." *Trap Door. Trans Cultural Production and the Politics of Visibility,* edited by Reina Gossett, Eric A. Stanley, and Johanna Burton, MIT Press, 2017, pp. 255–80.

Hegel, G. W. F.. *Aesthetics: Volume 1,* Translated by T. M. Knox, Oxford UP, 1998. *ProQuest Ebook Central,* <https://ebookcentral-proquest-com.libproxy.kenyon.edu/lib/kenyon-ebooks/detail.action?docID=5891731>.

Henke, Silvia. "Pornographie als Gefängnis—Elfriede Jelineks 'Lust' im Vergleich." *Colloquium helveticum,* vol. 31, 2000, pp. 239–264, <www.yumpu.com/de/document/read/4888156/pornographie-als-gefangnis-elfriede-jelineks-lust-im-silvia-henke>.

Irigaray, Luce. "And the One Doesn't Stir Without the Other." Translated by Helene Vivienne Wenzel. *Signs,* vol. 7, no. 1, 1981, pp. 60–67, *JSTOR,* <www.jstor.org/stable/3173507>.

____. *Marine Lover of Friedrich Nietzsche.* Translated by Gillian C. Gill. Columbia UP, 1991.

Jones, Jennifer. *Medea's Daughters: Forming and Performing the Woman Who Kills.* Ohio State UP, 2003.

Kallin, Britta."'Gut sei gewesen, was die Entfaltung alles Lebendigen gefördert habe': Feminist Mythmaking and Christa Wolf's *Medea. Stimmen.*" *Focus on*

Literatur, vol. 6, no. 1, 1999, pp. 39–55, <journals.uc.edu/index.php/fogs/article/download/178/149>.

Kaufmann, Hans. "Gespräch mit Christa Wolf. " *Weimarer Beitrage*, 20, no. 6, 1974, pp. 90–112.

Keeling, Kara. *The Witch's Flight: The Cinematic, the Black Femme, and the Image of Common Sense*. Duke UP, 2007.

Kelleter, Frank, and Ruth Mayer. "The Melodramatic Mode Revisited. An Introduction." *Melodrama! The Mode of Excess from Early America to Hollywood*, edited by Frank Kelleter, Barbara Krah, and Ruth Mayer, Universitätsverlag Winter, 2007, pp. 7–18.

Klocke, Sonja E. and Jennifer R. Hosek. "Introduction: Reading Christa Wolf in the Twenty-First Century." *Christa Wolf: A Companion*, edited by Sonja E. Klocke and Jennifer R. Hosek. de Gruyter, 2018, pp. 1–34.

Komska, Yuliya. "What to Do With Confederate Monuments: Seven Lessons from Germany." *The Washington Post*, August 17, 2017, <www.washingtonpost.com/news/made-by-history/wp/2017/08/17/what-to-do-with-confederate-monuments-seven-lessons-from-germany/>.

Koskinas, Nikolaos Ioannis. "Ist eine Medea ohne Kindermord überhaupt denkbar? Medea-Morphosen bei Euripides und Christa Wolf. Oder: Freispruch für Euripides." *Amaltea. Revista de Mitocrítica*, vol. 2, 2010, pp. 91–103, <revistas.ucm.es/index.php/AMAL/article/view/AMAL1010110091A>.

Künzel, Christine. "'Vielleicht kommt die Gewalt von innen': Dea Lohers Poet(h)ik der Gewalt." *Monatshefte*, vol. 99, no. 3, 2007, pp. 360–372, doi: 10.1353/mon.2007.0063.

Lorde, Audre. "The Master's Tools Will Never Dismantle the Master's House." *The Selected Works of Audre Lorde*, edited by Roxane Gay, W.W. Norton & Company, 2020, pp. 39–43.

Lü, Yixu. "Germany: Myth and Apologia in Christa Wolf's Novel *Medea. Voices.*" *Portal*, vol. 1, no. 1, 2004, pp. 1–19, doi: 10.5130/portal.v1i1.50.

____. *Medea unter den Deutschen: Wandlungen einer literarischen Figur*. Rombach Verlag, 2009.

____. "Transformations of Medea on the Eighteenth-Century German Stage." *Unbinding Medea: Interdisciplinary Approaches to a Classical Myth from Antiquity to the 21st Century*, edited by Heike Bartel and Anne Simon, Modern Humanities Research Association and Manly Publishing, 2010, pp. 148–160.

Luschnig, C. A. E. *Granddaughter of the Sun: A Study of Euripides' Medea*. Koninklijke Brill NV, 2007.

Marx Ferree, Myra. *Varieties of Feminism: German Gender Politics in Global Perspective*. Stanford UP, 2012.

McRuer, Robert. *Crip Times: Disability, Globalization, and Resistance.* NYU Press, 2018.

Messerschmidt, Astrid, and Eva Peters. "Kein Freispruch für Euripides: Zu den Medea-Romanen von Ursula Haas und Christa Wolf." *Weimarer Beiträge*, vol. 46, no. 4, 2000, pp. 524–546, <dialnet.unirioja.es/servlet/articulo?codigo=2638657>.

Mitrache, Liliana. "Von Euripides Zu Christa Wolf. Die Wiederbelebung des Mythos in *Medea. Stimmen.*" *Studia Neophilologica*, vol. 74, no. 2, 2002, pp. 207–214, doi: 10.1080/003932702321116217.

Neiman, Susan. *Learning from the Germans: Race and the Memory of Evil.* Farrar, Straus, and Giroux, 2019.

Oguntoye, Katharina, May Opitz [Ayim], and Dagmar Schultz, editors. *Farbe bekennen: Afro-deutsche Frauen auf den Spuren ihrer Geschichte.* Fischer Verlag, 1992.

Paul, Georgina."Schwierigkeiten mit der Dialektik: Zu Christa Wolfs *Medea. Stimmen.*" *German Life and Letters*, vol. 50, no. 2, 1997, pp. 227–240, doi: 10.1111/1468-0483.00053.

Pirro, Robert. "Situating a German Self in Democratic Community: Greek Tragedy and German Identity in Christa Wolf's Mythic Works." *German Politics & Society*, vol. 22, no. 1, 2004, pp. 31–52, *JSTOR*, www.jstor.org/stable/23740499.

Pizer, John. "From Pan-German Cosmopolitanism to Nostalgic National Insularity: A Comparative Study of Christa Wolf's *Kassandra* and *Medea.*" *Christa Wolf: A Companion*, edited by Sonja E. Klocke and Jennifer R. Hosek. de Gruyter, 2018, pp. 147–161.

Požárek, Marcela. "Mimesis, Moderne, Mythos: Dea Lohers *Manhattan Medea.*" *Germanica*, vol. 54, 2014, pp. 107–123, doi: 10.4000/germanica.2554.

Radulescu, Domnica. "Medea as Tragic Heroine: The Problem of Exile." *Sisters of Medea: The Tragic Heroine Across Cultures.* UP of the South, 2002, pp. 87–144.

Rétif, Françoise. "Die Lust am obszönen bei Georges Bataille und Elfriede Jelinek." *Elfriede Jelinek. Sprache, Geschlecht und Herrschaft*, edited by Françoise Rétif and Johann Sonnleitner, Königshausen & Neumann, 2008, pp. 107–118.

Roeben, Antje. "*Manhattan Medea*: Ein Mythos der Erinnerung?" *Zagreber Germanistische Beiträge*, no. 17, 2008, pp. 93–101, www.ceeol.com/search/article-detail?id=20497.

Rooney, Monique. *Living Screens: Melodrama and Plasticity in Contemporary Film and Television.* Rowman and Littlefield, 2015.

Roper, Lyndal. *The Witch in the Western Imagination.* U of Virginia P, 2012.

Rosenau, Maggie. "How to Deal With a Bully: Exhaustion, Crip-Time, and Radical Self-Care as a Temporal Practice." Coalition of Women in German

Annual Conference, October 19, 2019, University of the South, Sewanee, TN. Conference Presentation.

Sade, Marquis de. *The Crimes of Love: Heroic and Tragic Tales*. Translated by David Coward. Oxford UP, 2005.

Schmierer, Britta. *Motivation in Medeatragödien der Antike und der Neuzeit*. Verlag Königshausen & Neumann, 2005.

Schwarzer, Alice, editor. "Ich bitte um Gnade: Schwarzer interviewt Jelinek." *Emma. Das Magazin von Frauen für Frauen*, July 1, 1989, pp. 50–55, <www.aliceschwarzer.de/artikel/ich-bitte-um-gnade-264784>.

Scott, Claire E. "A Forcible Return to the Womb: Elfriede Jelinek's *Lust* (1989) and the Melodramatic Mode." *The German Quarterly*, vol. 91, no. 2 (2018): 108–122. doi: 10.1111/gequ.12062.

Sedgwick, Eve Kosofsky. *Touching Feeling: Affect, Pedagogy, Performativity*. Duke UP, 2013.

Sieg, Katrin. "Race, Guilt and *Innocence*: Facing Blackfacing in Contemporary German Theater." *German Studies Review*, vol. 38, no. 1, 2015, pp. 117–134, *JSTOR*, <www.jstor.org/stable/43555955>.

Spivak, Gayatri Chakravorty. "Can the Subaltern Speak?" *Marxism and the Interpretation of Culture*, edited by Cary Nelson and Lawrence Grossberg. U of Illinois P, 1988, pp. 271–313.

Stehle, Maria. "Pop, Porn, and Rebellious Speech." *Feminist Media Studies*, vol. 12, no. 2, 2012, pp. 229–247, doi: 10.1080/14680777.2011.597103.

Stephan, Inge. *Medea: Multimediale Karriere einer mythologischen Figur*. Böhlau Verlag, 2006.

Steskal, Christoph. *Medea und Jason in der deutschen Literatur des 20. Jahrhunderts: Aktualisierungspotential eines Mythos*. S. Roderer Verlag, 2001.

Struve, Ulrich. "'Denouncing the Pornographic Subject': The American and German Pornography Debate and Elfriede Jelinek's *Lust*." *Elfriede Jelinek: Framed by Language*, edited by Jorun B. Johns and Katherine Arens, Ariadne P, 1994, pp. 89–106.

Summers, Caroline. "Translating Subjective Authenticity from *Christa T.* to *Stadt der Engel* and *August*" Re-presenting Christa Wolf's Subaltern Voice." *Christa Wolf: A Companion*, edited by Sonja E. Klocke and Jennifer R. Hosek, De Gruyter, 2018, pp. 219–241.

Usborne, Cornelie. *Cultures of Abortion in Weimar Germany*. Berghahn Books, 2007.

"Was darf das Fernsehen?" *Panorama*. NDR fernsehen, 1974.

Weber, Beverly M. "Christa Wolf's Trouble With Race." *Christa Wolf: A Companion*, edited by Sonja E. Klocke and Jennifer R. Hosek. De Gruyter, 2018, pp. 163–180.

Weeks, Kathi. *The Problem with Work: Feminism, Marxism, Antiwork Politics, and Postwork Imaginaries.* Duke UP, 2011. *Project MUSE.* muse.jhu.edu/book/69362.

Wetmore, Kevin J., Jr. "Introduction: Medea the Outsider/ Medea as a Woman of Color." *Black Medea Adaptations in Modern Plays.* Cambria P, 2013, pp. 1–14.

Wilke, Sabine. "Die Konstruktion der wilden Frau: Christa Wolfs Roman, Medea Stimmen' als postkolonialer Text." *The German Quarterly,* vol. 76, no. 1, 2003, pp. 11–24, *JSTOR,* <www.jstor.org/stable/3252279>.

Williams, Linda. "Film Bodies: Gender, Genre, and Excess." *Film Quarterly,* vol. 44, no. 4, 1991, pp. 2–13, *JSTOR,* <www.jstor.org/stable/1212758>.

____. "'Something Else Besides a Mother': 'Stella Dallas' and the Maternal Melodrama." *Cinema Journal,* vol. 24, no. 1, 1984, pp. 2–27, *JSTOR,* <www.jstor.org/stable/1225306>.

Wogenstein, Sebastian. "'Meine Nachahmung eine Neuerschaffung'—Aneignung und Ent-Stellung in Dea Lohers Manhattan Medea." *Monatshefte,* vol. 99, no. 3, 2007, 298–315, doi: 10.1353/mon.2007.0077.

Wolf, Christa. "Lesen und Schreiben." *Lesen und Schreiben: Aufsätze und Betrachtungen,* Aufbau-Verlag, 1971, pp. 195–237.

____. "Subjective Authenticity: A Conversation with Hans Kaufmann." *Responses to Christa Wolf: Critical Essays,* edited by Marilyn Sibley Fries, Wayne State UP, 1989, pp. 55–75.

Zantop, Susanne. *Colonial Fantasies: Conquest, Family, and Nation in Precolonial Germany, 1170–1870.* Duke UP, 1997. *Project MUSE.* <muse.jhu.edu/book/68702>.

Index

German Studies in America

Edited by
Celia Applegate, Gail Hart, Kai Evers, Susan Gustafson, Peter Meilaender

German Studies in America publishes research across the field of German studies in the broadest sense, from literary criticism to cultural studies. The editors welcome scholarly work that takes an innovative approach to German, Swiss, or Austrian history, literature, politics, philosophy, national identity, religion, popular culture, film, music, and/or visual art. We are also eager to consider projects that adopt interdisciplinary and intersectional approaches as well as studies with theoretical approaches including psychoanalysis, gender studies, feminism, Marxism, critical race studies, etc. We publish scholarly monographs, translations and edited volumes of essays in both German and English. This series adheres to the highest academic standards and is peer reviewed.

STUDIENREIHE ZUR GERMANISTIK

Germanic Studies in America:

Vol. 1 Nordmeyer, Rubaijat von Omar Chajjam. 2. ed. 104 pages, 1969.
Vol. 2 Richards, The German Bestseller in the 20th Century. A complete Bibliography and Analysis. 276 pages, 1968.
Vol. 3 Germer, The German Novel of Education 1792-1805. A complete Bibliography and Analysis. 280 pages, 1968.
Vol. 4 Gerlitzki, Die Bedeutung der Minne in «Moritz von Craun». 132 pages, 1970 Vol. 5 Bowman, Life into Autobiography. A Study of Goethe's «Dichtung und Wahrheit». 162 pages, 1971.
Vol. 6 Putzel, Letters to Immanuel Bekker from Henriette Herz, S. Pobeheim and Anna Horkel. 108 pages, 1972.
Vol. 7 Geldrich, Heine und der spanisch-amerikanische Modernismo. 304 pages, 1971.
Vol. 8 Friesen, The German Panoramic Novel in the 19th Century. 232 pages, 1972.
Vol. 9 Novak, Wilhelm von Humboldt as a Literary Critic. 142 pages, 1972.
Vol. 10 Shelton, The Young Hölderlin. 282 pages, 1973.
Vol. 11 Milstein, Eight Eighteenth Century Reading Societies. A Sociological Contribution to the History of German Literature. 312 pages, 1972.
Vol. 12 Schatzberg, Scientific Themes in the Popular Literature and the Poetry of the German Enlightenment. 1720-1760. 350 pages, 1973.

Vol. 13 Dimler, Friedrich Spee's «Trutznachtigall». 158 pages, 1973.

Vol. 14 McCort, Perspectives on Music in German Fiction. The Music-Fiction of Wilhelm Heinrich Riehl. 154 pages, 1974.

Vol. 15 Motsch, Die poetische Epistel. Ein Beitrag zur Geschichte der deutschen Literatur und Literaturkritik des achtzehnten Jahrhunderts. 218 pages, 1974.

Vol. 16 Zipser, Edward Bulwer-Lytton and Germany. 232 pages, 1974.

Vol. 17 Rutledge John, The Dialogue of the Dead in Eighteenth-Century Germany. 186 pages, 1974.

Vol. 18 Rutledge Joyce S., Johann Adolph Schlegel. 322 pages, 1974.

Vol. 19 Gutzkow, Wally the Skeptic. Novel. A translation from the German with an Introduction and Notes by Ruth-Ellen Boetcher Joeres. 130 pages, 1974.

Vol. 20 Keck, Renaissance and Romanticism: Tieck's Conception of Cultural Decline as Portrayed in his «Vittoria Accorombona». 120 pages, 1976.

Vol. 21 Scholl, The Bildungsdrama of the Age of Goethe. 80 pages, 1976.

Vol. 22 Bartel, German Literary History 1777-1835. An Annotated Bibliography. 230 pages, 1976.

Vol. 23 Littell, Jeremias Gotthelf's «Die Käserei in der Vehfreude»: A Didactic Satire. 122 pages, 1977.

Vol. 24 Carels, The Satiric Treatise in Eighteenth-Century Germany. 168 pages, 1976.

Vol. 25 Lensing, Narrative Structure and the Reader in Wilhelm Raabe's «Im alten Eisen». 118 pages, 1977.

Vol. 26 Profit, Interpretations of Iwan Goll's late Poetry with a comprehensive and annotated Bibliography of the Writings by and about Iwan Goll. 202 pages, 1977.

Vol. 27 Hollyday, Anti-Americanism in the German Novel 1841-1862. 212 pages, 1977.

Vol. 28 Horwath, Der Kampf gegen die religiöse Tradition. Die Kulturkampfliteratur Österreichs, 1780-1918. 295 pages, 1978.

Vol. 29 Pantle, Die Frau ohne Schatten - By Hugo von Hoffmansthal and Richard Strauss. An Analysis of Text, Music, and their Relationship. 256 pages, 1978.

Vol. 30 Leckey, Some Aspects of Balladesque Art and their Relevance for the Novels of Theodor Fontane. 114 pages, 1979.

Vol. 31 Thomas, Ordnung und Wert der Unordnung bei Bertolt Brecht. 141 pages, 1979.

Vol. 32 Emmel, Weltklage und Bild der Welt in der Dichtung Goethes. Zweite, durchgesehene Auflage, 223 pages, 1979.

Vol. 33 Stern, Hilde Domin: From Exile to Ideal. 93 pages, 1979.

Vol. 34 Gellinek, Herrschaft im Hochmittelalter. Essays zu einem Sonderproblem der älteren deutschen Literatur. 180 pages, 1980.

Vol. 35 Weeks, The Paradox of the Employee. Variants of a Social Theme in Modern Literature. 160 pages, 1979.

Vol. 36 Mittelmann, Die Utopie des weiblichen Glücks in den Romanen Theodor Fontanes. 125 pages, 1980.
Vol. 37 Manyoni, Langzeilentradition in Walthers Lyrik. 128 pages, 1980.
Vol. 38 Helbig, G.E. Lessing: Die Erziehung des Menschengeschlechts. 77 pages, 1980.
Vol. 39 Schrader, A Method of Stylistic Analysis Exemplified on C.M. Wieland's «Geschichte des Agathon». 240 pages, 1980.
Vol. 40 Whiton, Der Wandel des Polenbildes in der deutschen Literatur des 19. Jahrhunderts. 208 pages, 1981.
Vol. 41 Fairy Tales as Ways of Knowing. Essays on Märchen in Psychology, Society and Literature, ed. by Michael M. Metzger and Katharina Mommsen. 200 pages, 1981.
Vol. 42 Beckett, The Reception of Pablo Neruda's Works in the German Democratic Republic. 251 pages, 1981.
Vol. 43 Wiswall, A Comparison of Selected Poetic and Scientific Works of Albrecht von Haller. 432 pages, 1981.
Vol. 44 Cervantes, Struktur-Bezüge in der Lyrik von Nelly Sachs. 144 S., Lwd., 1982. Vol. 45 Guthke, Erkundungen: Essais zur Literatur. 432 pages, 1983.
Vol. 46 Remak, Novellistische Struktur: Der Marschall von Bassompierre und die schöne Krämerin (Bassompierre, Goethe, Hofmannsthal). 130 pages, 1983.
Vol. 47 Laane, Imagery in Conrad Ferdinand Meyer's Prose Works. Form, Motifs, and Functions. 258 pages, 1983.
Vol. 48 Schaffner, The Apprenticeship Novel. A Study of the «Bildungsroman» as a Regulative Type in Western Literature with a Focus on Three Classic Representatives by Goethe, Maugham, and Mann. 178 pages, 1984.
Vol. 49 Gellinek, Pax optima rerum. Friedensessais zu Grotius und Goethe. 153 pages, 1984.
Vol. 50 Lewis, Eugene O'Neill, The German Reception of America's First Dramatist. 211 pages, 1984.
Vol. 51 Brüggemann, Drei Mystifikationen Heinrich von Kleists, Kleists Würzburger Reise - Kleists Lustspiel mit Goethe - Aloysius, Marquis von Montferrat. 220 pages, 1985.
Vol. 52 Weisstein, Links und links gesellt sich nicht. Gesammelte Aufsätze zum Werk Heinrich Manns und Bertolt Brechts. 517 pages, 1986.
Vol. 53 Allen, The Faust Legend. Popular Formular and Modern Novel. 178 pages, 1985.
Vol. 54 Hertling, Theodor Fontanes Irrungen, Wirrungen: Die 'Erste Seite' als Schlüssel zum Werk. 77 pages, 1985.
Vol. 55 Vogt, Vision und Revision: A Study of Inspiration in Thomas Mann's Fiction. 168 pages, 1987.
Vol. 56 Gillespie, Garden and Labyrinth of Time. Studies in Renaissance and Baroque Literature. 326 pages, 1988.

Vol. 57 Shirer, Difficulties of Saying 'I' The Narrator as Protagonist in Christa Wolf's Kindheitsmuster and Uwe Johnson's Jahrestage. 274 pages, 1988.

Vol. 58 Ammerlahn, Aufbau und Krise der Sinn-Gestalt: Tasso und die Prinzessin im Kontext der Goetheschen Werke. 170 pages, 1990.

Vol. 59 Bernhardt, Goethe's Römische Elegien: The Lover and the Poet. 220 pages, 1990.

Vol. 60 Neue Tendenzen der Arnimforschung, herausgegeben von Roswitha Burwick und Bernd Fischer. 320 pages, 1990.

Vol. 61 Markolin, Eine Geschichte vom Erzählen. Peter Handkes poetische Verfahrensweisen am Beispiel der Erzählung «Langsame Heimkehr». 268 pages, 1991.

Vol. 62 Clouser, Love and Social Contracts. Goethe's Unterhaltungen deutscher Ausgewanderten. 310 pages, 1991.

Vol. 63 Cicora, From History to Myth, Wagner's Tannhäuser and its Literary Sources, 217 pages, 1992.

Vol. 64 Denham, Visions of War, Ideologies and Images of War in German Literature Before and After the Great War. 197 pages, 1992.

Vol. 65 Velardi, Techniques of Compression and Prefiguration in the Beginnings of Theodor Fontane's Novels, 202 pages, 1992.

Vol. 66 Stoehr, Beyond the Zeus Principle: Two Hundred Years of Love and Politics in the Novel. 399 pages, 1993.

Vol. 67 Mommsen, Goethe und Diez: Quellenuntersuchungen zu Gedichten der Divan Epoche. 401 pages, 1995.

Vol. 68 Whaley, Johann Wolfgang von Goethe's Poems of The West and The East «West-Eastern Divan»–«West-Östlicher Divan»: Bi-Lingual Edition of the Complete Poems. Verse translation by John Whaley, with an introduction by Katharina Mommsen. 490 pages, 1998.

Vol. 69 Mommsen, Lebendige Überlieferung, George, Hölderlin, Goethe. 406 pa- ges, 1999.

Vol. 70 Brüggemann, Makarie und Mercurius, Goethes Wilhelm Meisters Wanderjahre ls hermetischer Roman. 158 pages, 1999.

Vol. 71 Hertling, Bleibende Lebensinhalte, Essays zu Adalbert Stifter und Gottfried Keller. 142 pages, 2003.

Vol. 72 Hertling, Adalbert Stifters Essays *Wien und die Wiener* (1841–1844) als verhaltenspsychologische „Studien" impressionistischen Kolorits. 128 pages, 2005.

Vol. 73 Moore, The Eye and the Gaze. Goethe and the Autobiographical Subject. 269 pages, 2015.

Vol. 74 Gustafson and Becker Malett, *Stella: A Play for Lovers* (1776) by Johann Wolfgang von Goethe. 118 pages, 2018.

Vol. 75 Meilaender and Rindisbacher, Writing Switzerland. Culture, History, and Politics in the Work of Peter von Matt. 288 pages, 2019.

Vol. 76 Pfeiffer and Tschepik, Meanings of Modern Work in Nineteenth- and Twenty-First-Century German Literature and Film. 182 pages, 2020.

Vol. 77 Roots, Fannish Folklore: Feminist Fan-Fiction Retellings of Germanic Fairy Tales. 256 pages, 2022.

Vol. 78 Scott, Murderous Mothers: Late Twentieth-Century Medea Figures and Feminism. 230 pages, 2022.